VENEZUELA:
A CENTURY OF CHANGE

Judith Ewell

Venezuela
A Century of Change

STANFORD UNIVERSITY PRESS
STANFORD, CALIFORNIA
1984

Stanford University Press
Stanford, California
© Judith Ewell, 1984
Originating publisher: C. Hurst & Co., London
First published in the U.S.A. by Stanford University Press, 1984
ISBN 0-8047-1213-1
LC 83-40093
Printed in Great Britain

CONTENTS

vi   *Contents*

PREFACE

Twentieth-century Venezuelan historiography has only begun to come of age in the last two decades. Venezuelans hesitated to write of current and very political events, and United States scholars were more attracted to the histories of Mexico, Brazil, and Argentina as nations which have played leading Latin American roles for a hundred years or more. Since the mid-1960s, United States social scientists have become fascinated with the political history of *Acción Democrática* and Rómulo Betancourt and with Venezuela's petroleum-based economy. More recently political scientists have studied pressure groups within the country and its international relations. Historians have been less eager to piece together a general history from the fragmentary monographs which exist. Edwin Lieuwen's *Venezuela* (1965) was one of the earliest general efforts, and John Lombardi's *Venezuela: the Search for Order, the Dream of Progress* (1982) is one of the most recent. Guillermo Morón's *A History of Venezuela* (1964) is the only comprehensive effort by a Venezuelan to be published in English.

This book (written at the request of the British publisher Christopher Hurst) seeks to fill the gap between the general histories, which have been relatively weak on the twentieth century — Lieuwen's work is an exception, but it is nearly twenty years old — and the more specialized studies on politics or economics since the Second World War. It disputes the assertion of Mariano Picón Salas that the twentieth century only began for Venezuela at the death of Juan Vincente Gómez in 1935. The more valid, if vaguer, turning point is the late nineteenth century when the uninterrupted trend toward national consolidation and centralization began. Neither Juan Vincente Gómez nor the foreign oil companies created Venezuela from whole cloth. They acted upon a cultural, economic, social, and geographic fabric which already existed by 1900.

I have made an effort to discuss a sampling of Venezuelan literature and art in this work. As Jean Franco argues,

Literature—and even painting and music—have played a social role, with the artist acting as a guide, teacher and conscience of his country. The Latin American has generally viewed art as an expression of the artist's whole self: a self which is living in a society and which therefore has a collective as well as an individual concern.[1]

Venezuelan writers have held an important position in their society even though Venezuelan literature has not received as much hemispheric and international recognition as that of some other Latin

American nations. Many Venezuelan writers merit further consideration as artists, but even more as spokespersons for national moods and perceptions.

Without the work of those scholars who have contributed monographs on Venezuela since the mid-1960s, this work would not have been possible. I have kept notes to a minimum, but I owe a great debt to the research and analysis of those authors listed in the bibliography. A synthesis such as this would be much more difficult without the opportunity to argue and discuss Venezuelan history with other friends and colleagues. The following people have afforded me such pleasant opportunities in the last few years: Oscar and Rosario Abdala, Susan Berglund, Steve Ellner, Robert Ferry, Mary Floyd, Edwin Lieuwen, Austin Linsley, John Lombardi, Carlos Romero, Ralph Van Roy, Kathy Waldron, and Winthrop R. Wright. The graduate students in my classes at the Universidad Católica Andrés Bello during 1979–80 deserve special thanks, as do my William and Mary students who have constantly challenged me and indulged me in my discussions of Latin America in general and "my" Venezuela in particular.

I am grateful to Barbara Fishbein and Carol Lingle and their colleagues at Practical Business Services for their patience and professionalism in typing another Venezuelan manuscript. Linda Merrell deserves special mention for her expert preparation of the map. Finally, I would like to thank Christopher Hurst for his support and helpful criticism. A special acknowledgement also goes to organizations which have financed my visits to Venezuela and provided me with the opportunity to know the country better: American Association of University Women (dissertation fellowship, 1969–70), Organization of American States (fellowship, 1974–5), Council for International Exchange of Scholars (Fullbright professorship, 1979–80). The College of William and Mary has also supported my research through a summer grant in 1978 and several semester leaves.

NOTE

[1]Jean Franco, *The Modern Culture of Latin America: Society and the Artist* (Harmondsworth and Baltimore: Penguin Books, 1970), p. 11.

ABBREVIATIONS

AD	*Acción Democrática*
AEV	*Asociación de Escritores Venezolanos*
ALALC	*Asociación Latinoamericana de Libre Comercio*
AN	*Acción Nacional*
ANAC	*Asociación Nacional de Autores Cinematográficos*
ANE	*Asociación Nacional de Empleados*
ARDI	*Agrupación Revolucionaria de Izquierda*
AVM	*Asociación Venezolana de Mujeres*
AVP	*Asociación Venezolana de Periodismo*
BAP	*Banco Agrícola y Pecuario*
BCV	*Banco Central de Venezuela*
Bs	*Bolívares*
CAP	*Comisión de Administración Pública (also Carlos Andrés Pérez)*
CCN	*Cruzada Cívica Nacionalista*
CIEI	*Comisión Investigadora contra el Enriquecimiento Ilícito*
Codesa	*Comité de Sindicatos Autónomos*
Codesur	*Comisión para el Desarrollo del Sur*
CONAC	*Consejo Nacional de la Cultura*
Conahotu	*Corporación Nacional de Hoteles y Turismo*
COPEI	*Comité de Organización Política Electoral Independiente*
Cordiplan	*Oficina Central de Coordinación y Planificación*
CSE	*Consejo Supremo Electoral*
CTV	*Confederación de Trabajadores de Venezuela*
CUTV	*Central Unica de Trabajadores de Venezuela*
CVF	*Corporación Venezolana de Fomento*
CVG	*Corporación Venezolana de Guayana*
CVP	*Corporación Venezolana del Petróleo*
Digepol	*Dirección General de Policía*
DIM	*Dirección de Inteligencia Militar*
DISIP	*Dirección de Servicios de Inteligencia y Prevención del Estado*
EVICSA	*Empresa Venezolana de Ingeniería y Construcción SA*
FALN	*Fuerzas Armadas de Liberación Nacional*
FCV	*Federación Campesina de Venezuela*
FDP	*Fuerza Democrática Popular*

Fedecámaras	*Federación de Cámaras y Asociaciones de Comercio y Producción*
FEI	*Frente Electoral Independiente*
FEV	*Federación de Estudiantes de Venezuela*
FND	*Frente Nacional Democrático*
FNP	*Frente Nacionalista Popular*
Fundacomún	*Fundación para el Desarrollo de la Comunidad y Fomento Municipal*
Funres	*Fundación para el Rescate del Acervo Documental Venezolano*
FVM	*Federación Venezolana de Maestros*
IAN	*Instituto Agrario Nacional*
INCE	*Instituto Nacional de Cooperación Educativa*
INCIBA	*Instituto Nacional de Cultura y Bellas Artes*
IND	*Instituto Nacional de Deportes*
INOS	*Instituto Nacional de Obras Sanitarias*
IVSS	*Instituto Venezolano del Seguro Social*
JRC	*Juventud Revolucionaria Copeyana*
LAFTA	Latin American Free Trade Area
MAC	*Ministerio de Agricultura y Cría*
MAS	*Movimiento al Socialismo*
MEP	*Movimiento Electoral del Pueblo*
MIR	*Movimiento de Izquierda Revolucionaria*
MOP	*Ministerio de Obras Públicas*
OAS	Organization of American States
OPEC	Organization of Petroleum Exporting Countries
ORVE	*Organización Venezolana*
PCV	*Partido Comunista de Venezuela*
PDN	*Partido Democrático Nacional*
PDV	*Partido Democrático Venezolano*
PRP	*Partido Republicano Progresista*
PRV	*Partido Revolucionario Venezolano*
PTJ	*Policía Técnica Judicial*
SELA	*Sistema Económico Latinoamericano*
SIC	*Seminario Interdiocesano Caracas*
SN	*Seguridad Nacional*
SUTISS	*Sindicato Unico de Trabajadores de la Industria Siderúgica y Similares*
UCAB	*Universidad Católica Andrés Bello*
UCV	*Universidad Central de Venezuela*
UNE	*Unión Nacional Estudiantil*
UPA	*Unión Para Avanzar*

UPM	*Unión Patriótica Militar*
URD	*Unión Republicana Democrática*
USB	*Universidad Símon Bolívar*
VBEC	Venezuelan Basic Economy Corporation

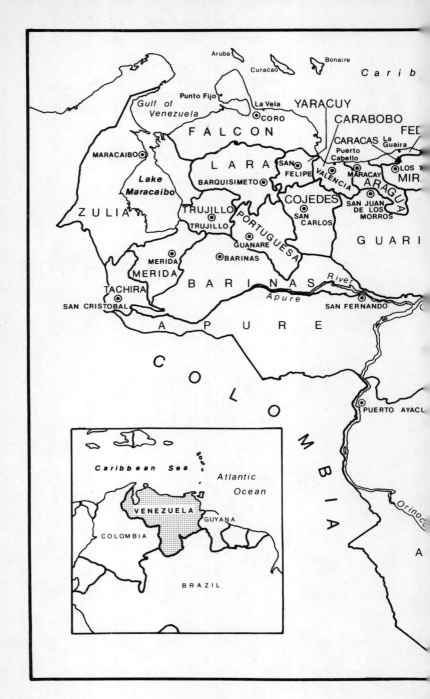

Sea

NUEVA ESPARTA

GARITA
SLAND

LA ASUNCION

Carúpano

Güiria

Trinidad and Tobago

Gulf of
Paria

ATLANTIC
OCEAN

to
ruz

CUMANA

S U C R E

RCELONA

MATURIN

MONAGAS

DELTA

NZOATEGUI

TUCUPITA

er

Ciudad
Guayana

A M A C U R O

CIUDAD BOLIVAR

VAR

G U Y A N A

Caroní
River

B R A Z I L

AS

LEGEND

States...............LARA
State Capitals......⊙CORO
Ports.................•Güiria

100   0   200

KILOMETERS

INTRODUCTION

The concept of "Latin America," although useful to scholars, may be more misleading than enlightening. Each country south of the Río Grande, or Río Bravo, is unique. Some of the uniqueness may be attributed to the colonial and nineteenth century experiences and to the speed, sequence, and timing of economic and demographic growth. Venezuela's historical pattern does not coincide with that of any other Latin American nation, although there are, of course, parallels. Like Chile, Argentina, and northern Mexico, Venezuela was hardly more than a defensive frontier during most of the three centuries of Spanish rule. None of these regions was known to have rich mineral deposits or dense populations of Indians suitable for labor. Unlike the other frontiers in the far south and the far north, however, Venezuela enjoyed a modest plantation economy based on cacao and tobacco. The plantation regions, supported by the labor of African slaves, developed societies not unlike those of some of the Caribbean islands or other coastal regions.

Alone among the frontier regions, Venezuela had a long and destructive War for Independence (1810–21), somewhat comparable to Mexico's struggle for independence. Off to a shaky start in the nineteenth century, Venezuela did not achieve the relatively early stability and economic growth enjoyed by Argentina and Chile. On the other hand, the Caribbean nation did not suffer from the foreign attacks which plagued Argentina, Chile, Peru, or Mexico during the first sixty years of national independence. The lack of external threats may have slowed down the development of a national consciousness and political consensus. Most of Venezuela's nineteenth century experience was characterized by poverty, a small population with a high mortality rate, and chronic civil wars. Only after the end of the Federal Wars (1859–63) did Venezuela initiate a slow and continuous tendency toward economic growth, political stability, and national consolidation. The development of the petroleum industry in the twentieth century quickened the pace of change. No other country in Latin America has been so entirely transformed in all aspects of national life as Venezuela has since 1900. An analysis of this transformation, and of the late nineteenth-century society from which it began, is most relevant to the understanding of present day Venezuela, its politics and its problems.

To stress the rapid and endemic change since 1900 does not deny the importance of colonial and early nineteenth-century history. The colonial period set the warp and woof of the fabric of Venezuela. The expanse of territory which we now call Venezuela

1

had little to recommend it when Columbus first discovered it in 1498. Named Venezuela because the Indian houses on stilts in Lake Maracaibo reminded the Europeans of Venice, the region bore no other resemblance to the fabled Renaissance city. Indian populations had not reached the highly developed state of the Incas of Peru or the Aztecs or Mayas of Mexico. Nor were there many Indians to exploit for labor, although some sixteenth-century Spanish settlers did make a business of selling Venezuelan Indians to the more economically developed regions of the Caribbean, such as Santo Domingo. Few minerals or precious jewels attracted the attention of the Spaniards, although the myth of El Dorado inspired some exploration of western Venezuela, and pearl fishing from the islands of Cubagua and Margarita drew some settlers to the east. Yet, after the conquest of Mexico in 1521 and the discovery and conquest of Peru in the 1530s, Venezuela became part of the abandoned Caribbean territories. Like Cuba, Hispaniola, Puerto Rico, and Central America, the Venezuelan mainland settled back into relative self-sufficiency and attracted little attention from the Crown or the *audiencia* (court) at Santo Domingo which held nominal authority over Venezuela.

Geography and the accidents of the location of early settlements did not facilitate a unified colony. The earliest settlements responded to the reality or the dream of wealth and maintained independent links to the particular territories which provided them with trade or markets. The early settlements in the east — Nueva Cádiz, Cubagua (1510) and Cumaná on the mainland (1523) — exploited pearls and salt and maintained closer contacts with Spain than with other Caribbean or other Venezuelan settlements. The western cities of Coro (1527), El Tocuyo (1545), and Maracaibo (1567) developed an early slave trade in Indians and an agricultural economy which would supply the mines of neighboring Nueva Granada (Colombia). In the central coastal region, the city of Caracas was founded in 1567, primarily to link the eastern and western settlements and to guard the central coast from the attacks of pirates. Caracas developed closer ties with the *audiencia* of Santo Domingo than with Spain directly or with the neighboring colony of Nueva Granada; strong Caribbean currents made the maritime communications among the three coastal population centers difficult. Until the eighteenth century, all the Venezuelan cities remained relatively self-sufficient and poor. Commerce with Spain was difficult and erratic, so the Venezuelans provided for themselves and conducted a lively contraband trade with the Dutch in the neighboring island of Curaçao.

The territory south of the coastal mountains and valleys was even more unattractive for Spanish exploitation or colonization. It was left to Franciscan, Dominican, and Jesuit friars to explore the *llanos* (plains) and the Orinoco basin and to begin the arduous job of pacifying the Indians and grouping them into missions. The interior missions had little contact with each other or with the coastal towns, but they did provide the first basis for a vision of a grander Venezuela beyond a few isolated enclaves of population along the coast and in the western Andes.

Like most of Spain's frontier colonies, Venezuela attracted few Spanish settlers and even fewer who could claim to be *hidalgos*, or nobles. Each city gradually developed its own class of *mantuanos* (literally, those who wore luxurious lace *mantillas*, or the élite), but their power, privileges, wealth, and patterns of consumption were poor indeed when compared to the élites of Mexico or Peru. Their position of high status rested upon their unsullied Spanish ancestry, their relative prosperity derived from plantations, commerce, or smuggling, and their access to political power in the municipal councils. Below them were the various middle strata, poor Spaniards or more frequently persons of mixed racial ancestry (*pardos*), who supported themselves through the exercise of crafts, petty commerce, some professions, or production of agricultural commodities for urban consumption. African slaves provided labor for the *haciendas* (plantations), and their possession also was a mark of status and a source of household labor for the urban élites. Frequently they too learned and practised skilled crafts in the cities. As a relatively poor colony, Venezuela could not afford to import large numbers of African slaves, although the prosperity of the eighteenth century did see an intensification of the slave trade before it was abolished in 1810. Most of the African population logically was to be found in the coastal plantation areas and in the major urban centers. The final, or more properly the first, component of the Venezuelan population was the Indian. Before the arrival of the Spanish, Venezuela had a great diversity of Indian linguistic groups with cultures typical of the ecological zones they inhabited: Andean highlands, Caribbean coastal valleys, Orinoco delta, or Guayana jungles. The Spanish invasion of the northern coastal areas quickly contributed to the death or flight of the Indians who had inhabited that zone. The greatest survival of indigenous population and culture was to be found in the Andean highlands and in the missions or unexplored regions in the south. In sum, the Venezuelan ethnic and social structure had all the components of Latin America in general. Yet, like most frontier regions, it had fewer African slaves, fewer Indians, and fewer Spanish *hidalgos*. The result was a more diversified society, compared with the vice-royalties of Mexico and

Peru, and a social pyramid in which there was relatively less distance between the top and the base.

The Spanish Crown and the *audiencia* of Santo Domingo paid little attention to Venezuela. After its settlement in 1567, Caracas began to assume a *de facto* and tentative leadership of the Venezuelan provinces. Neither Santo Domingo, Spain, nor the other provinces challenged Caracas's increasing hegemony in most matters. Caracas's dominance over the earlier settlements of Coro, El Tocuyo, and Cumaná came from several advantages the central city had over the eastern and western regions. At a higher altitude, and protected by mountains from pirate attacks, Caracas enjoyed a security unknown to the coastal cities. Yet there was also easy access to the Caribbean through the neighboring port of La Guaira. The altitude and the fertile valley of Caracas provided a more attractive and healthful climate than the hot, steamy cities of the coast. The good land in the valley allowed a diversified agriculture to feed the city's population, and the coastal cacao and tobacco plantations provided a source of status and income for the *mantuanos* of the colonial city. Small deposits of gold in the surrounding hills further sweetened the location for the early settlers.

Caracas assumed the leadership of the six provinces (Mérida de Maracaibo, Barinas, Cumaná, Guayana, Margarita, Caracas) by *ca.* 1800, but colonial institutions in general were weak or distant. The closest *audiencia* for most of the colonial period was in Santo Domingo or Nueva Granada, there was no central fiscal officer and no *consulado* (merchants' guild). The Catholic Church, seeing few Indians to convert or put to work and a relatively small and poor Spanish population, found little incentive to provide a complete network of ecclesiastical officials and little money to construct the grand cathedrals typical of Mexico and Peru. The provinces were not deemed worthy of an archbishopric until 1804.

The eighteenth-century rule of the Spanish Bourbon monarchs brought some unity to the Venezuelan provinces. Greater prosperity also followed some innovative economic policies. Dissatisfied with the amount of contraband conducted in Venezuela, the Crown encouraged the formation of the Caracas, or Guipuzcoana, Company, which received a monopoly of the cacao trade from Venezuela. The Basque shareholders also had the right to provision and administer the colony. The company simultaneously provided an impetus to the local economy and aroused a greater sense of unity, as Venezuelans railed against the arrogance of the Basque officials and the determination to end the lucrative smuggling trade with the Dutch. The ideas of the French and Spanish enlightenment further encouraged the Venezuelan élite to perceive and assert new economic and political rights.

Even after the failure of the Guipuzcoana Company in the 1760s, the Bourbon monarchs implemented more reforms which contributed to the unification of the provinces and to the ascendancy of Caracas. Spanish administration became more direct and efficient with the naming of an Intendant to centralize the fiscal administration of the provinces (1776) and with the appointment of a captain general to assume political and military control of the entire region (1777). In the 1780s, Caracas also became the seat of an *audiencia* and of a *consulado*; judicial and commercial affairs thus became more centralized and more orderly. The other provinces, accustomed to autonomy and independent trade ties, did not always accept graciously the greater prominence of Caracas, but the heightened status and prosperity of the entire colony were apparent.

Venezuela's tentative unification unfortunately gave way to the chaos of the Wars for Independence, which lasted from 1810 to 1821. The Wars were more than a simple struggle against Spanish rule and meant many different things: civil wars between different regions with different economic priorities, conflicts among classes and races, conflicts within élites and important families, and simple confusion at the vacuum of power caused by Napoleon's invasion of the Iberian Peninsula. Napoleon's conquest of Spain and his placing his brother Joseph on the Spanish throne in 1808 prompted a crisis of legitimacy in the entire empire. With the uncertainty of Spanish politics, American—and Venezuelan—local tensions burst into flame.

Led principally by the quixotic visionary, Simón Bolívar, Venezuela's Independence Wars broke old patterns and raised new dilemmas. Bolívar and the patriots dominated Caracas several times prior to the return of the Spanish Bourbon Ferdinand VII to the throne in 1814, but they were unable to hold the city and never secured a foothold in the *llanos* to the south where the royalist Tomás Boves held sway. The return of Ferdinand VII should have given the royalists the boost they needed to restore legitimacy and to retain the empire, but four years of warfare in addition to the ideological struggles between the Spanish liberals and Ferdinand VII made a return to the old order impossible. Bolívar, with his continental vision, finally hit on the notion of securing the *llanos* first, making ties with the patriots across the Andes in Colombia, and then taking Caracas. Aided by British legionnaires, who had been released by the end of the European struggle against Napoleon, and by *llanero* José Antonio Páez, Bolívar began the final stage of his campaign in 1816. By 1819 the last battle for the independence of Nueva Granada (Colombia) had been fought; the constitution which united Colombia, Venezuela, and Ecuador into Gran Colombia had been written; and in 1821 the last battle for Venezuela's independence was won. The geopolitical rationale of the Gran Colombian confederation gave way in 1829 to regionalism and to the centrifugal force which had begun with the Wars for Independence. Dominated by José Antonio Páez, Venezuela became an independent federalist republic in 1830. Simón Bolívar died the same year, a frustrated and disappointed national and international hero. Lesser Venezuelans were left to pick up the pieces and to forge a legitimate political system which would respond to the needs of the different classes and regions of the nation.

The length and violence of the Wars meant that Venezuela, like Mexico, would have difficulty in recapturing the late eighteenth-century momentum of growth and development. In contrast, for example, Argentina suffered less destruction and was able to rebuild the national economy and trade somewhat more easily than Venezuela. The Wars had also fed family and regional feuds in Venezuela enough to provoke many of the subsequent political conflicts of the nineteenth century. The Wars had also destroyed or impoverished many of the leading families of the colonial period, which opened the way for the rise of new élites, often *pardos* or *mestizos* who had shown military talent during the Wars, but who had had little experience of civilian politics. The men who ruled Venezuela between 1830 and 1870 were *caudillos* pure and simple, with little breadth of vision and less claim to the title of statesman.

Venezuela's political problems in the nineteenth century may have been accentuated, however, by the education and philosophy of the Independence generation. Constitutions and political institutions were often inspired by classical Roman law and tradition, by European political philosophy, or by the Constitution of the United States of America. Like the early Mexican leaders, Venezuelan politicians divided the nation into "states" which did echo the colonial provinces, but had less autonomy and reason for being after independence than did the states of the United States. They also grandly called for a separation of executive, judicial, and legislative powers in the North American and British style without a full consideration of the lack of such a tradition in the Hispanic political tradition. The unrealistic constitutions and the dominance of military leaders in the absence of a strong civilian political élite ensured that Venezuelans found little consensus on the issues of political legitimacy and presidential succession during most of the nineteenth century.

The political problems might have been solved more rapidly if the country had not been so devastated economically by the Wars. The traditional trade ties with Spain and Mexico were broken, and the protected market for export crops like tobacco and cacao disappeared. Cacao plantations and cattle ranches had been destroyed or abandoned during the Wars, and laborers had fled. In spite of the break from the economic growth of the late eighteenth century, Venezuela enjoyed some prosperity in the 1830s based on coffee cultivation. European demand for the product was strong, credit was available, and *hacendados* often chose to convert the ruined cacao plantations to coffee cultivation because coffee trees took less time to mature than cacao trees. Unfortunately, this switch to coffee and the government's accompanying enthusiasm for free trade and foreign credit placed the coffee planters at the mercy of the world market and their creditors when the world prices fell in the 1840s. Many planters who had enjoyed the short-lived prosperity plunged into bankruptcy in the 1840s.

International concerns had been of great importance during the Independence Wars but sank into secondary importance after 1830. Bolívar had had a vision of Latin American unity which had led him to hope for a spiritual—at least—confederation of all Hispanic America. He had also seen the value of cooperation with other Caribbean colonies and would have preferred to remove the colonial powers entirely from the Caribbean. But his force of will alone could not forge a unity among regions which had been related primarily through their ties to Spain. Nor could the new nations, exhausted by their own wars, continue the fight to eject Spain from Cuba and Puerto Rico. During the nineteenth century after the collapse of Gran Colombia, Venezuela remained nearly as isolated as it had been during the first hundred years or so of its colonial existence. The international ties which remained were principally economic and principally with Britain or other European mercantile states. These ties, logically, were stronger in Caracas, the seat of the government and the economic center of the nation, and later in Maracaibo where German merchants encouraged the cultivation of coffee in the Andean states.

The political nation, between 1808 and 1830, was dominated by Bolívar and his allies. From 1830 to 1848, the so-called Conservative Oligarchy endorsed the leadership of the *llanero* José Antonio Páez. An unschooled *caudillo* who had mastered the art of leadership and manipulation of men, Páez kept a firm hold on Venezuelan political life until 1848. His closest allies were foreign and local merchants and bankers. As the economic situation worsened in the 1840s and bankruptcies increased, opposition to Páez consolidated around Antonio Leocadio Guzmán, who called himself a liberal and found his support among planters, debtors, some local *caudillos*, and some Venezuelan families which had been allies of Bolívar during the Independence Wars and later considered themselves enemies of Páez. Páez snuffed out Guzmán's growing influence fairly easily by jailing him and condemning him to death for allegedly inciting popular uprisings in 1846. In 1848 Páez selected a new ally and president in José Tadeo Monagas; he expected that Monagas would continue to serve him and the Conservative Oligarchy.

Much to Páez's chagrin, Monagas and his brother José Gregorio kept control of the government until the Federal Wars began in 1858. Not recognizing their debt to Páez, the Monagas brothers allied with and supported the liberals and implemented a number of liberal reforms. They changed the penalty against Antonio Leocadio Guzmán to exile, they adopted a number of liberal proposals to aid the hard-pressed debtors and planters, and they decreed the abolition of slavery in 1854. Unfortunately for them, the liberal reforms neither revived the economy nor consolidated their power.

The conflagration known as the Federal Wars began in 1858 when liberals, conservatives, and local *caudillos* united to end the Monagas dynasty and to oust José Tadeo Monagas from office. For the six years that followed, no one was able to dominate the situation. Ezequiel Zamora, one of the most talented of the military leaders, died in the first year of fighting. José Antonio Páez had returned to the fray, but could not command a large enough following to impose his will on the nation again. Finally, Juan C. Falcón and his principal advisor, Antonio Guzmán Blanco, the son of Antonio Leocadio Guzmán, succeeded in bringing a tenuous order to the country. Since Falcón and the regional *caudillos* had advocated greater autonomy for the states, the winners wrote a new Constitution which divided the nation into twenty states. The new states—and incidentally the local *caudillos*—had a greater theoretical independence from the national government in Caracas than they ever had before or would again. The Constitution of 1864 thus became the extreme expression of local, or regional, political and economic power. The Wars had claimed 350,000 victims and left the nation exhausted. The economy and many élite families had again been devastated, opening the way for the creation and consolidation of a new national élite.

After the cataclysm of the Federal Wars, national leaders urged the way slowly away from localism and toward a more truly centralized government. It was as if the Federal Wars had constituted the last break from the past, and after 1864 a modern, national history could begin to take shape. Much of the story from 1870 to the present is that of an increasing concentration of power and population in Caracas and along the north central coast. Economy, society, politics, and culture all coalesced in the capital city. The states and the state *caudillos* could not unite to retain local control and autonomy. They could not overcome the centripetal force that drew them to Caracas. The *caudillos* had to capture the central government in order to ensure attention to local problems. Caracas always took revenge by absorbing the *caudillo* and making him a *caraqueño*.

The trend in the Western world in the last quarter of the nineteenth century was toward national and economic integration. A nation with such a small population and vulnerable coastline, and with gold and asphalt, could only hope to retain autonomy and stand off foreign threats through centralization. Antonio Guzmán Blanco (1870–88) epitomized the trend. He proved the most talented and skillful of the *caudillos*. His greatest flaw was his inability to choose a successor who could continue his rule with only minor challenges to his legitimacy. The vacuum of power caused by his self-imposed exile in Europe coupled with his constant long-distance meddling in Venezuelan politics provided an opportunity for Cipriano Castro from the western state of Táchira to seize power in 1899.

With the victory of Castro and his successor Juan Vicente Gómez, the pace of centralization quickened. Oil was discovered and began to be exploited in the second decade of the century. The president had to be strong enough not only to dominate the state *caudillos* but also to treat skillfully with the international oil companies and their home governments. The president firmly grasped power in his own hands, leaving little to Congress and much to his family and personal friends. Caracas power became more accentuated, but Caracas also reached its tentacles into the interior as lawyers, soldiers, spies, and other agents of the dictator supervised the oil fields, construction projects, and political activity. Venezuelans discovered their national identity in reaction to the highhandedness of the foreign oil companies and their employees. Government administrators needed more skills to survive the economic depression of the 1930s, to absorb the foreign technology demands, to control a growing government bureaucracy, and to stifle labor and student protests. National literature of the 1930s reflected the national consciousness as the writers turned from nostalgic *criollista* themes to a consideration of urban middle-class concerns, the impact of the foreigners and the oil boom, the abject misery of the poor, and the triumph of law and institutions over personalism and barbarism.

Middle groups, spawned by government service and oil company service, emerged and called for a greater voice in setting national priorities. They came together in professional associations, saw themselves reflected in literature, and avidly followed national themes in newspapers and the radio, especially after 1935. The small industrial working class, primarily in the petroleum camps and in Caracas, also pressed for dignity and a fairer share of the national income, but were too weak and isolated to succeed. The dictators had favored national entrepreneurs, but a greater awareness of the minimum requirements for economic development also made them impatient for change.

In 1908, and again in 1918, 1928 and 1936 some of the new groups tried to challenge the dictatorships. They failed, but each effort taught a new lesson. The predominant one was that a lightly populated, rural nation could not organize politically along class lines to combat a dictatorship and the foreign oil enclave. Ideologies of class conflict brought back memories of the contentious nineteenth century and merely divided the opposition. The idea spread that the opposition had to unite in multiclass, loose political alliance to demand a share in the exercise of power and a wider distribution of the national wealth. Political power, like the oil, should be sown more widely.

The scions of the Castro/Gómez dictatorship—Eleazar López Contreras and Isaías Medina Angarita—offered to share power with the emerging middle groups after 1935, but the offers were too miserly and too slow, especially in the context of the Second World War and the international desire to construct a postwar world free from dictatorships. A military and civilian coalition took charge in Venezuela in 1945 — as in several other Latin American countries — with promises of national economic development and political freedoms. The importance of oil, and of Venezuela as the primary world exporter of the commodity, forced the nation further onto the international stage. The Cold War accentuated security concerns that had been raised during the World War. The armed forces, the most organized and efficient national organization, became impatient with the squabbles of the civilian politicians. They abolished the new democratic institutions in 1948 and ruled until 1958, guided by their mission of national economic development and modernization. Civilians, middle groups, urban masses, and laboring groups would not be denied their opportunity to share in national decision making and in national wealth. For the first time in the twentieth century, the opposition united and forced the resignation of the dictator in 1958.

Since the fall of the dictatorship, Venezuela has enjoyed modern democratic elections, organized partisan activity, a thriving national economy, and an international role which seeks allies among the Western democracies and the nations of the Third World. A debate has arisen between the advocates of state capitalism and those of socialism. The socialists have made little headway either among the traditional peasants or with the more privileged workers and middle groups who fear that they would lose out under socialism. The majority believe that the compromises forged after 1958 have benefited the country. If and when that belief no longer seems tenable, the radical left or the radical right may enjoy more success.

Petroleum has not solved all the national problems. Indeed the roller coaster rise and fall of petroleum prices in the 1970s has prompted the national mood to oscillate between an arrogant confidence that the bonanza will never end and a fatalistic despair that the nation will return to the stagnation of the nineteenth century when the oil reserves disappear.

The concerns of post-industrial society have troubled a nation which has yet to enjoy all the fruits of full industrialization. Rapid urbanization has outstripped the services and the space needed to live comfortably in the capital city of Caracas. Glittering petrochemical complexes and national steel industries have not provided jobs for many of the population. The large middle-class population under the age of fifteen has grown up amid affluence with the expectation that affluence will continue for them. Yet, highly paying and acceptable jobs are limited, especially when financial exigencies cause the government to reduce the swollen and inefficient bureaucracy.

Political leadership since 1958 has been dominated by the generation of Rómulo Betancourt and those who came to political consciousness between 1928 and 1948. Most of these people remember the dusty and dictatorial nation of their childhood and marvel at the strides the nation has made. They have had patience and have set relatively modest, political goals. The youth who matured during the 1950s or the guerrilla struggles of the 1960s have taken the political democracy for granted and have set more ambitious economic and social goals. The questions for Venezuela's political future are several. Can the administrative and political structures swiftly remove the bottlenecks to development without losing the allegiance of the middle class? Can the nation exercise an autonomous international role when so closely linked to the United States? Can a nation of immigrants and new middle class people forge a national identity which will provide a cohesiveness for the society? Will the generation which takes political power in the 1990s prove as flexible and as skillful as those who have ruled in the two and a half decades since 1958?

Venezuela's fate in the next quarter of a century may help to answer the question of whether any new nations can securely join the developed world. Venezuela, still with a relatively homogeneous and small population, a favored location, and rich natural resources will have had perhaps three quarters of a century to "sow the petroleum." If they cannot resolve the economic and administrative problems, provide jobs and a decent living for all, develop a vibrant national culture with rich opportunities for the use of leisure time, encourage political efficacy and participation by a majority of the citizens, and experience international autonomy to the extent that that is possible in this interdependent world—then there may be but slight hope for any of the developing nations.

1

ON THE BRINK OF THE TWENTIETH CENTURY: THE 1890s

"Venezuela, its rivers and its peoples, its fevers and its paradises, the dreams of the multitudes which populate it, the experience of its *mestizaje*, the lands still to be discovered, the music of its immensity, is a theme too grand for a single poet."[1]

Mariano Picón Salas

Venezuela has probably experienced the most drastic changes of any Latin American country in the twentieth century. Petroleum revenues have affected nearly every aspect of national life. It has become a truism to state that Venezuela only entered the modern era in 1936 on the death of dictator Juan Vicente Gómez. Yet by 1900 Venezuela had existed as an independent nation for three quarters of a century. Economic patterns and social structures had crystalized. Political elites and opportunists competed for power through elections and armed revolts. An elite culture and a rich popular culture existed side by side. Sentiments of nationalism vied with regional loyalties as justification for actions. In short, the Venezuela of 1900 already contained the ingredients which would flavor the responses to foreign intervention and sudden wealth in the twentieth century. A survey of pre-petroleum Venezuela in the 1890s can heighten an appreciation of the continuities and changes in Venezuela up to the 1980s.

Geography, Resources, Economy

Venezuela ranks seventh in size among Latin American nations. In the nineteenth century, the country was surrounded by three larger, richer, more stable, and more heavily populated nations: Brazil to the south, Colombia to the west, and the British Empire (British Guiana) to the east. Although the geopolitical potential of the Caribbean location at the north of the South American continent was great, Venezuela's weakness and civil wars had precluded any realization of that potential. Each of Venezuela's three neighbors had expanded their frontiers at her expense by 1900. The only boundary that remained unchanged was the Caribbean Sea to the north; across that expanse of water, Venezuela faced the insular outposts of European powers.

Internally, Venezuela could be divided into four general regions, each with its distinctive climate, physiography, culture, populations, and economy: the coastal zone, the Andean west, the inland *llanos*, and the Guayana highlands. The uniqueness of the regions encouraged observers to idealize their characteristics. For example, Agustín Codazzi wrote in 1841 in his *Resumen de la geografía de Venezuela*:

No country in America has such distinctive zones as Venezuela. The first zone is that of cultivated land; the second is pasture lands, and the third that of forests. The three zones present, as Humboldt says, a perfect image of the three states of society: the life of the savage who lives in Orinoco jungles, that of the cowboy who inhabits the plains and that of the agricultural peoples who reside in the high valleys and at the foot of the coastal mountains.[2]

Codazzi's word picture suggests the difficulty that Venezuelans have faced in overcoming regional loyalties.

The most important region has always been the coastal strip, broadly encompassing the humid lowlands and the bordering foothills which stretch from Lake Maracaibo in the west to the Orinoco delta in the east. The major Caribbean ports — from west to east, Maracaibo, La Vela, Puerto Cabello, La Guaira, Barcelona, Cumaná, Carúpano, Güiria — had the role of integrating Venezuelan commerce and production into the Caribbean and Atlantic worlds. Coffee from the Andes, cacao and sugar from the central and eastern lowlands, tobacco from Barinas filled foreign ships in the colonial era and in the nineteenth century and journeyed to overseas markets. La Guaira remained the major port largely because of its proximity to the Venezuelan market for European luxury goods, but each Venezuelan port had close links to its own hinterland. Maracaibo was the chief port for the primary export crop of the late nineteenth century: coffee from the Andean states of Trujillo, Mérida, and Táchira. Puerto Cabello and La Guaira funneled the products of the more diversified central region to the exterior: cacao, coffee, sugar cane, cattle, and copper. Farther east, Carúpano exported the traditional crop of the *oriente* — cacao — and enjoyed a late nineteenth-century boom with the exploitation of the rich asphalt deposits of the Lake of Guanoco and the coal deposits of Naricual. President Antonio Guzmán Blanco (1870–88) took a major step in the economic integration of the nation when he forced each of the regional ports to turn over their customs revenues to the national government rather than to the state governments.

The economy of the coastal region rested firmly on plantation agriculture and commerce. Since the majority of the population resided there, small farmers also could make a reasonable living by selling their produce in local markets. Slavery had been abolished in the 1850s, leaving this region with the majority of the free blacks of the nation and an adequate labor supply. Some of the little towns of the coastal range had grown in the 1860s as a result of people seeking safe refuge from the Federal War (1858–63). Pockets of special economic zones existed, such as the salt mines of the Araya Peninsula or the local commerce between Coro and the Netherlands Antilles. As in most Latin American countries, *latifundia* was prevelant, especially along the coast which lay near the centers of political power and produced the lucrative export crops.

The little industry that existed in Venezuela in the late nineteenth century included food processing, textiles, tobacco processing, wood working; most of these light industries also were found in the cities of the central coastal area. Some foreign investment had gone into railroads, roads, and communications to link the coastal cities with the interior and with overseas markets. Such modernization was still pitifully scarce, even allowing for the small and scattered population. By 1892, there were only 875 kilometers of railroads, 5,600 kilometers of telegraph line, and 1,477 telephones. Port facilities badly needed expansion and improvements, since they remained in much the same condition as the Spanish had left them in at the end of the colonial period.

The attractive Andean states (the Venezuelan "provinces" have been so called since the Constitution of 1811), with their healthful climate and coffee prosperity, made up the second most important region of the country. Although isolated from Caracas because of the lack of roads, the Andean states enjoyed a relative ease of communication through the maritime route of Lake Maracaibo. Táchira, Trujillo, and Mérida basked in the prosperity brought by the export of coffee, although their economic dependence on the fluctuating international prices and the foreign bankers and merchants of Maracaibo limited their development. *Latifundia* was less common in the Andes, and the self-reliant family farm was typical. The industrious *andinos* raised many crops in the temperate zones of the lower elevations, often within the view of the snow-covered and isolated peaks. The *páramos* had an alpine vegetation, including the beautiful *frailejón* plant so beloved by residents of the area. People of the Andean states frequently turned west toward Colombian towns and valleys for education, trade, and, when politics became too tense in Venezuela, also for exile. The *andinos*, with their Spanish and Indian heritage, retained a distinguishing touch of traditional dignity and courtesy which made them seem closer cousins to the aloof Colombians than to the warm and impulsive

Venezuelans of the coastal cities and plantations.

The *llanos*, the flat, low plains that lie between the Orinoco River and the coastal foothills, comprise the third major region of Venezuela. The *llanos* suffer from an unrelenting climate, with alternating droughts and floods. Codazzi wrote:

It seems a great gulf which is found in the midst of the land; it is a sea of grass which forms the horizon as far as the eye can see; it is a mediterranean bordered by the foothills and the immense jungles of Guayana; it is the true cattle region, for there livestock multiply almost without man's attention; it is the great breeding ground which supplies the agricultural zone with draft animals and meat for the sustenance of their people.[3]

The region knew little economic activity aside from livestock raising; towns were small, few, scattered, and ephemeral. The exception was Ciudad Bolívar, which had long been the major Orinoco port for the export of hides and pastoral products. Just as *tachirenses* often felt closer to Colombia, the residents of Ciudad Bolívar had formed close ties, principally economic, with the British colonies of British Guiana and Trinidad. Discovery of gold in the far south of Guayana in the late nineteenth century had created a new surge of smuggling in Ciudad Bolívar. Like the coastal region, there are also sub-regions in the *llanos*, distinguished by rivers, elevation, type of soil and vegetation. The *mestizo llaneros* had become legendary from their participation in the Independence Wars, the Federal Wars, and their fierce individualism. As Codazzi wrote:

The *llanos* are a perennial field of military instruction for their intrepid inhabitants. Accustomed from youth to break wild horses, to fight with bulls, to swim the raging rivers and to conquer the alligator and tiger in solitary combat, the *llaneros* are used to laughing at danger. When war draws them from their ordinary occupations, the enemy finds them already to be hardened soldiers.[4]

Less romantically, Miguel Otero Silva was later to write of the desolation of the *llanos*, so vulnerable to plagues which swept over the country.

In that hot and still noon, the treeless desolation of Ortiz, the fearsome message of its relics impress the observer. From a miserable *rancho* comes the death rattle of a man who sweated out his fever supported by the filthy threads of his hammock. Flies silently hover around him, green flies, fat, glistening, the only flash of activity, and the only sign of life among the mounds of dead horses.[5]

Public and private health services were notably lacking all over Venezuela, but possibly the tough *llaneros* suffered the most from the combination of the fierce climate and frequent epidemics.

Finally, we have the heart of darkness and of hope, the Guayana jungles and highlands which inspired the myth of El Dorado and the lost world of Sir Arthur Conan Doyle. It continued to be the repository of the national hopes of Venezuelans, hope that seemed about to be fulfilled with the discovery and exploitation of the gold mines of El Callao. This immense region south of the Orinoco River reaching to the Brazilian border provoked scholar and politician César Zumeta in 1900 to write to President Cipriano Castro from Paris: "Guayana is our reserve and future. Exploit it, General, and neither fortune or history will ever forget your name."[6] Neither President Castro nor subsequent presidents have been able to follow Zumeta's advice. Over half of the national territory, the Guayana highlands have remained the mysterious preserve of Indians, scattered miners, prospectors, and missionaries. No naturalist has fully answered the challenge of cataloging the variety of birds and plants, just as geographers have improved but little upon the 1841 survey of Agustín Codazzi. The hydroelectric potential of the great rivers — Orinoco, Caroní, Caura, Ventuari — obviously could not be realized by the debt-ridden Venezuela of 1900.

Nationally, coffee, cacao, and cattle accounted for 90 percent of Venezuelan exports in the 1890s. Yet the *1894 Anuario Estadístico* (Statistical Yearbook) records significant production of corn, black beans, potatoes, sugar, tobacco, plantains, rice, onions, wheat, rubber, cotton, and tomatoes, among other agricultural and forest products. In addition, the census turned up 6,345,560 livestock, only a modest increase over Codazzi's 1839 figure of 4,617,582. Both estimates should be viewed with caution, but the increment might be considered more striking in view of the destruction of herds by the civil conflicts of the 1840s, 1850s, and 1860s. A number of minerals also were listed in the official statistics, but gold was the most important. In short, the nation produced a wide variety of agricultural products, although it depended chiefly on the cash crops of coffee and cacao for export earnings.

Population

Climate and geography affected the distribution of economic activities. Logically then, distribution, growth patterns, density, and characteristics of the population in the late nineteenth century also roughly corresponded to geographic and economic variations. Any discussion of population distribution and characteristics before World War II must be accompanied by a warning that the statistical sources are considered seriously deficient. The first national census of 1873 indicated a modern concern for statistical description. In 1894, the Ministry of Development published the first *Anuario*

Estadístico which compiled, organized, and summarized national figures. Obviously the summaries could be no more reliable than the government officials who gathered and analyzed them. In the absence of other sources, they will have to suffice for a demographic portrait of Venezuela in the 1890s.

In 1894, there were 2,444,816 Venezuelans, with slightly more women than men. The indigenous population had grown from the 1839 estimate of 221,400 to 326,000. Only 44,129 foreigners resided in Venezuela, nearly twice as many men as women. The most numerous groups were Colombians (11,081), Spanish (13,558), English (6,154) and Italians (3,179). Citizens of the United States (232) only outnumbered the Danes (82) among groups which were identified. Racial and ethnic composition of the population is difficult to verify. At the beginning of the nineteenth century, national percentages were estimated at 20.3 percent white or European, 18.4 percent Indian, 45 percent pardo or mixed, and 16.3 percent black.[7] In 1889, the Indian percentages had fallen to 14.6 percent of the population, although the Indian population had risen slightly in absolute numbers. All estimates are exceedingly suspect because of the fallibility of the statistics and the official decision to eschew racial and ethnic labels after the Federal War. We can only say with confidence that the majority of the population were of mixed origin and that by 1890 race was not an issue of overwhelming concern. Moreover, no single ethnic group could claim to be the major source of a cultural or political nationalism.

Most of the population lived in rural areas or small towns. Indeed, only three cities had a population greater than 10,000, according to the 1881 census; and only twelve towns had more than 4,000 inhabitants.

Cumaná	6,257
Coro-La Vela	9,373
Barquisimento	8,044
Valencia	36,145
Caracas	55,638
Maracaibo	22,209
Puerto Cabello	9,698
La Victoria	5,313
Barcelona	7,124
Carúpano	6,133
Cuidad Bolívar	7,719
San Cristóbal	4,313
Mérida	4,025
Guanare	4,538
Villa de Cura	4,934[8]

Most of the cities lay in the coastal highlands or were coastal ports.

All but four had been founded in the sixteenth century: Barcelona, Carúpano, Ciuaad Bolívar, Villa de Cura. Most had been political-administrative centers for their states or provinces, ports or both. The general population density of the republic was only 2.55 persons per square kilometer in 1891. The coastal area had the greatest population density, but the population of the Federal District itself only constituted about 3.7 percent of the national population.

Persons per square kilometer

Coastal	52.3
Andean	13.7
Llanos	30.8
Guayana	3.2[9]

In general, the population growth rate was very slow at least until 1926. The destructive Independence War, the constant civil wars, the epidemics, and the low level of medical knowledge and care all contributed to the slow natural growth and the high infant mortality, which did not begin to decline until the 1930s. In 1898 the worst smallpox epidemic of the decade hit the city of Valencia; 6,000 persons contracted the disease, and 1,900 died. In 1891, life expectancy at birth was only thirty-one years. Only about 9 percent of the population in 1891 was over the age of fifty years.[10]

Nor was the quality of life good for the statistically average Venezuelan in 1890s. Only about 19 percent of the population was literate although, surprisingly, the proportions did not vary much for women and men. About 18 percent of the women could read and write, while about 20 percent of the men could. Legal marriages were the norm for only about 12 percent of the population, and the illegitimacy rate was around 60 percent. Of course, the marriage and legitimacy rates tell us nothing about the stability or instability of consensual unions.

As one might expect, the vast majority of the working population was employed in agriculture. The *Anuario Estadístico* of 1894 provided the accompanying breakdown of employment.[11] Again, one is struck by the significant presence of women in categories such as merchant, artisan, liberal professions, and public administration. The large number of women in the personal service category is less surprising. We might speculate that the relatively poverty-stricken life of colonial Venezuela and the upheavals of the nineteenth century had done little to encourage stable family units, but had of necessity encouraged some economic self-sufficiency among the women.

Profession	Men	Women
Agriculture, livestock	348,103	28,053
Merchants	40,908	1,908
Artisans	50,386	85,302
Personal service	65,587	211,143
Liberal professions	6,696	1,046
Medical professions	1,207	273
Public Administration	3,317	3,675
Clergy and religious orders	456	72
Sailors and watermen	8,334	7
Miners	1,052	—
Public safety	5,501	—
Military officers	536	—
Unclassified	584,937	1,065,131

In very general terms then, the Venezuelan population on the brink of the twentieth century was unhealthy, illiterate, unmarried, rural, concentrated in the coastal belt, and numbered just over 2 million. These demographic patterns had been produced by climate, geography, pestilence, civil war, and the demands of plantation agriculture, dotted with mining enclaves and urban commerce.

Politics, Administration, Foreign Relations

Venezuela's geography, economic patterns, and population set the limits and the rationale for the politics of the late nineteenth century. The decade of the 1890s was a transitional period, in which elite groups—regional and national—and personalistic cliques vied for the presidential mantle that strongman Antonio Guzmán Blanco had abandoned in 1888. The significant conflicts underlying the trivial political squabbles were not new; should political and economic power be centralized in Caracas or divided among the states, and should the slight departures from *laissez-faire* liberalism favor the coffee and cattle *hacendados* equally with urban merchants and bankers? In a country in which all had claimed to be "liberals" since the destructive Federal War (1859–63), there were few if any advocates of industrialization, land reform, or socialism. There had been few European immigrants, no critical mass of *campesinos*, virtually no labor movement, and no intellectually radical tradition to spawn real dissent.

Before surveying the 1890 political clashes, it is useful to summarize some of the accomplishments of President Guzmán Blanco. During his eighteen years in power, he initiated the irreversible concentration of power in the central government at Caracas. Astutely, he allowed the *caudillos* to control political patronage and the disbursements of the Regional Development Juntas in their states. The regional *caudillos* received lucrative state monopolies and concessions. After 1881, their national prestige grew when they were called upon to "elect" the president through the Federal Council. The *caudillos* tacitly accepted a surrender of individual and state autonomy as long as they were permitted to share in the national wealth and power. It was a pragmatic, if tentative, solution in a sparsely populated nation where few *caudillos* could command sufficient force to rule the nation alone.

Guzmán's culminating efforts at control came in the Constitution of 1881, which replaced direct, popular, and secret suffrage with indirect suffrage. The new constitution reduced the number of states from twenty to nine, which meant that there were fewer *caudillos* to placate, and limited the presidential term to two years. Thus Guzmán's handpicked substitutes in the executive mansion would not have time to build up a personal following.

The policies which Guzmán implemented were not unusual for late nineteenth-century Latin America. He broke the already slight power of the Catholic Church in Venezuela, encouraged public education and foreign investment in railroads, roads, and telegraph systems, called for foreign immigration, and initiated an ambitious and ostentatious public construction program. He favored modernizing merchants and bankers over traditional or commercial planters. He expanded the size and scope of public administration. If the Ministry of Development was the first step away from classic liberalism in 1863, Guzmán accentuated the trend by creating the Ministries of Public Works (1874) and Public Instruction (1881). Except for the ephemeral existence of a Ministry of Mail and Telephones in the 1890s, the seven ministries remained virtually the same until the Ministries of Health, Agriculture and Livestock appeared in 1931.

Even with the expansion of public administration under Guzmán, the size and expenditures of the national government remained moderate. In 1894, total government revenues were Bs. 51,919,795.77 and were distributed among the ministeries as follows:

	Bolívares
Ministry of Interior Relations	10,688,192.15
Ministry of Development	3,009,729.42
Ministry of Public Instruction	3,183,918.16
Ministry of Treasury and Public Credit	4,402,394.36
Ministry of War and Navy	13,175,369.60
Ministry of Foreign Relations	2,380,550.34
Ministry of Public Works	4,449,641.74[12]

Guzmán Blanco did have opposition: spokesmen for the Church, farmers who futilely sought credit and protection from the government, and some regional *caudillos*. Representatives of Guayana and Zulia often bristled because their states had surrendered considerable state incomes—gold for Guayana and customs revenues for Zulia—in exchange for the national subsidies to the states. Other special interests at times resented Guzmán Blanco's disregard for their well-being; when Guzmán closed the port of Coro-La Vela in a squabble with the Dutch government, the merchants of the port understandably protested the interruption of their lucrative trade with Curaçao.

In spite of all the economic complaints, Guzmán had more to fear from other ambitious *caudillos*. After his more or less voluntary retirement in 1888, the competition to see who would succeed him began in earnest. Until his death in 1899 in Paris, Guzmán continued to intervene in Venezuelan politics, frequently through his kinsman and financier Manuel Antonio Matos, but his approval no longer carried the same weight. He might have averted some of the struggles of the 1890s by choosing and sticking with one strong contender. His first choice to succeed him as president was Dr Juan Pablo Rojas Paúl, who served from 1888 to 1890. A relatively enlightened intellectual who encouraged the founding of the National Historical Academy (*Academia Nacional de la Historia*), Rojas was too old and ill to consolidate an independent position in the face of some continuing loyalty to Guzmán and the rising star of the younger *llanero*, Joaquín Crespo. He named another civilian intellectual as his successor, and he hoped that Dr Raimundo Andueza Palacio would be loyal enough to return the presidential chair in 1892. Unfortunately, Andueza Palacio also tried to develop his own following and found in 1892 that most of Congress, Crespo, Rojas Paúl, "*El Mocho*" Hernández of Guayana and most of the other local *caudillos* opposed him.

Andueza's effort to revise the Constitution of 1881 provided the pretext for the seven-months *Revolución Legalista* (Legalist Revolution) of 1892, which Crespo hastened to lead before anyone else could. Andueza proposed to lengthen the presidential term to four years, to return to the twenty states of the 1864 Constitution, and to provide for direct, popular, universal suffrage instead of the indirect system that Guzmán Blanco had arranged. In fact, many of Andueza's opponents also favored the changes, but objected to Andueza's intention of remaining in power. The only *caudillos* of note who supported Andueza were young Cipriano Castro of Táchira and Manuel Antonio Matos; thus Crespo triumphed at the head of a diverse group of liberals, conservatives, regional *caudillos* and other opponents of Andueza. No coherent economic or political view predominated in the "Revolution."

The revolt did usher in the strongest and most skillful of the contenders for Guzmán Blanco's position. Crespo had held the presidency from 1884 to 1886 and then loyally turned it back to Guzmán. A *llanero* with wide military and political experience, he was also fortunate in the political and economic acumen of his wife Jacinta who had run the family businesses while he was in exile, and participated in military campaigns with him. Perhaps her forte was political intrigue, a skill she put to good use during the 1892 revolt. When her husband came to power, she enjoyed sitting in on cabinet meetings and frequently offered advice. Dr Juan Pietri, Secretary of State of the Revolution, in 1893 boldly, and unwisely, objected to Crespo that women's opinions were not welcome in the councils of state. Pietri soon tendered his resignation, to be replaced by José Antonio Velutini who valued Doña Jacinta's opinions more highly.

. Crespo was provisional president from 1892 until 1894, presiding over a Constituent Congress (1893) which effected the very reforms that he had ostensibly revolted against. In 1893, he was elected to a four-year presidential term in a universal, direct, and secret vote. In the adroit management of competing *caudillos* he proved a worthy successor of Guzmán.

Crespo realized that many would-be revolutionaries would lay down their arms if the price were right. He refused to form a narrow government only of his friends and of the "yellow" faction of the liberal party. When the financier and kinsman of Guzmán Blanco, Manuel Antonio Matos, headed a conspiracy in 1895, Crespo sent him a tempting message: Matos could enter the cabinet as Minister of the Treasury and could, if he wished, name all the other ministers. Matos could not resist. In general Crespo exercised what his contemporary, César Zumeta, called "*cesarismo plebiscitario*"; when one minister was criticized, Crespo replaced him with another. Thus, in the manner of Emperor Pedro II of Brazil, Crespo appeared to respond to the popular will and could escape some criticism himself. He also took care not to favor one potential successor or colleague over another. His caginess meant that the competitors schemed against each other rather than against him.

Those who could not be won over could expect exile, jail, or military action, although there were relatively few armed revolts against Crespo. Yet, the President was a generous rather than a vengeful *caudillo*. Jail or exile might be followed quickly by amnesty and even, as with Matos, an offer of a position in the government. The most severe action taken by Crespo occurred when he first came to power in 1892 and still heeded the advice of Juan Pietri. The government charged functionaries and *caudillos* of previous governments with misdeeds in office, and initiated a series of trials to establish their guilt. Caracas University students and José Manuel Hernández, *"El Mocho"* (see below), lauded the trials as a means of enforcing administrative honesty. Doña Jacinta Crespo, with a sharp political sense and with wide family and social contacts, showed less enthusiasm; she supported José Antonio Velutini, who called for clemency toward the former officials, and was instrumental in Velutini's rise and in the decision to drop the trials.

Mass opposition was virtually unknown in Venezuela, but the first organized protest of 3,000 unemployed artisans did take place in Caracas during Crespo's presidency in January 1895. The Governor of the Federal District announced that socialism would not be tolerated in Venezuela and promptly arrested the artisans.

Crespo's most effective opponent was José Manuel Hernández, nicknamed *El Mocho* (the maimed) because of several missing fingers. The son of a Caracas carpenter and immigrant from the Canary Islands, Hernández had mixed in local politics in the state of Guayana and become associated with the state's local resistance to Guzmán Blanco's centralization. *El Mocho* had little ideological consistency, and at times his political acumen faltered. Yet his personal and oratorical appeal gained a great following among small businessmen, farmers and priests of the rural interior who wanted more attention paid to their problems or "new faces" in the government. During the 1893 Constituent Assembly, Hernández appealed to the students of Caracas University as well when he opposed clemency for the functionaries of the Andueza government, called for the elimination of monopoly concessions to government favorites, and a return to the 1864 Constitution with its twenty states. He especially opposed Guzmán's economic centralization and charged that the channelling of national wealth through Caracas was one of the sources of administrative corruption and peculation. *El Mocho* objected to the increasing power of the President and preferred strengthening Congressional power. Logically, he also resisted the placement of national military forces in the provinces. The quirks of Venezuelan political history decreed that *El Mocho* be termed a "conservative," since the followers and heirs of Guzmán Blanco claimed the mantle of liberalism that fell upon the winners of the Federal War. Further research may answer more fully the question whether Hernández wished to "conserve" the traditional and reactionary power of the local *caudillos* or to "liberate" small businesses of the interior (Venezuelans refer thus to the nation outside

Caracas) from the overpowering, and wasteful, control of the central Government.

At any rate, Hernández's presidential candidacy in the 1897 election broke with tradition. Sponsored by the Liberal Nationalist Party, *El Mocho* conducted the first "modern" presidential campaign in Venezuelan history. He realized that the Constitutional reform which had revived direct, universal suffrage would allow him to apply some of the tactics he had witnessed during the 1896 election in the United States. He traveled widely in Venezuela, organized local juntas to support his candidacy, and fired off letters even to people he did not know asking for support. At least forty-two newspapers sprang up to endorse his candidacy and advertise his program in an election which attracted more popular excitement than any since 1846. He endorsed widening the suffrage to eighteen-year-olds, and he speculated to a friendly newspaper editor on the advisability of allowing women to vote. The editor quickly responded that that would be too revolutionary even for *El Mocho*. Perhaps *El Mocho* was more naive than revolutionary, since he apparently did not believe that President Joaquín Crespo would control the electoral process to ensure victory of his chosen candidate, Ignacio Andrade.

After Crespo's forces seized the municipal plazas in the first stage of voting, the outcome was predictable. Andrade won 406,610 votes, and Hernández 2,203, with minority candidates Rojas Paúl (203), Guzmán Blanco (152), and Nicolás Rolando (31) dividing up a few other votes. Genuinely surprised and disappointed, rather like Francisco Madero of Mexico in 1910,* Hernández issued the *Proclama* of Queipa in rebellion against *continuismo* and centralism. The *Proclama* reiterated most of his earlier views.

Crespo determined to ratify his position as strongman and

*Francisco I. Madero, a liberal and rather naive politician, ran for the presidency of Mexico in 1910. His opponent was the incumbent dictator, Porfirio Díaz, who had held power since 1876, except for the years 1880–84. Madero lost the obviously staged election and challenged the results. Díaz's courts upheld Díaz's election. Madero was, however, allowed to escape from prison where he had been placed at the conclusion of the election. He fled to Texas and announced that he was leading a revolt against Díaz. The action, much to the surprise of Díaz, precipitated a major national revolt which finally unseated the old dictator in 1911. As he went into exile, Díaz is rumored to have said: "Madero has unleashed a tiger; let us see if he can control it." Madero ruled from 1911 until 1913 before being overthrown and assassinated by his enemies. Full-scale civil war ensued again until General Venustiano Carranza gained control in 1916 and allowed the radical Constitution of 1917 to be promulgated. The civil wars between 1910 and 1917 are known collectively as the Mexican Revolution.

incidentally to assure his return to the presidency in 1902. He quickly volunteered to lead a military force against the Hernández rebellion. On 16 April 1898 at La Mata Carmelera, not far from Cojedes, Crespo died in battle at the age of fifty-seven.

Crespo's death threw the country into a paroxysm of warring factions again. The official yellow liberals divided into *crespistas*, *andradistas*, and various other minor groups. *El Mocho* Hernández did not capitalize on the opportunity by marching on Caracas, and his delays allowed President Andrade time enough to rally some forces. *El Mocho* was captured and imprisoned less than two months after Crespo's death. The elimination of the two men who could easily command a large following — Crespo and Hernández — cleared the stage for the appearance of a new star and hero.

Andrade tried, but he was not adequate for the role. He followed the example of Crespo and tried to identify himself with the Hernández issue of returning to the twenty states of the federation. His motives were not only to be identified with the reform, but a canny judgment that twenty state *caudillos*, checked by twenty military commanders, would be easier to dominate than nine powerful ones. As always, constitutional reform responded to chosen tactics for control of the nation rather than to ideological, or legal, rationale. Predictably, many who opposed Andrade's constitutional change did so not because they objected to the change, but because they rejected his political ambitions. Among those who had returned from exile at the death of Crespo was the Táchira *caudillo* Cipriano Castro.

Castro had supported Andueza's government in 1892, and when Andueza lost, Castro retreated into self-imposed exile in Colombia. He made a tentative effort to rejoin the fray in 1897 when he sent word to President Crespo that he opposed the liberal candidacy of Andrade. Crespo laconically replied: "Too late for advice, too early for threats."[13] In late 1898, Castro would find a more propitious time both for his advice and his threats.

Venezuelan leaders in the 1890s devoted most of their attention to internal politics. The nation could hardly be said to have had a foreign policy. In most cases, the Caracas government simply reacted to European pressures or initiatives. Yet Venezuelan leaders chose carefully among alternative actions, assuring a small measure of control over events. The major disputes between the powers and Venezuela concerned Venezuela's foreign debt and foreign claims, economic and political relations with European Caribbean colonies, defense of national territory against foreign encroachment, and treatment of foreigners who wished to conduct business in

Venezuela. The resolution of these issues was fated to be played out in the context of the struggle between the United States and European nations for control of the Caribbean and the isthmian passageway. The major pawns in this competition proved to be Cuba, Venezuela, Colombia and Panama. It is worth noting that Venezuela alone secured United States protection without a formal loss of national sovereignity or territory.

As with the domestic political structure, President Guzmán Blanco had set in motion the events which would generate the crises of the late nineteenth century. He had actively sought European loans, frequently under unfavorable conditions for the Venezuelan government. While Guzmán personally became wealthy from the commissions he raked off on these negotiations, the Venezuelan debt increased far beyond the ability to repay, especially when customs revenues or coffee prices dropped.

President Guzmán Blanco also refused, with reason, to satisfy foreigners who registered claims against the Venezuelan government. Perhaps the most serious case was that of the *Compañía de Transporte por Vapor de Venezuela*, a New York company which had secured the concession for steam navigation on the Orinoco River in 1869. Some of the company's ships were captured or damaged during the revolutionary activity and blockades which accompanied Guzmán Blanco's rise to the Presidency. Guzmán pointed out that the 1869 decree which had authorized foreign navigation of the river had specifically denied the concessionaires the right to international reclamation in the case of losses or disputes. Nevertheless, the US Department of State insisted until President Crespo in 1894 agreed to accept the decision of an international arbitration committee. The Committee in 1895 awarded the company $141,500, still short of the $360,000 asked for. More serious international problems required the Venezuelan government to yield the legal point in order to secure the assistance of the United States government.

In the 1890s, the British government threatened Venezuelan sovereignity, security, and territory. Great Britain, eager for possession of the gold mines in Venezuela's Guayana and for control of the vital mouth of the Orinoco River, asserted that British Guiana's boundary reached west of the mouth of the Orinoco; Venezuelans countered that the original Spanish boundary had been at the Esequibo River, 160 miles to the southeast. The British refused to arbitrate or to back down. Venezuelans feared an alliance between Colombia to the west and Great Britain in which Venezuela would lose control of the Orinoco and be cut off from the vast, resource-rich Guayana south of the great river. After the Venezuelan government settled the outstanding claim with the United States, Washington forced the British to accept arbitration of the Guiana boundary. The US Secretary of State Richard Olney brashly announced that "the United States was practically sovereign in this hemisphere," but the British government was probably more influenced by the practical problem of the Boer War in South Africa. The 1899 arbitration decision set the boundary just to the east of the Orinoco, assuring Venezuelan control of the river's delta but conceding to British Guiana 60,000 square miles of Venezuelan territory. As a weak and relatively unstable nation, Venezuela could do nothing but accept the decision.

By no means were Venezuelan relations with the United States to be harmonious during the next century. Yet the wisdom of requesting US intervention was clear; Venezuela, alone among the Latin American nations, faced a strong European nation across a border which offered no geographical barriers to expansion. British Guiana and Trinidad were British sentinels looking toward the western gold and asphalt in the lightly populated Venezuelan territory. The United States could not, or would not, guarantee the Esequibo territory to Venezuela, but did ensure the more important objectives of control of the Orinoco and Guayana.

Indeed, Venezuela even occasionally wielded a "little stick" in the region. Again due to an initiative of Guzmán Blanco, the Venezuelan government complained that the Caribbean islands encouraged smuggling and harbored dissident Venezuelan exiles. When the islands refused to cooperate with the Venezuelan government, Guzmán Blanco issued a 30 percent tax on all goods imported from the Caribbean. The tax remained in force with few breaks until the 1960s. Guzmán's action damaged the island economies and angered island leaders, but it was intended not as an anti-Caribbean gesture, but as an anti-European one. Guzmán's true Caribbean objectives were probably best revealed by his encouragement of Cuban revolutionaries. Despite protests from the Spanish Consul in 1871, the Venezuelan President permitted Cuban exiles to organize in Venezuela an expedition which planned to overthrow the Spanish government in Cuba. The expedition failed, but the Venezuelan role pointed up a lingering dream of a Caribbean which would be free of European colonies.

If it was impossible to force the foreign powers to leave the region, the next-best policy was to try to play them off against each other. Around 1880 President Guzmán Blanco had invited the General Transatlantic Steamship Company of France to exercise a number of concessions in Venezuela, one of which would give them the monopoly to establish a mint in Ciudad Bolívar on the Orinoco.

They would control the mining region, a lucrative enough proposition to attract a sizeable French colony to the region. The resident British Minister to Venezuela saw the objective as one to establish a strong French presence on Venezuela's weak eastern flank which faced the British colonies. The scheme was unpopular with Venezuelans, and perhaps not attractive enough to the French, and failed. It does suggest that Guzmán Blanco saw the merits of checking one foreign power by means of concessions to another.

Encouraging United States investment and commerce in Venezuela accomplished the same purpose of countering the traditional dominance of the British and Germans. Mercantile families of British origin controlled trade with the Orinoco and eastern Venezuela; the Boulton family in particular held sway over commerce at La Guaira. Many Germans controlled the financing and marketing of Táchira coffee from the western ports of Maracaibo and Coro-La Vela. Individual United States citizens began to trickle in, and in 1896 the National Association of Manufacturers (NAM) opened an office in Caracas. Even more important as signaling a new era, the New York and Bermúdez Company, a subsidiary of General Asphalt of Philadelphia, in 1887 began to exploit the asphalt concession in the eastern area of Guanoco. The advantages and disadvantages of allowing foreign companies to compete for trade and mineral concessions would be seen more clearly in the petroleum epoch yet to come.

In sum, by the end of the 1890s, Venezuelans had already tentatively chosen some political, administrative, and foreign patterns which they would continue to strengthen in the century to come. Caracas had won control over the politics and economics of the nation; neither state *caudillos* nor regional economic entrepreneurs would be able to act without securing the patronage and consent of the national government. The national government also initiated the timid beginnings of the state commitment to a responsibility for national economic development. The Ministry of Development represented a logical move, for an underpopulated and divided nation, away from classical laissez-faire. These choices naturally facilitated an accretion of power to the President rather than to the Congress. Bureaucracy began to burgeon with the creation of the new ministries, and provided the President with a potentially loyal group of intellectuals, advisers, and followers. With the defeat of *El Mocho* Hernández and with the other centralizing tendencies, the need for a national army to replace the state militias gained in importance. Finally, the Venezuelan government chose to welcome foreign investment and tried to prevent any one external power from becoming too omnipotent. The nearly inevitable favorite protector was the United States, which presented less of an immediate threat than neighboring Great Britain.

Other paths remained open and subsequent patterns were indeed much influenced by the rise of petroleum. Statesmen had to find a way to lessen national vulnerability to international economic fluctuations when the economy depended on exporting primary products such as coffee, cacao, gold, asphalt, and eventually oil. What roles would industry, commerce, agriculture, extractive minerals, foreign trade and balance of payments have in the future? Should *laissez-faire* economics give way to socialism or state capitalism? These questions could not be answered quickly.

A related choice yet to be made was the decision of how the national wealth was to be distributed. Which groups should benefit from government protection and sponsorship? The national government would channel the revenues through Caracas, but to whom? To the elite and friends of the governing party? Should the opportunity be open to persons of talent from the lower ranks of society? What decisions should be made with respect to artisans, labor, *campesinos*? How should the national wealth be distributed between the capital and the interior? Which areas of the national economy would foreigners be allowed to enter freely? What percentage of the national revenues should be allowed to go to foreigners? Under what conditions? These questions would become more intense when the national wealth became greater.

Finally, there remained the question of the Venezuelan role in the Caribbean. Would a quiescent attitude toward United States protection continue to guarantee national sovereignty? Would belligerence toward the European colonies in the Caribbean facilitate the exit of the European nations from the region, or result in reprisals from Europe?

Venezuelan twentieth-century Presidents and parties would experiment with different answers to these questions of national development. Politicians who had grown up in the Venezuela of coffee and cacao reacted differently from those who reached adulthood in the first flush of the post-World War I oil boom.

Intellectual attitudes and styles, interpreted by Venezuelan cultural elites, influenced the development of national identity. Perception of national identity and role flavored the subsequent political choices. As with many Latin American nations, nationalism first appeared in *criollista* literature, which sought to portray the essence of the nation and its cultural tradition.

Literature, Art, Science, Culture

When Don Arístides Rojas died in 1894, the news of his death occupied more space in Caracas newspapers than did the simultaneous election of Joaquín Crespo to the presidency. Rojas, an outstanding writer and intellectual, had begun to popularize Venezuelan historical and poetic themes in *Leyendas históricas de Venezuela* (Historical Legends of Venezuela), *Estudios históricos* (Historical Studies), and *Origenes Venezolanos* (Venezuelan Origins). The veneration that he received testified to the beginnings of *criollismo* in Venezuela.

The Venezuelan government had already assumed some responsibility for patronage of the arts, just as it had with economic development. The late nineteenth century saw the founding of the National Library, the *Instituto de Bellas Artes*, the organization of the national archives, the creation of the *Academia Nacional de Historia*, and provision of funds for the collection and publication of historical manuscripts. The Director of the *Instituto de Bellas Artes* was also responsible for the scenic arts in the 1870s. Chairs of art and sculpture appeared at the *Universidad Central de Venezuela* as did chairs and societies for the promotion of science. Scientific research received some government support in the 1890s and also reflected a new national concern; doctors and laboratory technicians such as José Gregorio Hernández and Rafael Rangél initiated research and treatment of Venezuelan tropical parasites and diseases.

The late nineteenth century was, of course, the age of positivism all over Latin America. Dating from about the 1860s, Venezuelan intellectuals had seized upon the tenets of Auguste Comte, mixed with generous doses of the social Darwinian notions of Herbert Spencer. Arturo Uslar Pietri argues that the Venezuelan positivists before 1900 were relatively optimistic, liberal and reformist; after that time they became more pessimistic and disillusioned about Venezuelan progress.[14] Of course, Venezuelans had some hope in the 1890s that the successors of Antonio Guzmán Blanco would be able to institute a stable and legitimate government. The death of Joaquín Crespo dashed those hopes, and the succession of foreign crises in the first decade of the twentieth century further contributed to a national loss of confidence.

In painting and the visual arts, three great muralists of the Guzmán Blanco epoch all died around 1900: Martín Tovar y Tovar (*d.* 1902), Arturo Michelena (d. 1898), and Cristóbal Rojas (*d.* 1890). Only Antonio Herrera Toro was to see the end of Cipriano Castro's rule; his death in 1914 truly ended the cycle of early nationalistic painters. The paintings of the four had been a magnificent celebration of the Venezuelan national spirit and heroes. Their subjects naturally were elite leaders like Simón Bolívar and the generation of independence leaders. Mexican artist David Siquieros thought that Venezuela had the greatest muralists of the nineteenth century; he especially admired Martín Tovar y Tovar's two famous works: the battle of Carabobo and the signing of the act of independence.[15] Art historian Alfredo Boulton argues that these murals aided the development of a national consciousness and pride among the illiterate population that lived in or passed through Caracas. Subsequent generations of painters showed more interest in the varied landscape of Venezuela, perhaps in unconscious agreement with the literary positivists that national heroes after Bolívar's generation had proven unworthy of the Liberator's mantle.

The heroic muralists came to prominence at the same time as a new generation of novelists. The 1890 publication of Manuel Vicente Romero García's (1865–1917) *Peonía* marked the effective beginning of the authentically Venezuelan novel. For the first time Venezuelan readers encountered the themes of the struggle of man against nature or against social organization, the conflict between barbarism (usually rural) and civilization (usually urban), and the quest for modernization. Romero García had also gained fame as a man of action for his journalistic opposition to Guzmán Blanco, which had earned him a record fourteen or fifteen visits to the prison La Rotunda by 1888. He was also a founder of the organization *Unión Democrática* (1889), which loosely mixed positivism and romanticism with political reforms such as proportional representation of minorities.

The newest of the arts — film — appeared in Venezuela in 1897. Following a performance of the opera in Maracaibo, an entrepreneur presented two locally made films. Venezuelan film-maker Manuel Trujillo Durán must have been gratified at the enthusiastic reception that *Muchacho bañándose en la Laguna de Maracaibo* (Boy bathing in Lake Maracaibo) received.

Unfortunately, there was little meeting of the popular and elite cultures during the 1890s. The strong folk traditions of the rural areas with their mixture of Indian, Spanish, and African roots found expression in fiestas, folk tales, and song, especially the *contrapunto* of the *llanos*. The elite applauded the classical career of Teresa Carreño (1853–1917), a prodigy and pianist who took Europe by storm, but the rural people kept alive the true folk music and dances such as the *joropo*.

The traditional folktales of the *campesinos* perhaps give a clue to the popular mentality of late nineteenth century. The ever-present figures of Tío Conejo (Uncle Rabbit) and Tío Tigre (Uncle Tiger) were the most popular of the animal protagonists of country tales. Most of the tales celebrated the triumph of a peculiarly Venezuelan *astucia* or *viveza* (cleverness). Strangely, the rabbit usually outwitted the more powerful and rapacious tiger and earned popular sympathy. Other constants of Venezuelan folktales were the abhorrence of pure power, the admiration of cleverness and deceit, the beliefs that wealth or other advantages arrived through a stroke of luck, that equality was more important than liberty, and that the purpose of justice was not to remedy the wrong, but to punish and castigate the powerful.

Some tales did have human protagonists rather than animals, but no important ones were female. The typical males were Juan Bobo, the country yokel, and Pedro Rimales, the sharp city slicker. The sympathy usually lay with Rimales who, like Tío Conejo, possessed the *viveza* to outwit his challengers. Thus, inherent weakness or strength mattered less than the possession of *viveza*, the characteristic which linked the weaker rabbit and the stronger urbanite.

As with the *contrapunto* music of the *llanero*, the narrative technique which expressed these tales was dramatic. The teller acted out the sayings and the plot. These folktales might have been the source for a rich and varied national theatrical tradition, if there had been a meeting between the countryside and the city. Without meaningful contact, the folk culture would languish, nearly forgotten in the rural areas, while the urban elite seized and formalized the urban folk traditions or received inspiration from brief visits to the rural *haciendas* or *llanos*.[16]

Folk religion also expressed folk wisdom and tradition. Variations could be found from region to region in accord with the peculiar distribution of Indians, Africans, Spaniards, and missionary orders. Various syncretisms maintained some vitality in the small towns and countryside, at the same time as President Guzmán Blanco attacked the Catholic Church, making way for the dissemination of more secular universal values in the cities. The cult of María Lionza, the dances of the day of San Juan, the dancing devils of Yare, the dance of El Carite in the Oriente and Margarita, and folk Christmas music and traditions continued to be strong in the small towns and rural areas.

The cult of María Lionza differed from many of the rural and folk traditions in its strength and its ability to thrive also in urban Venezuela. Based on the legend of an Indian girl who became a protector of animals and nature, the cult's principal sanctuary was near Chivacoa in the state of Lara. Shamans or mediums of the cult would fall into a trance, often induced partly by smoking cigars.

They used their magic to solve personal problems or to cure illnesses among cult members. María Lionza was often portrayed as a beautiful young woman who rode on the back of a tapir.

Rural sports also varied from region to region. The *llanos* became known for the *toros coleados*, a form of bullfighting in which the bull is thrown by his tail. The game which was eventually to capture the enthusiasm of Venezuelans — baseball — originated in the 1890s, as a recreation of the Caracas upper classes. Some Venezuelan students who had been studying in the United States taught their cohorts the game and provided the balls, bats and gloves. In 1895, the first baseball club was formed in Caracas, signalling the triumph of US baseball over British cricket. But not even baseball could withstand the upheavals of 1897–9, and the game went into a brief eclipse in Caracas until its revival on the new field of El Paraíso in 1902.

Venezuelan culture of the 1890s displayed a new vitality after the exhaustion of the civil wars of the nineteenth century. Some new currents, such as *criollismo* or positivism, corresponded to similiar trends in other American nations, although the expression was uniquely Venezuelan. Hope or despair for the future derived from Venezuela, its political system, its economy, its landscape, its intellectuals, its people.

Continuity with the past was to be broken in the 1890s largely because of the untimely death of the talented Joaquín Crespo and because of the increasing interest of the imperial powers in the resources and strategic value of the Caribbean nation. Major political and international events between 1899 and 1903 would set the tone for Venezuela's twentieth century. The vacuum left by the death of Crespo would be filled by *tachirense* Cipriano Castro and his colleague Juan Vicente Gómez. Further, the boundary dispute with the British and the English-German-Italian blockade of 1902–3 compelled Venezuelan leaders to seek assistance and protection from the United States.

The ascendency of the Táchira *caudillos* and the United States dominance in the Caribbean provided the background against which the subsequent financing and development of the Venezuelan petroleum industry would be played out. In abstract terms, the events of the 1890s cleared the way for the development of the Venezuelan political system, economy, and international role. Yet, it is important to stress that Venezuela in 1899 was no *tabula rasa* on which oil magnates and foreign governments would be able to scribble freely. It was already the nation of Martín Tovar y Tovar, of Simón Bolívar, of César Zumeta, of Cipriano Castro, Teresa Carreño, of *Peonía*, Doña Jacinta, of films, the *Academia de*

Historia and of the *Universidad Central de Venezuela*, of *El Mocho* Hernández, María Lionza, baseball, and Tío Conejo and Tío Tigre.

NOTES

1. Mariano Picón Salas, *Comprensión de Venezuela* (Caracas: Monte Avila, 1976), p. 101.
2. Agustín Codazzi, *Resumen de la geografía de Venezuela* (Caracas: Ministerio de Educación Nacional, 1940), Vol. I, p. 62.
3. Ibid., p. 78.
4. Ibid.
5. Miguel Otero Silva, *Casas Muertas* (1955; reprinted, Caracas: Editorial Tiempo Nuevo, 1973), pp. 135–6.
6. Francisco Salazar Martínez, *Tiempo de Compadres* (Caracas: Librería Piñango, 1972), p. 58.
7. Chi-Yi Chen and Michel Picouet, *Dinámica de la población: caso de Venezuela* (Caracas: Edición UCAB-ORSTOM, 1979), p. 21.
8. Ibid., p. 20.
9. Ibid., p. 45.
10. Ibid., pp. 33–4.
11. Venezuela, *Anuario Estadístico* 1894, pp. 120–4.
12. Ibid., p. 271.
13. Manuel Alfredo Rodríguez, *El capitolio de Caracas* (Caracas: Ediciones del Congreso de la República, 1974), p. 423.
14. Arturo Uslar Pietri, *Letras y hombres de Venezuela*, 4th edn (Madrid: Editorial Mediterraneo, 1978), p. 235.
15. Alfredo Boulton, *Historia abreviada de la pintura en Venezuela* (Caracas: Monte Avila, 1971), Vol. II, pp. 53–4.
16. Uslar Pietri, pp. 245–51.

2

THE FAILURE OF THE GENERATION OF REINALDO SOLAR AND THE TRIUMPH OF THE TACHIRENSES, 1899–1922

"There is my destiny! My homeland! The incomparable beauty of my homeland cries out, calling me in the light and the color of its landscape, in the desolation of its poverty, in the infinite joy of the sunlight! In the sadness of its dead cities, without a past! In the fascination of its mirages; in the silence of its deserts. In the restless, tragic wind which floats over the abyss of shadows in the buried soul of my race. In the shout of horror of one who is ambushed; in the wail of one who is consumed by barren lust; in the delirium of one who embraces the invisible flame of fever; in the lost voice in the plains that sings homesickness for forgotten homelands; of those who came in caravels and in slave ships, and of those who saw their tribes destroyed and their gods replaced!"[1]

Rómulo Gallegos

The year 1899 signaled an end to the confidence and relative stability of the 1890s. In that last year of the century, civil war again swept the country, this time headed by *andinos* of Táchira. The price of Venezuela's major export, coffee, dropped drastically in the international market. The Paris Tribunal handed down its decision in the boundary dispute between Great Britain and Venezuela, and Britain won nearly 90 percent of the territory claimed. Finally, rising interest in the Panama Canal and Spain's ejection from the Caribbean lured other European nations to expand their influence in the region. Venezuela, at least indirectly, would be a pawn in the final challenge launched by European nations toward United States domination of the Caribbean.

Even with the inauspicious beginning of the twentieth century, the two Táchira *caudillos*, Cipriano Castro and Juan Vicente Gómez, directed Venezuela toward its first real modernization. They completed the centralization which Antonio Guzmán Blanco had begun. Between 1899 and 1922, they prevailed over and virtually eliminated the strength of the regional *caudillos*, and Gómez destroyed the remnants of the traditional political parties. Prompted by foreign threats and inspired by the centennial celebration of the nation's independence in 1910–11, they built up the armed forces. Gómez oversaw the organization and rationalizing of national accounts and tax collection. Two relatively new self-conscious national elites acquired importance: the Caracas financial barons and the intellectuals. The *caudillos* used men of talent,

36

education, and expertise as long as they were loyal. Physical order and civil order were both served by the new network of roads that the government constructed. By 1922 — before petroleum wealth became the major dynamic force in the nation — Venezuela had wiped out some of the sources of the political instability, poverty, and insecurity which had plagued it in the nineteenth century.

Tradition did however, remain, as debilitating to society as it was invigorating to the *criollista* novels and paintings. A laissez-faire philosophy and a relatively meagre national income meant that little money was spent on public health, education, or other public services. Disastrous epidemics swept the nation, most notably in 1908 and 1918. The inadequate schools and universities that existed were often closed in retaliation for student demonstrations. Gas, electricity, and public transportation remained in the control of national or foreign entrepreneurs. Congress, the courts, and government ministers served at the whim of the President. Critics could choose martyrdom, prison, or exile. The Gómez prisons, especially those in Caracas, Puerto Cabello, and Maracaibo, became notorious throughout the hemisphere, as did his torture and mistreatment of political prisoners. Rural areas received few benefits from the nascent order and prosperity. Urban workers' feeble protests evoked no response but police violence and long prison terms. The friends and family of the dictator received lucrative government concessions, monopolies, and perquisites. Castro, Gómez, and their colleagues continued to believe that they were entitled to any personal wealth which they could accumulate from their positions of power. Gómez's system and his prisons shaped two generations. The liberals of 1908 and 1918 failed and fatalistically accepted the dictatorship. Yet their example and their teaching helped to unite and to inspire the youth who would challenge Gómez in the second quarter of the century.

The quarter-century from 1899 to 1922 can be divided into three periods. From 1899 to 1908, Cipriano Castro aggressively and usually successfully challenged foreign and domestic enemies. When Juan Vicente Gómez took over in December 1908, he provided a respite from the excesses of Castro's last years in power, and so from 1908 to 1914, some semblance of peace and order returned, fomented by Gómez's efforts to placate potential foes until he could be sure that he was in firm control. Between 1912 and 1914 Gómez became indisputable master of the nation and ushered in the period of his greatest power. Five new constitutions defined these stages in the Venezuelan political drama — 1901, 1904, 1909, 1914, 1922 — as the *caudillo* or his notions of government changed.

Both Cipriano Castro and Juan Vincente Gómez were autocrats, but they differed greatly in style and personality. Castro was a mercurial, outgoing, lascivious *bon vivant*, as famous for his enthusiastic dancing as for his ostentatious spending. Gómez was a taciturn, parsimonious, hard-working *andino* who was more at home discussing his cattle herds than French wines. Gómez naturally took as much pleasure in bringing order and organization to diplomatic relations, the armed forces, and the national treasury as Castro did in humiliating Caracas bankers and foreign investors and governments. Castro's closest collaborators were those who shared his tastes for dancing, debauchery, and fine food. Gómez sought out men who resembled him in their fiscal conservatism, predictability, asceticism, and devotion to work. Castro's strident nationalism contrasted with Gómez's willingness to placate foreigners and his slight regard for long-range national interest.

The Era of Cipriano Castro, 1899–1908

Cipriano Castro was born on October 12, 1858, the third of eight children. His father was a small merchant who traded between his Táchira home of Capacho and Bogotá, Colombia. Like many Táchira youth, Cipriano received much of his education in Colombia. He also became enamored of politics in Colombia and pledged to return "true" liberalism to Venezuela. His newspaper articles, commanding personality, and participation in a local political skirmish in Táchira in 1886 won him some fame as a local politician. He held several positions in the state government of Táchira, and from 1890 to 1892 he was the deputy from the state of Los Andes to the national Congress. In Caracas Castro espoused two noble, but losing causes: protection of Venezuelan rights in the dispute with the British and support of President Andueza Palacio's unsuccessful bid to continue in the presidency beyond 1892. When Joaquín Crespo marched into Caracas, Cipriano Castro retreated to his ranch in Colombia to write of liberalism, read military strategy, and wait for his opportunity.

Táchira's economic crisis caused by the falling coffee prices at the end of the decade helped Castro's star to rise after the death of Crespo in 1898. President Andrade's government could or would do little to alleviate the distress of the mountain state. Many of the educated young men of the Táchira towns and cities began to listen more closely to Cipriano Castro.

Castro launched his "*Revolución Liberal Restauradora*" (Liberal Restorative Revolution) on May 24, 1899. For a pretext, he objected to President Andrade's tactic of having Congress rather than the state legislatures ratify a constitutional change to revive the twenty state division. The real issue, of course, was that the change would enable President Andrade to replace Joaquín Crespo's men with his own appointees and thus consolidate his own position. If Cipriano Castro wanted to seize national power, he had to do so quickly.

Castro's revolution, which swept from the Andes to Caracas in 153 days, took more than 3,000 lives. His *tachirenses* fought forty-two engagements without losing a battle.[2] In spite of the impressive military statistics, Presidente Andrade remained in control of most of the country until he left Venezuela on October 19.

In the end, Castro's victory was more political than military. Andrade had sent the kinsman of Antonio Guzmán Blanco, Manuel Antonio Matos, to negotiate peace terms with Castro in Valencia. Rather suddenly in the midst of these negotiations Andrade left the country, perhaps deciding that the fight could not continue without money, credit, or the support of the hard-pressed mercantile elite. The interim government hastened to welcome Castro as he entered Caracas on crutches. His new friends from Valencia and many of Andrade's allies participated in the triumph. A nearly perfect revolution since, as historian Ramón Velásquez remarked, "Poor President Andrade is the only loser."[3]

Castro announced his program of "new men, new ideals, new methods." He then appointed to office men who represented an accumulated three hundred years of public careers including two former Presidents — Juan Pablo Rojas Paúl and Raimundo Andueza Palacios — and José Manuel *"El Mocho"* Hernández. Strangely enough, the people who were left out of this feast of national unity were Castro's military companions from Táchira. In the short run, Castro's inclusion of all political factions, even many of the Liberals that he had fought to overthrow, gave him time to consolidate his position without major opposition. In the long run, the slighting of the *tachirenses* would give Castro's colleague, Juan Vicente Gómez, the opportunity quietly to build his own following among the *andinos*.

A number of major conflicts with foreign powers limited the attention that President Castro could devote to internal affairs. In some cases, Castro provoked the conflicts. For example, he aroused the suspicions of Colombian leaders with his grandiose plan to recreate the Bolivarian state of Gran Colombia (Ecuador, Colombia, and Venezuela) and to mold a liberal alliance that would also include Central America. Yet Castro's more serious clashes occurred largely in spite of his actions.

The first bad omen for Venezuelan international relations came on October 3, 1899, just three weeks before Castro entered Caracas.

The Tribunal of Paris, as we have seen, allowed Venezuela to retain control of the mouth of the Orinoco, but awarded the major part of the disputed Guiana territory to Great Britain. At the time, Castro could not challenge the decision. Subsequently, the Venezuelan government charged that they had been cheated by British suborning of Russian delegates on the Tribunal.

Great Britain, Germany, and Italy posed a more serious threat to Venezuelan stability and independence in 1902 and 1903. Venezuela's finances had long been in chaos, and the drop in coffee prices in 1899 made the situation worse. Foreign governments and investors continued to press claims for damages suffered in various civil wars. Former President Guzmán Blanco had incurred a number of costly loans from foreign bankers which had not been repaid. The German, British, and Italian governments demanded immediate settlement of their claims just at the time that Castro's finances were most shaky. Castro maintained his characteristic belligerence toward the foreign governments at first, but finally agreed to make a settlement. In fact, he had no choice. Banker Manuel Antonio Matos had begun a revolt against Castro with the tacit backing and financial assistance from various foreign investors. Castro could agree to the terms imposed by the foreign governments, or he could fall to another *caudillo* who had the help of the foreigners.

Unmoved by Castro's offer to settle, the foreign powers blockaded Venezuela in December 1902. The European blockade represented a challenge to United States hegemony in the Caribbean more than it did a sincere attempt to settle claims, but the United States government, none too happy with Castro's hostility toward United States investors, originally did not object to the aggression.

A pawn in the imperial game, Venezuela influenced the outcome when Castro asked the US ambassador, Herbert Bowen, to negotiate on behalf of the Venezuelan government. The ambassador arranged the terms for Venezuelan payment of claims and for the European lifting of the blockade. Thus, the United States ambivalence about Cipriano Castro did not preclude coming to his assistance when the alternative might have left Britain or Germany in control of the southern rim of the Caribbean. In 1904, President Theodore Roosevelt further confirmed US policy when he enunciated the Roosevelt Corollary to the Monroe Doctrine: In the event of "chronic wrongdoing" by the Latin American nations, the United States government would administer the necessary punishment. It would brook no direct interference by the European powers.

After the blockade, Castro's relations with foreign nations

continued to be stormy. Like Guzmán Blanco, he took vengence in the Antilles for the actions of the European leaders. In 1904, he ordered the Venezuelan ports of Ciudad Bolívar, Caño Colorado, Güiria, Puerto Sucre, and La Vela de Coro closed to trade; all imports had to go through either Puerto Cabello or La Guaira, which meant that the Antilles trade suffered longer and more expensive routes. Castro also imposed an additional surtax on Antillean commerce and forbade any imports or exports on ships smaller than 40 tons, which effectively prohibited most of the trade from the islands.[4]

Cipriano Castro recognized the special relationship of Venezuela to the Dutch island of Curaçao. In 1904, he tried to acquire the island in exchange for a commercial treaty with the Dutch. The Dutch colonial minister evaded the proposal by suggesting a plebiscite of island residents and reminding Castro that neither the United States nor Germany would be pleased by such a transfer. Wisely, Castro decided that the island was indeed better off in Dutch hands. His preference for the Dutch, however, did not prevent tensions or the breaking of diplomatic relations in 1908. In the same year, Castro's government was barely on speaking terms with France and the United States. Some of his irascibility after 1905 may have been caused by his failing health. Nonetheless, in most of the foreign conflicts, Castro did defend the strongly nationalistic thesis that foreigners who worked or lived in Venezuela were subject to Venezuelan laws and courts. Foreign newspapers portrayed Castro in caricature as a child to be disciplined, as a monkey, or as a stereotypical Latin revolutionary — sometimes complete with Mexican sombrero and *serape*. In the early twentieth century, proponents of the Drago and Calvo Doctrines* drew only ridicule from the imperialistic powers.

Foreign pressures and Castro's recalcitrance encouraged a national unity in Venezuela. So too did Castro's domestic program, which continued the centralization that Guzmán Blanco had begun.

---

*The Argentinian jurist Carlos Calvo (1824–1906) is known for his doctrine which challenged European legal rationale for intervention in Latin America in the nineteenth century; he asserted that the interventions had been based purely on the superior force and will of the European countries. A Calvo clause, often inserted in a contract between a government and a foreign firm, requires the foreigner to settle any legal claims in the host country and not to ask for diplomatic assistance from his country of origin. Another Argentinian jurist, Luis María Drago (1859–1921), formulated the doctrine named for him in 1902 when German and British ships blockaded Venezuelan ports. The Doctrine argued that collection of foreign debts by force violated the juridical equality of states and that such rule by force should not be tolerated.

The 1901 constitution augmented the executive's power and extended the term of office to six years. An indirect method of voting assured the victory of the *caudillo*. Castro appointed or confirmed local officials and state governors but his principal collaborators continued to be the Caracas and Valencia "doctors." Portrayed as the initiator of the *andino* hegemony in the nation, Castro in fact reserved the highest government positions for the old liberals.

Military challenges consumed much of Castro's attention, and military expenditures took the largest share of the national revenues. Castro purchased foreign arms and gunboats and steam launches for the navy. He decreed the construction of a military academy and had a Superior Board of Military Instruction to coordinate the educational programs for new recruits. Soldiers' rations tripled, and they were paid in coin rather than in food. Recognizing the importance of geographic knowledge, Castro had detailed national maps drawn to help formulate military strategy. A new military code based promotion on time in grade and on passing an exam. A decree divided the armed forces into infantry, artillery, and maritime battalions. Some of the reforms were little more than formalities, but they expressed an intention to build a strong national armed force to dominate and eventually replace the state militias and personal armies.

Financial constraints destroyed many of Castro's ambitious plans. Falling coffee prices and a new French tariff which discriminated against Venezuelan coffee hurt national revenues in general and Castro's state of Táchira in particular. Unemployed Táchira workers flooded into Caracas looking for work. Castro's own "war surcharges" on imports and exports even further reduced revenues, as trade dwindled. A specie crisis in 1900 and 1901 also aggravated the situation, and abundant silver nearly caused gold to disappear. Lack of revenues meant that public works could not begin and that the national government was frequently unable to pay either the salaries of state officials or the normal state subsidies. Small wonder that ambitious *caudillos* readily found troops to follow them.

Castro made few economic reforms of note. Consistent with his nationalism, he did try to draw in the reins on foreign businesses in Venezuela. His mining code of 1904–5 would govern the granting of concessions for petroleum exploration in 1907. The early concessions still sought asphalt more than petroleum, but Castro's code clearly made the awarding and administration of future concessions an executive prerogative. Some of the foreign claims made against the Venezuelan government had originated from multiple grants on the same land. Presumably such confusion might be avoided if the executive were the only one authorized to grant concessions.

Castro's general hostility to foreign investment might have spurred a nascent industrialization in Venezuela. Yet, like Guzmán Blanco, Castro did not envisage an industrialized national economy. He also preferred the time–honored tradition of granting monopoly concessions for various businesses to his friends. There were concessions for firearms and dynamite, sugar cane, textiles, flour mills, guano, tobacco, liquor, matches, meat. These national monoplies often wiped out local artisans and factory owners and displaced laborers. Three thousand miners in Maracaibo lost their jobs in 1905 as a result of the nationalization of the salt mines.[5] Local economic elites lost out to the men who obtained the national monoplies at the same time that the local political bosses were losing out to national politicians. The goal, of course, was not so much to centralize the economy as it was to enrich Castro and his colleagues.

Castro turned his back on demands for public services, but carefully guarded his public image. Bubonic plague broke out in Macuto and La Guaira in 1908, and Castro dispatched the young bioanalyst Rafael Rangel to the coast to investigate the situation and try to remedy it. Publicly, Castro denied that there was any major health problem, and Rangel's herculean work in diagnosing and checking the epidemic was never acknowledged. Subjected to criticism and attacks by other scientists and politicians, Rangel became depressed and committed suicide in August 1909. Venezuelan scientist Marcel Roche wrote, "It [Rangel's career] causes us to reflect on the relationship between the Venezuelan society at the beginning of century and the man of science, on the effects of politics when they become involved with scientific affairs, and on the obstacles to conducting research among us, some of which we have inherited."[6]

The situation was little better for other intellectuals and writers. Castro closed the *Universidad Central de Venezuela* and the universities of Zulia and Carabobo several times for political reasons. Writers often retreated into romantic aping of foreign fiction, or *criollista* attention to local customs and landscapes, or they went into exile. However, in spite of the hostile intellectual climate, several key works appeared during Castro's years in power. Rufino Blanco Fombona and Manuel Díaz Rodríguez were probably the best known novelists. César Zumeta's *El continente enfermo* (The Sick Continent, 1899) became famous throughout the continent for its warning that Latin American nations must unite to defend their territory and resources from the greed of the imperialist powers. The two most representative works to appear were Pío Gil's (Pedro María Morantes) novel *El Cabito* (The Little Corporal) and José Gil Fortoul's three-volume *Historia constitucional de Venezuela* (Constitutional History of Venezuela, 1907-9).

Both Pío Gil and Gil Fortoul reflected on Venezuela's political instability, much as their contemporary Francisco I. Madero did in Mexico with *La sucesión presidencial en 1910* (The Presidential Succession in 1910). Madero had praised the stability brought to México by the dictator Díaz, and had merely proposed that Díaz choose a responsible and talented vice presidential candidate as his running mate in 1910. *El Cabito*, the more critical and more pessimistic of the two works, sketched out a debauched and corrupt President and the squabbling, greedy *canaille* that competed for his favor. To Pío Gil, those who abandoned principle to fawn over the latest dictator bore a great share of the blame for the corrupt government. The author expressed little hope that progress or institutions could remedy the baseness and selfishness of the elite. Gil Fortoul, on the other hand, found cause for some optimism in the study of the evolution of Venezuelan law and institutions. Even in the two volumes which covered the chaotic period from 1830 to 1863, Gil Fortoul claimed that the republic, which had been born in the mind of the hero and liberator Simón Bolívar, had evolved. "The soul of the national organism," he asserted, "is eternal."[7] The greatest threat to the national organism had been the partisan competition of the nineteenth century; once parties and rivalries had been eliminated from national life, progress would be assured. Appropriately, Gil Fortoul, like other Venezuelan positivists, saw no necessary contradiction between an individual dictator and the long-range progress toward civilization. He served in the governments of Castro and Gómez; Pedro María Morantes went into exile.

Intellectuals proved no match for the autocratic Castro. Other *caudillos* challenged the *andino* more seriously, but he confirmed his hold on the nation by defeating them all. "*El Mocho*" Hernández, General Antonio Paredes, and Manuel Antonio Matos headed the major movements to unseat Castro. Hernández refused to accept the cabinet office he had been offered, made the charge that Castro had violated the principles of the revolution, and reiterated his call for true state autonomy. Castro quickly routed him and threw him in prison, only to release him at the end of 1902 so that he might join the national forces which were fighting against the foreign blockade. He was then rewarded with the position of Venezuelan representative in Washington to arrange some of the details following from the Protocol of Washington in 1903. Ever true to principle, "*El Mocho*" wrote a critical letter to Castro. By return telegraph, Castro took him off the national payroll leaving him in Washington in precarious economic straits.

Paredes had been one of the few to remain loyal to President

Andrade when Castro launched his revolution. For his refusal to surrender, he was in prison between 1899 and 1903. From jail, he initiated a popular literary genre in twentieth century-Venezuela; his *Diario de mi prisión en San Carlos* chronicled his years and companions in the hated Maracaibo prison. His luck had not improved when he led a group of exiles to invade Venezuela from Trinidad in 1907. Quickly isolated and captured, he received no mercy from Castro. In accordance with traditional *"ley fuga"* (law of flight), Castro's men shot Paredes and two of his comrades as they "tried to escape" and threw their bodies into the Orinoco River.

The most serious rebellion against Castro brought together an impressive coalition: foreign investors, popular masses, some regional *caudillos*, Caracas bankers, and the wealthiest man in Venezuela, Manuel Antonio Matos. Castro precipitated the revolt in December 1900, when he pressed Matos and other financiers to make a loan to the government. When they refused, Castro marched them through the streets of Caracas to jail. The loan followed shortly thereafter, but so did the rebellion. Matos could not forgive the insult or forget his own ambitions to achieve the position attained by his brother-in-law, Guzmán Blanco. The *Revolución Libertadora* received considerable help from Castro's enemies. The Orinoco Steamship Company loaned ships to Matos; the French cable company scrambled or turned over to him the government's telegrams; the Germans of the *Gran Ferrocarril de Venezuela* protected the rebels and blocked the government troops; the New York and Bermúdez Company provided money; even Trinidadian and Colombian government officials assisted the rebels.

Despite the resources at his command, Matos was neither skilled nor charismatic enough to triumph. Each regional *caudillo* issued his own *proclamación* which gave his reasons for revolting, reminiscent of the local revolts which precipitated the Mexican revolution. Cipriano Castro was more determined than Porfirio Díaz of Mexico, and in what has been called the "largest, longest, and most decisive battle in Venezuelan history,"[8] Castro defeated Matos' forces at La Victoria in November 1902. The fighting continued into 1903, but the outcome was not in doubt. Castro announced to Congress in 1903, with some justification, that he was proud of "the glory of having conquered the famous historic caudillism, killed by my own hand, in the field of battle itself, on the point of my sword, because thus I have paved the way for a lasting and abundant peace. . . . The annihilation of savage caudillism . . . is the best present that any patriot could offer his country, subjected to the heavy yoke of its cursed domination."[9]

The nation paid a heavy price for the armed conflicts between 1901 and 1903, which were the most extensive since the Independence Wars. Over 12,000 were killed in over 210 armed encounters. Livestock and crops were destroyed. The old political parties virtually disintegrated. *Tachirenses* came to dominate the bureaucracy and the national army, which replaced the state militias. Although Castro took credit for the destruction of the old *caudillo* system, the physical destruction of the civil wars and the foreign blockade probably did more to wipe the slate clean than did Castro himself. Castro's greatest accomplishment may have been merely surviving these tumults.

A romantic might judge that Castro could conquer all but his own nature and his chief ally, Gómez. His heavy drinking, use of aphrodisiacs containing strychnine, and venereal disease aggravated infections of the urinary tract and brought about fever, renal failure, and uremia. Very possibly the physical disorders damaged his brain tissues and central nervous system, and contributed to the behavioral aberrations and paranoia that became more marked after 1906.[10] Suspicious that Juan Vicente Gómez was conspiring against him, Castro set a trap for his ally in April 1906. He appointed Gómez as Acting President, while he retired to Los Teques. Gómez proved either too clever or too loyal to fall into the trap, and he humbly insisted that Castro should return to office. Gómez bided his time and also made a firm ally of Castro's wife, Zoila. Castro's suspicions were quelled for the moment, but his health continued to get worse. In December 1908, he left his trusted ally in charge while he sailed for Europe to seek medical advice.

Ironically, Pío Gil and *"el cabito"* left Venezuela on the same ship. Neither was ever to return to his homeland. Pío Gil died in Paris in 1918, and Cipriano Castro died in Puerto Rico in 1924.

The Era of Juan Vicente Gómez: the Early Years, 1908–1922

If Gómez had waited a long time for his opportunity, he did not immediately move to exploit it. He watched mutely from the balcony of the Casa Amarilla while a crowd cheered the end of the Castro regime on December 13, 1908. A former Castro supporter, Juan Pietri, raised Gómez's arm and yelled *"Viva Gómez!"* The crowd followed and then rushed off to sack the properties of Castro and his few loyalists. As in 1892 and again in 1899, supporters of the losing President hastened to aver their loyalty to the new leader.

Progressives and liberals who applauded the fall of Castro had little reason to expect that Gómez would guide the nation to the modernization they hoped for. Born in 1856, the oldest of thirteen children, Gómez became the head of his Táchira family at age fourteen when his father died. He taught himself to read, write, and keep his account books. Necessity, native shrewdness, and the *andino* tradition of hard work enabled Juan Vicente to accumulate a substantial estate in livestock and agriculture. He avoided gambling, drinking, and politics. He never married, but began to enlarge his clan by siring illegitimate children. His many women had little hold or influence over him, and he only legally recognized the children of Dionisia Bello. His first political action was to serve Cipriano Castro as commissary in the struggle in 1892 to defend President Raimundo Andueza Palacio's move to continue in office. When that movement failed, Gómez and his large family joined Castro in exile in Colombia. The years of exile brought Gómez closer to Castro and to his inflated political plans. In 1899 when Castro judged the time right to challenge President Ignacio Andrade, Gómez went along as commissary and field general. At the age of forty-two, he was seeing Caracas for the first time: hardly a promising background for a twentieth-century President, and many of Castro's enemies who rallied around Gómez in 1908 did so in the expectation that they could quickly control or unseat him.

Gómez may not have been a *brujo* (witch), as his fellow *andinos* claimed, but he was no fool. He accepted the support of the old Castro followers, the Liberal Nationalists of *El Mocho*, and anyone else who chose to join the government, but he watched them very carefully. He called for United States warships to come to prevent an uprising or a Castro invasion; in exchange he signed the Buchanan protocol, which absolved the New York and Bermúdez Company from fines for their participation in the 1903 *Revolución Libertadora*. Before the celebration of the New Year, he had quietly removed the most dangerous Castro loyalists from their military commands. He accused Castro of plotting to kill him and charged him with the murder of Antonio Paredes. The Gómez government then threatened that it would try Castro for murder if he ever came back to Venezuela. The wily *andino* hedged his bets by constructing a network of spies to watch Castro's movements and by enlisting the help of the US government. Several times US authorities turned Castro around as he sailed toward the Venezuelan coast. The ex-President became a man without a country until his death in 1924.

The legal and constitutional formalities followed in 1909. The Constitution of 1909 reaffirmed the twenty-state system, which was to remain unchanged although the states would never again have any degree of autonomy. Gómez conveyed the illusion of shared power by establishing an advisory Council of Government; the Council disappeared from the 1914 Constitution because it had given too much advice. The Congress elected the President, as it would continue to do till the Constitution of 1947, and a President could serve only one term. The Congress, of course, elected Gómez President for the first constitutional term which ran from 1910 to 1914. Gómez proved to have quite an affection for constitutions and had new ones written in 1914, 1922, 1925, 1928, 1929, and 1931. Small wonder that students at UCV referred to the course on constitutional law as mythology.

In 1909, however, Venezuelans still hoped that constitutional regularity would prevail. There were some ominous signs that made an early appearance, such as the defection and exile of Gómez's former allies Leopoldo Baptista, West Point graduate General Linares Alcántara, and a few other Castro loyalists or opportunists. Yet a general wave of euphoria hit Venezuela in Gómez's first year in power. As coffee prices rose, the economic crisis eased. Trade improved along with diplomatic relations. Thirty thousand exiles returned. Artists and intellectuals delighted in the relative freedom and discussed programs for national and artistic rebirth. Conditions for the first time encouraged the emergence of a loose "clique" of intellectuals, who believed that they had a special role to play in their nation. Somewhat similar to the Generation of 1898 in Spain who deplored their nation's "invertebrate" condition, this Venezuelan generation of 1908 had been formed by the blockade of 1903, the loss of Guayana, and the extravagance and irresponsibility of Cipriano Castro. Like Rómulo Gallegos' fictional hero Reinaldo Solar, they lacked experience, a coherent ideological program to unite them either in art or in politics, and genuine ties to the rural or urban masses.

The celebration of the centennial anniversary of Venezuelan independence in 1910 and 1911 inspired a new national spirit in literature, the arts, and history. Historian Francisco González Guinán had rediscovered the 1811 declaration of independence. With great ceremony, the *Academia de Historia* authenticated the documents, and they were placed in the *Salón Elíptico* of the National Congress. Artists were commissioned to portray heroic scenes from national history. The young painter, Tito Salas, returned from Paris in 1911 bearing a triptic of Bolivarian scenes to go in the *Salón del Gabinete* of the *Palacio Federal*.

Some optimistic movements toward national renewal threatened the Gómez mania for consensus or fell apart from personal or philosophical differences. For example, novelist, satirist, and caricaturist Rufino Blanco-Fombona (1874–1944) tried to found a new political party in 1909. Already disillusioned with Gómez and cognizant of the virtual disappearance of the traditional parties,

Blanco-Fombona hoped for "a new political party, radical, civilian, civilizing, honest, just, which will fight martial barbarism, restore a rigorous political morality, reform the national economy, establish a new social justice, awaken in the country a confidence in itself, in its forces, in its future, and confront the farce of the old liberals and the stagnation of the hard or anachronistic conservatism."[11] The vague aspirations seemed harmless, but Gómez imprisoned and then exiled Blanco-Fombona. In 1932, the novelist commented bitterly that, with two exceptions, all of the men who had so hopefully subscribed to his new political movement had ended by serving Gómez.

Also short-lived was the weekly magazine, *La Alborada* (The Dawn), founded in 1909 by novelist and teacher Rómulo Gallegos and three of his friends. The magazine spoke of emerging from the dark night of tyranny into the dawn. For the three months of its existence it carried essays on politics as well as on literature and art. Gallegos criticized the traditional political parties for being personalistic groups with no convictions or ideals. He called for a greater respect for law and for more power to go to the legislative and judiciary branches of the government. Gallegos continued to write for other journals after *La Alborada* was closed. In 1920, he even won Gómez's approval for an issue of *Actualidades* (Topical Events) which featured the state of Aragua, where Gómez lived. Unlike those with whom Blanco-Fombona was so disgusted, however, Gallegos was never comfortable with the dictator's favor.

In a 1912 newspaper article, Leoncio Martínez (1889–1914) called for a rebirth in the arts to match the newly organized and outfitted army. Artists and writers responded by founding the *Círculo de Bellas Artes*, a cultural organization which also invited the general public to come and discuss art and beauty. Young student artists had been carrying on a feud with the more conservative *Academia de Bellas Artes*, both because of disagreements with the new director and because Gómez's budget cuts had eliminated some student scholarships. Within the *Círculo*, they defended variety in artistic movements and the value of some of the recent European experiments. Despite their interest in European innovation, the most famous of this group began the first serious study of light in the Venezuelan landscape. Manuel Cabré and Armando Reverón were two of the most successful artists associated with the *Círculo*. Essayists, novelists, and poets included Rómulo Gallegos, Laureano Vallenilla Lanz, Fernando Paz Castillo, Leoncio Martínez. By 1916, the group had lost most of its initial fire, although it did not vanish until 1929.

Whether they served or fought Gómez, the intellectuals of the *Círculo de Bellas Artes* shared a mood of pessimism. Exiles believed that they could not work productively in Venezuela, a country so racked by backwardness and civil strife and presided over by the nearly-illiterate Gómez. Gallegos's fictional creation, Reinaldo Solar, pondered as he watched the Venezuelan coast disappear on his voyage to Europe: "How beautiful you are, my country, and how you make us suffer! We all nourish ourselves with the same thought: to abandon you."[12] Some neutrals like Gallegos tried to concentrate on their own work and avoid politics. The collaborators like Laureano Vallenilla Lanz believed that Gómez was the "necessary caesar," the strong hand that Venezuela had to have in order to conquer its inherent anarchy and individualism. A later generation could take heart from the Mexican and Russian Revolutions, but the pessimism or escapism of the 1908 generation permeated their art and their politics. Their success as a group would be in the influence they had on younger generations as teachers and exponents of a *criollismo* which yearned to join the modern world without losing authentic national values.

Gómez accepted the adhesion of the positivist intellectuals, perhaps delighting in the economic hold that he had over them. Yet he probably valued more highly the greater sincerity of his natural allies: the economic elite, the Táchira military officers, and his own irregular extended family. Gómez did not make the mistake which Cipriano Castro made in his choice of political enemies. He carefully cultivated Manuel Antonio Matos and the Caracas entrepreneurs. The *andino* had more in common with the goals and objectives of bankers, financiers, and businessmen than he did with the lavish spenders who had so befriended Castro. His own intention to settle foreign quarrels, encourage foreign investment, rationalize state finances, maintain internal order, and expand the national network of roads found favor with the first modernizing elite of the country. Luck, in the form of rising coffee and cacao prices, was on Gómez's side if he wanted to curry favor with *hacendados*, merchants, and bankers. He built on that luck by abolishing the war import/export taxes imposed by Castro and thus promoted a revival of trade. Gómez's grasp of the principles of money and banking or international finance may have been rudimentary and intuitive, but returning prosperity placated the economically powerful. *Hacendados* were later to become alienated by his abandonment of them in the 1920s, but they found little fault in the expansive pre-war years.

The three families which best represented the rational, entrepreneurial values which Gómez admired were the Boultons, the Vollmers, and the Zuloagas. These families parlayed modest family holdings into unprecedented wealth during the Castro/Gómez period. By the end of Gómez's reign in 1935, they dominated the classic fields of commerce, land speculation, public services, and light industry. Their investments, business acumen, and head start made them the core of the small group of millionaires who have influenced economic decisions in Venezuela down to the present.

The English Boultons arrived in Venezuela early in the nineteenth century and developed a modest import-export business, facilitated by their contacts with British bankers. World War I assured their final victory over the strong German commercial firms in Venezuela, and they expanded to become a truly national firm. Subsequently, they diversified into aviation, public services, and light industry. The German Vollmers also entered Venezuela in the nineteenth century. A modest and unpretentious family, they put their cash into the safest of investments: land. Losing *caudillos* sold their land cheaply, and the Vollmers astutely acquired parcels on the outskirts of Caracas and other major cities. They had also invested in two of the most lucrative industries of pre-industrial Venezuela by 1901: Santa Teresa rum and the *Cervecería Nacional*. After the turn of the century, the new roads, the urban transportation system, civil wars, and some prosperity encouraged urban growth; the Vollmers took their profits from the urban land sales they made and fed them into their growing industrial empire. Finally in Caracas, the Zuloagas, a Basque family, had been modest and middle-class from the eighteenth century until the 1890s. Ricardo Zuloaga earned a university degree in engineering in the 1890s and immediately put it to work in founding the first electric plant in the Caracas valley. The *Electricidad de Caracas* began with a capital of Bs 1.5 million at the beginning of the century and grew to Bs 7 million by 1917. The size of the investment and the importance of the service made it the most important industry in the country. Like the other successful family empires, the Zuloagas reinvested their profits and diversified their holdings. In 1914, they created the first Venezuelan insurance company, *La Previsora*, and subsequently they turned to beer, cement, glass, and other light industries.

These families became some of the first to move to the fashionable new suburb of Caracas, El Paraíso. No doubt many of them spent their fair share on French wines and imported foods. Yet they became the prototype of the hard-working, competitive, ascetic "robber barons" of Venezuela. Competition in organized sport also became important. They financed baseball playing-fields, tennis courts, and a new race track in El Paraíso. The first horse race had taken place in Venezuela in the 1890s, but the construction of the new track in 1908 certified the sport as a new national mania. The early baseball teams consisted of sons of Zuloagas, Boultons,

Vollmers, Machados, and other El Paraíso elite families. In the first national tennis cup, Ricardo Sanabria Boulton defeated his brother Gustavo in 1908. Soccer and tennis continued to be elite games, learned and practiced in the private *colegios* and clubs. Baseball, however, was surrendered to the popular classes after the aristocratic team called *Los Samanes* (*lit.* The Rain-Trees) scattered after its humiliation in being unable to defeat some of the younger, tougher street teams that began to dominate. After the 1918 visit of the intimidating Puerto Rican Borinquen Stars, Venezuelan teams acquired even more discipline and direction. They recognized that the baseball teams had to be directed and managed on the same rational lines as their new industries.

In short, Gómez and the wealthiest families in Venezuela shared the values of hard work, progress, investment, saving, competition, and "healthy" use of leisure time. Gómez's three principal domestic advisers also shared these values: Félix Galavís, who reorganized the armed forces; Román Cárdenas, who modernized the national treasury and tax system; and Vicente Lecuña, who as director of the Banco de Venezuela and president of the Caracas Chamber of Commerce, became a kind of minister without portfolio mediating between Gómez and the economic elite. These three bore witness to Gómez's intuition in choosing men who were loyal, hardworking, and able to rationalize the national administration. A fourth man, Gumersindo Torres, played a key part in formulating the petroleum legislation which was to govern the first quarter century of exploitation; he proved to be ahead of his time, however, in a degree of economic nationalism that neither Gómez nor the foreign oil companies were willing to accept.

In his early years in office, Gómez relied for support on the Catholic Church and the United States in addition to the economic oligarchy. He once again encouraged religious education, in contrast to the anticlericalism of Antonio Guzmán Blanco and the Liberals in the 1890s. He sought good relations with the Vatican and in 1916 received a decoration from Pope Benedict XV as his reward. As Gómez repudiated the cantankerousness of Cipriano Castro, relations with all nations slowly became more cordial. By 1912, he had paid off the claims which had issued from the 1903 blockade, and to give further reassurance to foreign investors, the Venezuelan Government through executive decree modified the Calvo Doctrine (see p. 41, fn.). Gómez would allow foreign nations who did not like the arbitration of Venezuelan courts to appeal to their own national courts or to international organizations.[13] In 1912, US Secretary of State Philander Knox paid a cordial visit to Venezuela.

After Woodrow Wilson came to the US presidency in 1913, and

especially after the beginning of the first World War, Gómez's relations with the United States cooled somewhat. Gómez insisted on strict neutrality during the war, but he openly admired the Germans. Rumors circulated that he intended to sell or lease Margarita Island to them or that he hoped that a German victory would allow Venezuela to recover the Guíana territory lost to the English. Woodrow Wilson consulted his Secretary of State, Robert Lansing: "This scoundrel ought to be put out. Can you think of any way in which we can do it that would not upset the peace of Latin America more than letting him alone will?"[14] Apparently Lansing could not, although the US Ambassador to Venezuela from 1913 to 1922, Preston McGoodwin, mildly encouraged some of Gómez's opponents. Gómez's affection for the Germans aroused opposition in Venezuela as well, for most Venezuelans sided with the Allies, in spite of the effective propaganda of the German ambassador and colony in the country. At the conclusion of the war, Venezuelan students took to the streets to celebrate the victory of the democratic nations and indirectly to attack Gómez as an ally of the fallen Kaiser's government. Gómez proved more talented than the Kaiser in suppressing dissent, and a new generation of Venezuelans filled the jails or went into exile. Venezuela did join the League of Nations, asserting that Caracas had supported the principle of neutrality throughout the War.

The adherence of the economic elite and the Church and the relative isolation provided by the First World War gave Gómez time to build up the true bulwarks of his twenty-seven year reign: the Army and the Treasury. The vulnerability of Venezuela to foreign attack and the patriotic fervor which accompanied the preparations for the centennial celebrations provided an ample pretext to modernize the armed forces. The key to modernization proved to be the post of Inspector General of the Army, created in January 1910. Its first holder, Felix Galavís, was another no-nonsense *andino* like Gómez. He called in the Prussian-trained Chilean Colonel Samuel McGill to supervise the organization of a national armed forces. McGill's appraisal of the Venezuelan situation prompted a recommendation for armed forces which could simultaneously allow maximum centralization to repel foreign attacks and maximum agility to quell far-flung domestic revolts. As long as he was assured of being able to check revolts quickly in the key regions of Zulia, Táchira, and the central coast, Gómez assented to the plans. Military expenditure, high under Castro, rose by 180 percent between 1908 and 1914.[15]

Military professionalization received a considerable impetus with the opening of the *Academia Militar* in 1910. Although *tachirenses* remained in control of the school, it aspired to be a national institution and invited state governors to nominate young men from their states. Officers received higher salaries than their civilian counterparts, but officers of the same rank often received different compensation, depending on the degree of trust reposed in them by the dictator. The new national army then was born in a situation which encouraged cleavages within it: *tachirenses* and Gómez loyalists would rise in rank more quickly than men, no matter how skilled and well trained, from other states. Older, more traditional officers, established few ties with the Caracas oligarchy. On the other hand, younger cadets like Isaías Medina Angarita, a *tachirense* who graduated from the Military Academy in 1914, frequently attended Caracas *tertulias* and enjoyed some popularity with social and intellectual circles of the city. After Gómez's death, Medina proved to be one of the few in his generation who was trusted by military and civilians alike.

In the new national armed forces more attention was paid to the hitherto neglected navy and the beginnings of an air force. The *Academia Militar* initially provided formal training for naval officers, but the *Escuela Naval* was subsequently moved to Puerto Cabello, site of the dry dock and other naval installations. Training in naval mechanics and engineering technology became part of its curriculum. In 1920, a law of aviation entered the books, and the *Escuela de Aviación Militar* came to Maracay as a branch of the army. Venezuela purchased three combat planes from France and enlisted the services of a French military mission to train pilots. There was a major setback in 1923, however, when a series of accidents wiped out the small flight, and some interservice rivalries left the air force without strong support. Gómez shared some of the *campesino* distrust for these *"bichos"* (creatures) that flew although his tiny air force had intimidated his enemies.

Gómez intended to ensure that his armed forces had a monopoly on the use of force. In 1919 he issued a law which prohibited the carrying of arms. Government officials confiscated any guns which could be found. The 1914 Constitution created the office of Commander in Chief of the Army, a position which Gómez would hold until his death. In 1925 Gómez inserted a clause in the new constitution forbidding the states from raising or supporting their own armed forces. Henceforth, serious challenges to the President would come from within the national institution of the armed forces rather than from a rival *caudillo*.

Two major military conspiracies occurred in these early years and failed, thus providing Gómez with the excuse to jail or exile any officers whose loyalty he doubted. General Román Delgado

Chalbaud launched the first of his efforts to unseat Gómez in 1913, ostensibly in reaction to the cancellation of the 1914 elections. At about the same time, there were rumors that Cipriano Castro had launched an invasion effort. Gómez announced that these threats justified his assumption of emergency powers, and Delgado Chalbaud languished for fourteen years in the hated La Rotunda prison of Caracas. A military conspiracy also accompanied the civilian revulsion against the germanophile Gómez in 1919. Gómez's spies enabled him to discover and arrest the alleged conspirators before the movement could begin. His son, José Vicente Gómez—"Vicentico"—took charge of the torture of the prisoners, confirming his reputation as a sadist. From this time on, the Gómez regime could not shake off the unsavory reputation of being one of the most brutal and repressive dictatorships in the Americas. Gómez's newly organized army and his willingness to intimidate and torture suspected enemies ensured that no armed movement would come close to unseating the old "catfish."

Another efficient *tachirense* put the national accounts in order, lessening any foreign threats to Venezuelan sovereignity on the pretext of debt collection. This fiscal conservatism also completed the wooing of the Venezuelan economic elite and some foreign investors. Román Cárdenas, an engineer who as Minister of Public Works from 1910 to 1913 had planned the national network of highways, became Minister of the Treasury from 1913 to 1922. He centralized all tax collection and eliminated the old system of farming out the tax concession on liquor, cigarettes, salt, public lotteries, and the like. A firm believer in a balanced budget and in an internationally standardized system of accounting, Cárdenas drastically cut salaries and expenditure at the outbreak of the First World War. Thus, in spite of the disastrous effect of the war on Venezuelan trade, the nation could maintain the essential administrative expenditures and the amortization of the foreign debts, an obsession with Gómez. The wage cuts and the slow-down in public works expenditure prompted strikes and protests from Venezuelan workers. Gómez's response was typical and intimidated protestors at the same time as it provided free labor for public projects. He passed the law of *tareas* (labor) in 1916, which required political and common prisoners to labor on public works without pay and excused rural people from military service if they put in two days of work a month on highways or other national construction.

Cárdenas's measures, had resulted by 1922 in a great increase in national income from domestic taxes. Falling agricultural prices after 1920 and the beginnings of income from petroleum concessions also contributed to the relative importance of internal revenues, but Cárdenas's service gave Venezuela an orderly system of national accounts before the oil wealth had become significant. Domingo Alberto Rangel writes: "Our history in terms of fiscal order can be divided into two epochs: that of the most protean and spectacular disorder between 1830 and 1914 and the almost cartesian order after the latter year. What do Descartes, Juan Vicente Gómez and Román Cárdenas have in common? The order that in the French is rationality and in the two *tachirenses* an instinct of a suspicious young bull and the mandate of a fox who knows how to hoard."[16]

Another of Gómez's intimates contributed to the fiscal order without holding a formal position in the government. Historian Vicente Lecuna had two passions: the study of the life of Simón Bolívar, and money and banking. As director of the Banco de Venezuela and president of the Caracas Chamber of Commerce for much of the Gómez period, Dr Lecuna had his finger on the economic pulse of the nation. He visited Gómez weekly in Maracay to explain the intricacies of budgets, international monetary exchange, and the gold standard. Other ministers came and went, but Lecuna continued to act as a go–between for the Caracas financial and mercantile establisment and Juan Vicente Gómez.

The ascendancy of Cárdenas and Lecuna accompanied the last period in which the Venezuelan economy was dominated by agricultural exports. Prices for the two principal crops, coffee and cacao, remained fairly stable from 1908 to 1922, and the areas under cultivation expanded. Yet soil exhaustion, failure to modernize equipment, the distance of coffee plantations from ports, and the growing concentration of land ownership by Gómez and his cronies meant that Venezuela would increasingly have trouble in competing with Brazilian coffee. Venezuela's unique sweet cacao, a product preferable to the semi-bitter or bitter variety which dominated the market, was not marketed aggressively by the Government or the planters. Gómez also made sins of commission such as allowing the imprisonment of those who would not sell land to his allies. Soldiers or goats sometimes invaded cacao *haciendas* to encourage the owners to sell. A third export, cattle, also fell prey to Gómez's greed, to civil conflicts and to diseases so common to the *llanos*. In 1888 there were over 8 million cattle in Venezuela, but by 1922, the number had dropped to just under 3 million, only 33 percent higher than an estimate of 1839. Gómez himself grabbed up the monopoly on the slaughter and distribution of beef for the important urban markets and for export. Thus, signs of distress were present in Venezuelan agriculture even before the fall in prices after 1920 and the disturbing effects of the petroleum boom.

Petroleum may not have been a major export by 1922, but decisions had been taken which were to dominate the industry for the next half century. Some Venezuelans, most notably Gumersindo Torres and César Zumeta, argued for a degree of nationalism closer to that reflected in the Mexican Constitution of 1917, but Gómez chose a more cautious path. The first Venezuelan refinery was built in 1917, but most Venezuelan oil would be refined in Curaçao or other areas. The President clearly established his authority to negotiate concessions and terms with the companies, without the intervention of Congress. The administrative bureaucacy began to swell to deal with the new national activity; an Office of Mines appeared in the Ministry of Development in 1909 to be followed in 1913 by a Technical Office of Mines and an Inspector General of Mines. Consistent with Gómez's preference for foreign investment and with a pragmatic desire to encourage rapid development of petroleum deposits, the terms offered were some of the most generous in America. Most of the debate within Venezuela centered on the optimum length of concession time and size of parcels for exploitation, the size of the taxes and royalties, the advisability of trying to force the companies to develop their concessions more rapidly, and, to a lesser extent, the question of Venezuelan presidential control.

Development Minister Gumersindo Torres (1918–21) with the mining law of 1918 and petroleum code of 1920 took a firm position on limiting the companies' freedom of action, although he characterized his stand as a moderate one between those who wanted to surrender all to the foreigners and those who wanted such stringent terms that the companies would avoid Venezuela altogether. Torres's relatively moderate package fell prey to a formidable series of enemies: the 1920–1 recession which halted foreign exploitation and appeared to give the foreigners the whip hand in negotiations, Venezuelan critics of both extremes, and US ambassador Preston McGoodwin, who had Gómez's ear and pressed the views of the foreign companies. Torres was dismissed in 1921, and the Venezuelan Congress passed a law which expunged some of the offending clauses of the 1920 law. Oilmen were still not happy and demanded the enactment of a less ambiguous code. Gómez caved in, and called in three US companies and company lawyers to draw up new legislation. They did so, basing it mostly on US practice in Mexico in the years before the Revolution, and the Venezuelan Congress obediently enacted this law in 1922. Petroleum spokesmen praised the law as the best in Latin America. The companies enjoyed low taxes and royalties, less pressure to initiate exploitation rapidly, no Venezuelan congressional input, and no restriction on the amount of land that one company could hold.

The concessions which these laws were to regulate had begun with the general mining concessions granted by Cipriano Castro in 1907. Gómez gave out more concessions in 1909 and again in 1912, under slightly more restrictive terms than Castro's. These grants continued to be transferred from one investor to another, with most of them ending up in the hands of British companies. The 1907 and 1912 concessions, with renewals, ran until 1943, and their terms were considerably more generous than those under which US operators were later to work. After World War I, the competition between the US and British investors increased, and was focused exclusively on petroleum. The combination of the Mexican Revolution and Venezuela's first commercial strike in the Maracaibo Basin in 1914 lured the foreigners to Venezuela. McGoodwin's skills and contacts ultimately ensured that the United States companies would receive the major portion of the concessions after 1918.

Gómez's generosity to the oil companies was consistent both with his earlier obsession to placate foreign governments and investors and with his reactions to the events of 1918 to 1922. The immediate postwar years were not good ones for Gómez and apparently threw him back on his earthy, peasant-like nature. Whatever initiatives and creativity he had shown earlier in politics and administration gave way to retrenchment and reaction. His most faithful collaborators were growing older and less innovative with him; they feared any criticism of the familiar traditional order. Except for the unremarkable sons of Gómez, younger men largely found themselves frozen out of influential government posts.

Gómez had also suffered personally from the influenza epidemic which raged in Caracas in 1918; his favorite son, Alí, died along with about 22,000 other Venezuelans and the old dictator lost face publicly when he retreated to San Juan de los Morros while the disease ran its course. Some of the young Caracas students who voluntarily helped victims of the disease forged one of the first authentic links of sympathy between the oligarichic elite and the urban masses so abandoned by the government. In 1921 Gómez himself became ill, awakening hopes that he, like Castro, would fall without a fight; but he recovered, to preside over the government for another fourteen years.

The end of the war also brought political and economic problems to Gómez. The demonstrations and the military conspiracy of 1918-19 were the most serious that he had faced since his methodical consolidation of power between 1912 and 1914. After 1920, coffee and cacao prices dropped drastically, causing *hacendados* to grumble and government revenues to fall. Gómez protected his economic standing by his pact with the foreign oilmen, and his political dominance by bringing his family members into positions of power. The 1922 Constitution provided for two Vice-Presidents: Gómez's brother Juancho and his son José Vicente, "Vicentico." The toughness of the foreigners and the weaknesses of the relatives made a nearly impenetrable phalanx around Gómez until his death.

By 1922, then, Gómez had built a new national administration which was stronger and more unified than anything Venezuela had experienced since the colonial period. He counted on support from the army, the emerging economic elite, the Church, the foreign oil companies, and his family and other loyal *tachirenses*. In a series of moves, he had eliminated the traditional political parties, the old *caudillos*, and the leadership of some groups which would prove more troublesome in the future. Numerous exiles dreamed of, and occasionally launched, quixotic invasions to unseat Gómez, but they were as divided in exile as they might have been back in Venezuela, and Gómez was never in danger of being turned out by an armed movement.

By 1922, the forces which were ultimately to replace Gómez and his clique were as unformed as their future leaders. In that year Jóvito Villaba and Rómulo Betancourt were fourteen, Raúl Leoni sixteen, and Rafael Caldera only six. Caracas had gained in national prominence with the centralization of political power, but it still remained a city of only 92,212 inhabitants. Students and intellectuals had little ideology to unite them, and they often remained physically isolated by the closing of their natural meeting place, the University. The national army had cleavages between the old officers and the new, but the Táchira domination of most of the command positions meant that military conspiracies had little chance to develop. Labor organizations began to appear in Caracas and in the Zulia petroleum camps, but there was little labor militancy and no ability to withstand the dictator's attacks. Some cultural and economic nationalism had appeared, but could not be widespread when most of the population was illiterate. Elite or labor protests still received little support from urban masses. Even less could the scattered, malnourished, and miserable rural laborers provide any backing for a national movement against Gómez.

The period from 1922 to 1943 witnessed some of these groups forming a still shaky unity around a nationalistic and socially reformist ideology. Venezuelan society was being transformed, first by the Castro/Gómez centralization and later by the wealth, technology, and values of the oil companies.

NOTES

1. Rómulo Gallegos, *Reinaldo Solar* (Caracas: Monte Avila, 1972), p. 67.
2. William M. Sullivan, "The Rise of Despotism in Venezuela: Cipriano Castro, 1899–1908" (Ph.D. diss., University of New Mexico, 1974), p. 132.
3. Ramón J. Velásquez, *La caída del liberalismo amarillo*, 2nd edn (Caracas: n.p., 1973), p. 242.
4. Sullivan, pp. 425–7.
5. Ibid., p. 537.
6. Marcel Roche, *Rafael Rangel: ciencia y política en la Venezuela de principios de siglo*," 2nd edn (Caracas: Monte Avila, 1978), pp. 17–18.
7. José Gil Fortoul, *Historia constitucional de Venezuela*, 5th edn, 3 vols. (Caracas: Librería Piñango, 1967), 2:14.
8. Sullivan, p. 192.
9. Velásquez, pp. 285–6.
10. Sullivan, p. 558.
11. Naudy Suárez Figueroa (ed.), *Programas políticas venezolanos de la primera mitad del sigle XX* (Caracas: Universidad Católica Andrés Bello, 1977), 1:44.
12. Gallegos, p. 118.
13. Sheldon Liss, *Diplomacy and Dependency: Venezuela, the United States, and the Americas* (Salisbury, NC: Documentary Publications, 1978), pp. 66–7.
14. Quoted in ibid., p. 68.
15. Domingo Alberto Rangel, *Gómez el amo del poder* (Caracas: Vadell Hermanos, 1975), pp. 202–3.
16. Ibid., pp. 235–6.

3

OIL AND THE FEVER OF POLITICAL FREEDOM, 1923–1945

"Petroleum is the fundamental and basic fact of the Venezuelan destiny. It presents to Venezuela today the most serious national problems that the nation has known in its history. It is like the minotaur of ancient myths, in the depths of his labyrinth, ravenous and threatening.

"The vital historical theme for today's Venezuela can be no other than the productive combat with the minotaur of petroleum.

"Everything else loses significance. Whether the Republic is centralist or federalist. Whether the voters vote white [that is, for AD] or any other color. Whether they build aqueducts or not. Whether the University is open or closed. Whether immigrants come or don't come. Whether schools are built or not built. Whether the workers earn five bolívares or fifteen bolívares. All those issues lack meaning.

"Because they all are conditioned, determined, created by petroleum. They are all dependent and transitory. Dependent and transitory.

"Petroleum and nothing else is the theme of Venezuela's contemporary history."[1]

Arturo Uslar Pietri

By 1922, Gómez had set his system into place, and his successors, Eleazar López Contreras (1936–41) and Isaías Medina Angarita (1941–5) continued it. Petroleum revenues paid off the national debt in 1930, financed road building and subsidies to the states during the economic depression, and supported the growing armed forces, government workers, and friends of the dictator. Indirectly the relative prosperity contributed to improved nutrition and health for many Venezuelans. The system seemed secure, and López and Medina relaxed some of the repression and introduced some modern social reforms.

In retrospect, we can see that the security which petroleum wealth brought to the Gómez system was a false one. At the same time petroleum provided the government with the means to annihilate old enemies, it encouraged the development of new ones, more enduring and less understood. The new jobs in the petroleum camps encouraged a fresh unity and class consciousness among workers. They demanded training for more advanced jobs, respectful treatment, a living wage, safe working conditions, and the right to press such demands as a group. They coveted the services provided for foreign employees: schools, hospitals, clubs, houses with gardens, stylish imported clothing, baseball equipment. The company lawyers, frequently Venezuelans, who mediated between the companies and

61

the government were no less struck by the material comforts of the Anglo-Saxons and were frequently hurt and insulted that the foreigners did not wish to mingle with them socially or treat them as equals.

The oil wealth had paid for an extensive new highway system and for automobiles to travel them, for radio broadcasting, and gradually for newspapers and magazines. News of events in Zulia or Anzoátegui could eventually reach much of the Venezuelan population, increasingly concentrated in Caracas and along the northern coastal cities. The growing middle and professional classes became concerned with national problems, history, and culture — seen through the prism of rapid changes wrought by petroleum. They fed a new literary boom of novels and stories still Venezuelan at heart, but enlarged by universal themes. These middle groups thrown together in universities, work, and social clubs also formed or strengthened professional associations which would speak out on issues of professional or national interest. They had often traveled, or read, or communicated with those who had experience in other countries. Students and intellectuals often pointed to the example of Mexico: a nation which had had a social revolution, an oil industry, frequent conflicts with foreigners, and in 1938 had nationalized its oil industry. Many Venezuelans were intrigued by the model, but frustrated by their own pragmatic assessment that Venezuela was not modern enough, educated enough, diversified enough, or strong enough to be able to emulate Mexico and control its own resources. The tiny economic élite, which would form *Fedecámaras* (see below, p. 133) in 1944, longed for the industrialization and economic development which would signal modernity; by and large, it preferred a government which would provide all support, but which would leave economic decision-making to the businessmen and entrepreneurs.

The most impatient of these groups influenced by oil were, of course, the young. Like Rómulo Gallegos — or Reinaldo Solar — who had hoped for a political rebirth in 1908, the generation of 1928, or 1936, sensed a new opportunity with the declining health and eventual death of Gómez. Their associations were not limited to professional or student groups. They were intent on creating political parties and movements which would aggregate the power necessary to effect the responses which the oil industry demanded.

Thus we come full circle. The new wealth which could have strengthened the dictatorship insidiously brought forth forces which would destroy it. For if much of the resentment and envy was directed toward the three dominant oil companies — Shell, Gulf, and Standard — it increasingly became directed toward the Venezuelan government which catered to the foreigners more carefully than to Venezuelans. The old pessimism and fatalism among the population was giving way to a new optimism, born from the awareness of the potential of petroleum. The optimism was channeled into groups of people who wanted, and believed, that Venezuela could become modern and strong, could protect its citizens from foreigners, could eliminate many of the evils of the old *caudillo* system, could invest in human resources of the nation. Gómez, López, and Medina and the Gómez system were not adequate for the task. A new age and new hopes required truly new men — and not the same sort of system which came from the days of the *Revolución Liberal Restauradora* of Cipriano Castro.

Petroleum and Change, 1922–1945

The period from 1922 to 1945 saw Venezuela become the world's first great exporter of petroleum and the world's second producer, after the United States. The oil revenues contributed greatly to the ability of the Táchira generals to remain in power. In the long run, petroleum exploitation produced changes in Venezuelan society which required a different form of political control. The changes became obvious and prompted the political revolution of 1945.

The figures of petroleum export and production are quickly told in statistics. Venezuela produced 1 million barrels of oil in 1921 and 323 million barrels in 1945. By 1930, it surpassed Mexico in production, became the world's first exporter, and paid off the foreign national debt. Most of the exported oil was heavy crude, of relatively low value and quality; little petroleum was refined in Venezuela. As a rule it went to the Dutch Antilles to be refined and was then transhipped to the east coast of the United States, which was its principal consumer. Less than 3 percent of Venezuelan petroleum was consumed domestically, and in 1930 there were complaints that the domestic product commanded higher prices for consumers in Venezuela than it did in the United States or Chile.

Foreign companies exploited nearly all of the Venezuelan oil. In 1928, there were 107 companies operating in Venezuela, but only five of them exported and the big three — Dutch Shell, Gulf, and Standard Oil controlled 98 percent of the market. The Dutch and British Shell companies dominated the area in the 1920s, but by the mid-'30s, Standard Oil's Venezuelan subsidiary had surpassed Shell and by 1945, was producing over half of the petroleum in Venezuela. The US companies were especially affected by the fact that exploitation cost less in Venezuela than in the United States.[2]

The foreign-directed petroleum exploitation affected Venezuelan society in a number of ways. The foreigners, generally in enclaves in Zulia and later in the Monagas and Anzoátegui states in the east, created a demonstration effect. Roads, health care, housing, sports and entertainment, religion, and working customs all followed the foreigners' preferences; most oil camps had clearly differentiated living areas for foreigners and Venezuelans. The companies which provided housing for Venezuelans did so reluctantly and what they provided was of inferior quality. Foreign attitudes to Venezuelans were frequently arrogant, enthnocentric, and condescending. For example, William T. Wallace, vice president of Venezuelan Gulf, doubted that the companies should provide housing for Venezuelan workers in the petroleum camps. "It is impossible to expect the native mind to conform to the accepted method of living in highly developed countries after centuries of dirt and unsanitary living. This change can only come slowly and when demands are made for exactly the same houses, they are based except in rare cases, not on a real desire to conform to American practices, but from a desire to try to get something for nothing, and if granted, the demand always is never satisfied if there is any chance of obtaining that something for nothing."[3]

Petroleum exploitation contributed to a changing distribution of population in Venezuela and intensified the rural migration either to the cities or to the petroleum areas. The town of Cabimas, where the La Rosa fields were, rose from a population of 1,940 in 1920 to a figure of 21,753 in 1936. Maracaibo saw the greatest change; its 1920 population of 40,000 had doubled by the end of the decade. Petroleum occupied 0.3 percent of the labor force in 1920 and 1.2 percent in 1936. Although the petroleum companies themselves were not highly labor-intensive, the surrounding areas quickly provided shops, bars and entertainments, prostitutes and other services typical of a boom area. Most of the migrants to Zulia came from neighboring Falcón and Trujillo states, but *margariteños* also came in large numbers. Additionally, the companies brought in black workers from Trinidad, the Dutch islands, and other parts of the Caribbean. By 1929, some 10 percent of the unskilled labor force was Antillean.[4] Racial and cultural tensions heightened. Some of the earliest strikes in Zulia were prompted by the high-handedness of Dutch overseers toward Venezuelan workers. Ramón Díaz Sánchez in his petroleum novel *Mene* (1936) recounts the firing and blacklisting of a black Trinidadian worker who used a restroom designated for whites only. The Trinidadians often felt superior to the Venezuelans, and the Venezuelans resented and discriminated against the blacks. The resentment was based on some racist sentiment and on a belief that jobs should not be going to foreigners. In 1929, Gómez issued a decree that no more Antilleans should enter Venezuela and that those already in the oil fields had to register with the authorities and carry identification cards.[5]

The companies affected the ecological balance of Zulia and the east in other ways. The drilling in the 1920s was rapid and messy, as the British and United States rushed for short-term production and for advantage over the other companies. Offsetting wells, fires, and waste were typical. The once beautiful lake and its shores were covered with a film of oil. Houses, vegetation, clothes, birds, and animals all suffered their coating of "the Devil's excrement." Oil derricks were set up in the middle of towns like Lagunillas and Cabimas with slight concern for fire hazards or the lives and property of the citizens of the towns. The Motilón Indians, in the southwest area of the lake, saw their winter hunting ground and food supply threatened by the roads and jungle clearings. They frequently attacked the camps, and by 1926 prompted Gómez to send a small army to the area to harry them back. The companies put up sentinels to protect the camps. Some spokesmen for the companies would have preferred a wholesale extermination of the Indians, but they settled for a piecemeal campaign.

The economic depression also made an impact in Venezuela, although it was not as severe or as long-lasting as in much of the Americas. Yet Venezuelans could perceive the dependent relationship between the marketing and production of their natural resources and the international economy, largely dominated by the United States. The slower expansion after 1928 meant that over 40 percent of the total 1929 work force was dismissed in 1930. The US government made matters worse in 1932 by enacting a tariff on imported oil; refined products were hurt more than Venezuela's crude oil, but astute Venezuelans could conclude that this new product would place Venezuela more at the mercy of foreign prices and the whims of foreign governments than had the exporting of coffee and cacao.

Not surprisingly, the petroleum exploitation by the foreign companies contributed to a rising feeling of nationalism among Venezuelans. They could focus on the foreigners as the source of racial and class tensions, as destroyers of the Indians and of the vegetation of the Lake, as supporters of Gómez, as masters of the Venezuelan economy, and as destroyers of the traditional agricultural economy. Of course, many of the complaints against the foreigners were exaggerated and overlooked the complicity of Venezuelans in many matters. Nonetheless, the variety of changes which the foreigners caused or with which they were closely associated could arouse a cross-section of the Venezuelan population to unite against them. Gómez seldom tried to use the hostility toward the foreigners, but both López and Medina astutely drew on the mild xenophobia to win popular support for actions they wished to take to curb the excesses of the oil companies. Thus, in spite of themselves, the foreigners inspired both the first surge of modern economic development and the first displays of an assertive nationalism.

Relationships between the Venezuelan government and the foreign oil companies between 1922 and 1945 were affected by world economic conditions, the *caudillos'* personalities, World War II, the parallel progress of the Mexican petroleum industry, and the rise of popular nationalism in Venezuela. By and large Gómez's relations with the companies remained in the spirit of the 1922 law in which the companies had secured generous concessions. The Venezuelan government had very little control or influence over the activities of the companies. More often than not, the dictator supported the foreigners against his own countrymen, especially the workers. Yet Juan Vicente Gómez could also manipulate and subtly threaten the companies. He watched them as closely as he did his Venezuelan exiles and critics. Zulia governor General Vincenio Pérez Soto reported to Gómez in August 1926 that the US ship *Niagara* was serving as a sentinel of US interests, just as US warships had done in Mexico in Baja California in 1914. The ship had direct communications with the United States and obviously intended more than topographic surveys.[6] Gómez always refused to allow the companies to dredge a channel in the bar at the mouth of Lake Maracaibo, which would have facilitated transportation of the crude oil. The examples of Panamanian independence and other landings of marines in the Caribbean were not lost on Gómez, and he did not intend to lose western Venezuela.

On the other hand, Gómez and his colleagues could exploit foreigners' fear of the nationalism which had driven them out of Mexico. When General Vincenio Pérez Soto tried to persuade the petroleum companies to correct some of the worst abuses in Zulia, they referred to him as a "civilized Pancho Villa" and subtly referred to the "chaos" that nationalism had brought in Mexico.[7] Both the *gomecistas* and the companies could play the Mexican card to try to intimidate the others throughout this period.

Gómez was also canny enough to play the companies off against each other and to seek benefits for himself and his friends. A friend and colleague set up the *Compañía Venezolana de Petróleo* which offered to sell concessions to the foreigners. Foreigners at first resisted, but when Gómez circulated rumors that the Germans had options on one quarter of the holdings, the US companies rushed to buy, even at the inflated prices which Gómez and Baldó had set.[8] There was no pretense that this income would go to the nation, but it was an example in which the bargaining game with the companies was played to the benefit of Venezuelans.

Finally, Gómez reinstated Gumersindo Torres as Minister of Development in the period 1929–31. Having lost little of his fire, Torres publicized the companies' misrepresentation of costs, especially of transportation. The doctored figures greatly reduced the royalties that they owed to the Venezuelan government. Torres calculated that between February 1927 and January 1931, Standard Oil of Indiana had bilked the Venezuelan government of Bs 26 million and Gulf Oil had saved themselves Bs 30 million. Torres presented a bill, and, despite strong Venezuelan press support, again lost his position in response to company protests. Torres, like the Mexican card, served to remind the companies that their preferential treatment could be altered.

From 1936, López Contreras was in a stronger position but found that the obdurate companies would play a waiting game that would defeat him. In his favor, he had the eruption of popular nationalism, as revealed by the masses which rioted in the petroleum areas after Gómez's death. Some oil camps were evacuated, as buildings were burned and foreigners were threatened. López quickly quelled this threat to his authority and to the companies when he subsequently dictated an end to the December 1936-January 1937 strike, leaving the workers' demands largely unmet.

The European war and the Mexican expropriation of petroleum companies in 1938 helped to reinforce López's position. His Development Minister, Néstor Luis Pérez (1936–8), revived many of Torres's arguments and formulated a new petroleum legislation. Supported by the courts, López and the press, the Congress passed the new law in July 1938. It provided for more government control and supervision of the industry and greater revenues for the government. Unfortunately, it remained largely a paper tiger, since the companies refused to surrender the privileges they had under previous or existing law. They simply ignored the new legislation. The Mexican example was chilling to them, but they could see that Venezuela's economy was more dependent on the single product of oil, and that the population was smaller and more dependent on the petroleum revenues.

It would finally fall to the Medina government to cash in on the parallel circumstances of the Second World War, the Mexican expropriation, Venezuelan nationalism, the fears of the US State Department, and the benefits of the Good Neighbor "give-them-a-share" approach. The State Department urged the US oil companies to be more responsive to Venezuelan demands in order to forestall any major problems in the Hemisphere during the War. The

Venezuelan government could also be more conciliatory than in the First World War, for now the Venezuelan economy was linked more firmly to that of the United States. Moreover, the recent advances in military technology and the increased strategic importance of oil rendered the long Venezuelan coastline particularly vulnerable to an attack by one of the great powers. The reduced petroleum activity in Venezuela meant less government revenue, and an accompanying political insecurity.

Still Medina pushed at the companies. In July 1941, he set a new exchange control which was less beneficial to the companies; they could now exchange a dollar for Bs 3.09, while exporters of coffee and hides and cacao received more than Bs 4 for a dollar. He passed an income tax law in 1942, which affected the companies. Agricultural subsidies could be phased out, the government treasury benefited, the companies protested.[9] Medina had more of a flair for rousing public sympathies than had López, and he was confident that his campaign to explain and justify actions taken toward the companies would be acceptable. The final step came in March 1943, when the Congress passed the petroleum law which lasted with minor revisions until the 1976 nationalization. The law unified and updated all previous petroleum legislation, provided for higher royalties, greater exploration and surface taxes, high initial exploitation taxes, the promotion of domestic refining, a broadening of the government's influence and powers, and an end to the customs exemption privileges. In exchange for accepting these more stringent rules, the companies were promised a lowering of tariff schedules so that imports would not be discouraged. The government agreed to drop an investigation into disputed titles, and promised that the concessions which would have ended in the 1960s would be extended. Thus the companies exchanged greater security of their concessions for greater government participation in the revenues and administration of the industry.

Delegates of the newly-formed *Acción Democrática* party in Congress protested that the new law did not go far enough in protecting the government rights and patrimony. It is difficult to guess whether the government could have achieved a more stringent legislation. It appeared, however, that the government's will to enforce and supervise even the legislation that existed was more crucial than the laws themselves. This had been the case since the beginnings of the asphalt and oil industries. But the international companies still had most of the information, and sufficiently powerful allies in their more powerful governments, to be able to subvert most efforts at economic nationalism. A country such as Venezuela in the 1940s, with few close ties to other oil-producing nations, with major national and social dilemmas still unresolved and with few experts in petroleum to advise them, could hardly hope to wring the maximum benefits from the companies.

The Gómez System

The Gómez system built a political bridge between the personalistic *caudillo* system of the past and the modern bureaucratic state of the future. Gómez himself presided over a government which moved away from a *laissez-faire* philosophy. Power became increasingly centralized in Caracas and in the presidency, and Gómez had to exercise that power more actively in relatively new fields, such as labor relations, banking, and subsidies for agricultural exports. There is no doubt that Gómez himself was a traditional *caudillo*, ruling a personal empire through friends and relatives. Yet the new actors on the scene — the petroleum companies — forced Gómez and his advisors to take new measures to maintain the order they had so carefully constructed between 1908 and 1922. Within careful limits, the companies and the foreigners had also to abide by and accommodate themselves to that order. After Gómez's death, the governing elite increasingly perceived that the Venezuelan people were allies rather than enemies in the search for national autonomy and economic independence.

The petroleum industry also indirectly provided another pressure to which Gómez had to respond. As the Venezuelan economy became more linked with the Caribbean and North Atlantic economy, foreign governments and groups sometimes criticized his actions. José Vasconcelos of Mexico attacked him for repression of labor organizations and political opposition. The Pan American Federation of Labor and the International Labor Organization both investigated and criticized the Gómez government. The Caracas diplomatic community urged Gómez to release the students imprisoned after the 1928 revolt. Such protests were mild, of course, compared to the 1902–3 foreign blockade, but Gómez appreciated the importance of avoiding foreign criticism and countered the assaults as best he could. Foreign critics had to be heeded not only because they blackened the nation's reputation, but also because they gave support to Venezuelan exiles and to dissident groups within the nation.

Venezuela's action in the world community still remained insignificant during Gómez's lifetime. Yet the nation did join and participate actively in the League of Nations. Warned not to alienate the great powers by votes within the League, Venezuelan ambassadors still gained valuable experience in diplomatic negotiation and

César Zumeta served as an elected non-permanent member of the Council in 1929–31. One principle which Venezuela consistently supported in the League was that of restricting League activities to political matters; Venezuelan delegates openly objected to the expense of maintaining economic and technological missions, and privately wanted to avoid having multilateral groups intervening in their country's domestic affairs.[10] Bilateral relations were also limited; in 1926, Venezuela had diplomatic relations with only nineteen countries: the United States, the Vatican, nine Latin American and eight European states. There were forty-three employees of the Foreign Ministry in Caracas, forty-nine diplomatic officers, and forty-seven consuls. The figures did not change much in the period up to 1939. Diplomats were generally outstanding intellectuals, friends of Gómez, and their diplomatic dispatches often provided information about the activities of Venezuelan exiles, sycophantic praise for the dictator, and pleas for money. In their correspondence with the dictator, Pedro Arcaya, César Zumeta, and Laureano Vallenilla Lanz frequently expressed their gratitude to Gómez for past gifts and delicately informed him when they again found themselves without sufficient funds. Sometimes the diplomats also gave intelligent advice which went unheeded. César Zumeta wrote a series of memoranda to Gómez recommending an aggressive support and marketing of Venezuelan sweet cacao in Europe. The product had an eager acceptance there, especially in Germany, over the more common bitter cacao. Gómez displayed no enthusiasm for the proposal, and the unique sweet cacao suffered the same decline as other agricultural products during the depression.

Gómez did depart somewhat from a traditional *laissez-faire* attitude to provide some subsidies and support for some sectors of the Venezuelan economy. He was able to do so because, even during the depression, government revenues remained high, compared to what he had known when he first assumed office in 1908 (see the accompanying table). With adequate revenues, Gómez could afford to take some measures to support Venezuelan agriculture during the depression. The emergency measures could not permanently restore health to an agricultural structure already weakened by increased appropriation of land by the dictator and his friends and by the shocks rendered by the petroleum economy. Coffee and cacao exports had fallen immediately after the First World War, but had recovered somewhat by the mid-1920s. Oil for the first time replaced coffee as the primary export crop in 1926, and *hacendados* complained bitterly of their credit problems and of the loss of workers to the petroleum camps. Gómez responded to the complaints with two unprecedented measures. First, he established the

VENEZUELAN GOVERNMENT INCOME[12]
(*thousands of bolívares*)

1921–2	70,927
1922–3	87,691
1923–4	102,249
1924–5	120,165
1925–6	172,098
1926–7	182,148
1927–8	186,752
1928–9	230,415
1929–30	255,445
1930–1	210,229
1931–2	185,096
1932–3	171,889
1933–4	171,829
1934–5	202,980
1935–6	189,125
1936–7	274,003
1937–8	330,137
1938–9	340,043
1939–40	353,548
1940–1	345,683

Banco Agrícola y Pecuario (Agriculture and Livestock Bank) in 1928 to issue mortgages to the hard-pressed farmers, and this was the first autonomous government institution, the forerunner of dozens of specialized government agencies which were to blossom in the 1970s. Even during the depression, the *bolívar* remained surprisingly strong, especially after 1933 when the United States devalued the dollar. The strength of the Venezuelan currency exacerbated the problems both of export agriculture and of the oil industry within Venezuela. Gómez attempted to manipulate the exchange rate to favor both oil and agricultural interests, but the measures failed to satisfy the farmers. Finally, in 1934, Gómez decreed outright subsidies for export agriculture. The measures may have been too little and too late for the growers, but they did acknowledge government responsibility for the economy. Moreover, as noted previously, the Venezuelan coffee and cacao growers had not displayed an urge to modernize. Nor were they blessed by an abundance of good land near good ports and railroads. One Venezuelan critic claims that they used government susbsidies and mortgages to enrich themselves rather than to promote agricultural exports, and indeed many apparently took the mortgage credit and transferred their assets to commerce and urban land. By 1937, the *Banco Agrícola y Pecuario* held 22 percent of the total value of all farm property as collateral, a situation which owed as much to the short-sightedness and greed of the *hacendados* as it did to the international economic crisis or Venezuelan government errors.[11]

Gómez also took extraordinary measures to save one of the largest Venezuelan commercial firms from the effects of the depression. The Boulton firm had replaced several German firms in coffee exporting after World War I. Bolstered by the high demand for consumer goods in the petroleum camps, the Boultons had greatly expanded their commercial outlets during the 1920s. In 1929, they were caught with a great deal of coffee and merchandise in their warehouse. Coffee prices plunged, but the Boultons still had to pay for the merchandise they had imported. *Andinos* who had used the firm as a bank in Maracaibo demanded their money. Gómez and his advisers feared that a Boulton collapse would damage Venezuelan government credit and the entire economy. Like Cipriano Castro denying that there was a plague in La Guaira, Gómez proudly denied that the depression was affecting Venezuela. The Venezuelan government bought the Boulton family mansion in El Paraíso, Caracas, and several other of their buildings, which allowed the Boultons to weather the crisis. Inveterate risk-takers, they turned from coffee to representation of major shipping lines like Grace and Alcoa, and became associated with the new Pan American Airlines Company, which had begun to operate in Venezuela. In 1942 they received a license to form their own airline, Avensa, which would compete with the state owned Aeropostal. Thus, both with agriculture and with commerce, the Gómez efforts to protect some major economic units contributed to their ability to rearrange their assets to take better advantage of the new economic scene.

The petroleum companies and entrepreneurs received favorable treatment, and the coffee and cacao growers were bought off. Gómez obviously tolerated few complaints from the lower end of the economic scale, but he apparently did recognize that repression might be mixed with some minor concessions to prevent large-scale labor problems. The oil regions experienced their first strikes in 1925, with a demand for higher wages and the removal of the hated Dutch supervisors. Gómez decreed an end to the strike, sent troops, and urged the companies to introduce a slight raise in wages. Strike leaders were jailed, or mysteriously disappeared from Zulia.

In 1928, the Gómez government passed a labor bill, which on paper provided minimal guarantees to workers. It also established the second autonomous institute, the *Banco Obrero* (Workers' Bank), which supplied funds to finance construction of workers' housing. Critics alleged that the Bank simply provided one more means for Gómez's cronies to enrich themselves. The US consul in Maracaibo estimated that houses worth Bs 8,000 were sold to workers for Bs 15,000[13] Gómez tolerated no autonomous union activity, which showed mild signs of developing in oil camps of Zulia and in Caracas. An insignificant government union became in 1926 the *Federación Obrera de Venezuela* (Workers' Federation of Venezuela), but Gómez's labor policy still rested more heavily on the use of force and repression than on persuasion or paternalism. The absence of an industrial base or large numbers of industrial workers, of national communications, and of European traditions of syndicalism or anarchy made the job relatively easy. Government expenditures on public works — 27 percent of the national budget in 1928–30 — helped absorb some of the workers displaced by faltering agriculture. When the oil companies dismissed workers in 1930, Gómez provided funds for the men to return to their home states.

Gómez's constitutions (1922, 1925, 1928, 1929, 1931) also expressed the move away from *laissez-faire* liberalism. For example, the 1925 document gave the President the authority to enforce conservation of natural resources; thus the absolute right of property ownership was limited by public utility considerations. As in any *caudillo* system, of course, constitutions, congresses, and courts were less important than Gómez's will. The wily dictator maintained control over the minute details, as his correspondence in the Miraflores Archive shows. Engineer José N. Arguello wrote to Gómez on June 19, 1924 to inform the dictator of the construction progress on the Transandean highway. He complained that the Ford which Gómez had sent him the previous year was a lemon and *"inservible."* He requested a new car for the opening ceremonies for the highway. A Buick, Arguello suggested, would be much preferable and more *"resistente."*[14]

Other aspects of the Gómez regime remained equally traditional. In the 1920s, he relied heavily on his family for support and potential successors. A series of accidents, feuds, and disloyalties embittered the old man and left the succession question for a time in doubt. Alí, the favorite son, had died in the 1918 epidemic. The 1922 Constitution provided for two Vice Presidents: son José Vicente and brother Juancho. In 1923, Juancho was assassinated as he slept in Miraflores palace. José Vicente and his mother Dionisia were implicated, although no firm evidence ever became public. Dionisia went into exile, and José Vicente followed after becoming suspected of involvement in another plot. Cousin Eustoquio, one of the most hated men in Venezuela for his cruelty and high-handedness, hovered around in various posts until Gómez's death in December 1935. He then made a bid for power, but was unable to pre-empt

Minister of War Eleazar López Contreras and died in a futile assault on the presidential palace. By the 1930s, Gómez clearly preferred that López Contreras succeed him, and his preference probably bestowed some degree of legitimacy on López, supported by the army, while it avoided the internecine fighting which might have resulted had one of the Gómez clan been drafted into the presidency.

Gómez's family and the army were the only viable contenders to succeed him in 1935. Yet signs appeared in the late 1920s that other Venezuelans intended to enter the fray. The newly organized *Federación Venezolana de Estudiantes* (Federation of Venezuelan Students) turned a celebration of student week in February 1928 into a veiled criticism of the dictator, to which Gómez responded typically and promptly by jailing the students. Much to his surprise, working-class Venezuelans turned out in Caracas and all over the nation to demand the release of the students. Shortly thereafter, some young officers in Caracas garrisons initiated a conspiracy, and, as in 1918, enlisted the support of some civilians. Unfortunately, the alliance of officers, students, and urban masses enjoyed little co-ordination and discipline, and Minister of War López Contreras quickly jailed the military ringleaders. López did not order the wholesale assassination, torture, and detention which had followed the 1918 conspiracy, but he did order the imprisonment of his son, who had participated in the military conspiracy. Young López became ill in prison and died shortly thereafter. Gómez nevertheless suspected General López Contreras of undue generosity toward the conspirators and banished him to the Andes for a brief period. He regained the dictator's confidence and returned to Caracas in 1931 as Minister of War.

In 1928 and 1929, López demonstrated that he would tolerate no disorder, but also that he preferred to exercise moderation in the use of force. He was put to the test again in January 1936, when protests, looting, and vandalism broke out after Gómez's death. The violence that broke out then in the cities and oil camps was the most extensive that Venezuela had experienced in a quarter of a century. López was in a touchy situation. He had quickly asserted his authority over the armed forces, especially after the death of Eustoquio Gómez, and had lifted some of the rigid censorship and repression of the Gómez regime. Yet he chose not to repudiate Gómez completely, as Gómez had Castro in 1908 or as Castro had Andrade in 1899. With the *gomecista* hard-liners glowering from the right and the urban masses, workers, and student pressing from the left, López chose to reimpose censorship and to order Federal District Governor Félix Galavís and the army to control the popular movements in Caracas and the oil zones.

Popular demonstrations in Caracas' Plaza Bolívar on February 14 protested the reimposition of censorship. Governor Galavís' police became trigger-happy and fired on the crowd, killing and wounding several people. López recognized that he was dealing with a new situation, and he employed two new tools to maintain control: the radio and the February Program. The latter was a package of social and economic reforms unlike anything previously promised by a Venezuelan executive. The first Venezuelan President to speak to the nation over the radio pledged the government's responsibility for economic development and the welfare and health of its citizens. Venezuelans could expect constitutional legality, labor rights, public health and social assistance, a reorganization of education at all levels, reform of a corrupt public administration, encouragement of foreign immigration, a major effort to create a national communications and transportation infrastructure, and tax and banking reforms. The plan had something for everyone and signaled López's intention to check the army's strength with populist appeals. The young intellectual Arturo Uslar Pietri coined a term in 1936 to express the government's commitment to invest the oil wealth more widely in the human material of Venezuela. The government must, Uslar argued, *"sembrar el petróleo"* — sow the petroleum. The wealth which came from the viscous liquid should cause a healthy, literate, and modern nation to bloom.

More surprising than the promises of reform was the effort to implement the February Program. A Chilean mission helped to establish the teacher training institution, the *Instituto Pedagógico* (Teachers' Training Institute) in 1936. A National Labor Office and a new labor law also appeared in 1936. The *Consejo Venezolano del Niño* (Venezuelan Children's Council, 1939), the *Instituto Preorientación para Menores* (Preorientation Institute for Minors, 1939), and the *Casa de Maternidad Concepción Palacios* (Concepción Palacios Maternity Home, 1938) expressed a concern for the nourishment and care of children. López announced the first three-year development plan in 1938. New cabinet ministries were created: the *Ministerio de Agricultura y Cría* (Ministry of Agriculture and Livestock) and the *Ministerio de Trabajo y Comunicaciones* Ministry of Labor and Communications). The government assumed greater control over the economy and monetary policy after it established the *Banco Industrial* (Industrial Bank), the *Oficina Nacional de Cambios*, (National Exchange Office), and the *Banco Central de Venezuela* (Central Bank of Venezuela). The more extreme petroleum law of 1938 was aimed at exercising more control over the oil companies. The bureaucracy grew and changed as

López tried to replace some of the old *andinos* with *caraqueños*.

López emulated Gómez in his rabid anti-Communism and suspicion of all political parties. He did not honor his pledge to restore full civil liberties and in 1937 he used alleged Communist activities as a pretext to exile a number of labor and political leaders and to refuse to legalize some of the nascent political movements. The new 1936 Constitution retained the Gómez clause that defined Communism as treason against the nation. The President also retained his blanket authorization to expel or imprison anyone suspected of leftist tendencies.

One traditional method of administrative reform served López well. The 1936 Constitution contained a clause which confiscated all of Gómez's extensive holdings in Venezuela. Those who had suffered at the hands of the dictator had first claim on the Gómez property. With that one action, López distanced himself from Gómez and fed some of the popular repudiation of him. He also garnered some political allies among the grateful recipients of the largesses, many of whom were members of the elite or the emerging middle groups. In the 1930s, there was not enough political advantage to be gained from using the confiscated land to begin an agrarian reform program among scattered, unorganized, and largely inarticulate peasants. The confiscation applied only to the property of Gómez and his family, so it won great approval without arousing the kind of protests which Crespo had faced in 1892 when he wanted to confiscate his predecessor's goods.

López further contributed to the development of political legitimacy when he reduced the presidential term from seven years to five and surrendered power to his chosen successor, Minister of War, Isaías Medina Angarita. The Congress which elected the new President in 1941 theoretically had a choice between Medina and the rival candidate proposed by the civilian opposition, novelist Rómulo Gallegos. The Gallegos candidacy was in fact only symbolic, but it represented another slight thaw in the old *caudillo* system.

Medina Angarita, one of the first graduates of the Military Academy in Caracas, came from a different generation of Táchira military leaders from those who had been with Cipriano Castro when he and his cohorts had seized control of Caracas in 1899. Medina had spent little time in Táchira and felt at home with the economic and social elite of Caracas. The new President proved much more tolerant than any of the previous *andinos* and earned the respect and indeed the love of many of his compatriots.

The period from 1941 to 1945 saw more political discussion, organizing, and activity than had occurred at any time since the nineteenth century. Medina formed an official government party, the *Partido Democrático Venezolano*, in 1943, but allowed other political parties, including the Communists, to operate openly. Rómulo Betancourt's and Rómulo Gallegos' political followers formally united to found *Acción Democrática* in September 1941, and this became the principal opposition party. Freedom of the press and of Congressional debate intensified the feverish political enthusiasm.

Several issues naturally prompted heated discussion. Medina's government proposed Venezuela's first income tax law in 1942. A new petroleum law in 1943 went further than that of 1938, and the government announced its intention to require compliance. The law provided that the Venezuelan government should receive 50 percent of the oil industry's profits. The timing was good, and the US State Department urged the companies to work with the Medina administration during the tense war years. *Acción Democrática* opposed the law, objecting that it did not go far enough, and in so doing earned a reputation for strident nationalism.

Other measures proved less divisive. The government and the economic elite could agree on the advisability of creating the *Instituto de Seguro Social*. Two troublesome boundary disputes were settled. In 1941, Colombia and Venezuela established mutually agreeable boundaries on the Guajira Peninsula at Castilletes. No mention was made at the time of how the territorial seas of the Gulf of Venezuela would be divided, an issue over which the two countries were to disagree bitterly in the 1970s. Maritime frontiers did, however, receive delimitation in the East, since Britain surrendered the island of Patos to Venezuela, and the Gulf of Paría Treaty was signed in 1942, which divided the shelves and waters of that Gulf between Venezuela and Trinidad.

When the time came for Medina Angarita to choose a successor, he proved even more liberal than López Contreras. He chose the man, and the Congress would dutifully elect him. Nonetheless, Medina discussed his choice with the civilian politicians who called for free elections and a wider suffrage. Medina's candidate, the Venezuelan ambassador to the United States, Diógenes Escalante, pleased *Acción Democrática* leaders since they believed that he would move more quickly toward a democratic system. Escalante then became ill and Medina's second choice, Angel Biaggini, was not acceptable to the civilians. A succession crisis loomed.

Medina's authority had been further eroded by a division within the armed forces. General López Contreras and the right wing of the *andinos* deplored the open activity of leftists and wanted to restore López to the presidential chair. On the other hand, younger officers like Marcos Pérez Jiménez chafed at Medina's unwillingness to move more quickly to modernize the nation and the armed forces.

Gómez, López, and Medina had shaped their politics in the shadow of the new petroleum wealth, the increased foreign presence in the nation, and the lingering traditions of the *caudillo* system. Simultaneously, the petroleum wealth had encouraged new groups and classes to protest that *caudillo* politics were an anachronism in a nation so intimately linked through trade and alliance with the Western democracies.

Transportation, Communication, and Organization

Arturo Uslar Pietri remarked that the issue of centralism or federalism was irrelevant in Venezuela after it became a petroleum nation. In fact, changes which accompanied the development of the oil industry and the expanding wealth and responsibilities of the Caracas government encouraged a stronger national identity. The petroleum industry affected some regions more than others, but it was a national industry. In spite of Gómez's perceptions being rooted firmly in the nineteenth century, the new industry demanded modernization of the national infrastructure. The petroleum camps and Gómez's new road network permitted easier population movement within the country. *Andino* and *margariteño* came together in the oil fields of Zulia as they had never done before.

The largest portion of the government's share of the new wealth undoubtedly went to Gómez and his friends. Yet a wider group of lawyers, doctors, engineers, journalists, teachers, and merchants also benefited from the flourishing economy. The government did not spend a great amount on social programs, but it did relinquish more than it had done before in agricultural subsidies, bureaucratic and military salaries, funds for *Banco Obrero* construction, and public works. The Venezuelan population had stabilized and begun to grow slowly in the 1930s, but not so rapidly as it did after the Second World War. Thus by 1940s the modest government expenditures and modernization probably had a measurable *per capita* impact on the three and a half million Venezuelans. Arguably, the 1930s marked Venezuela's entrance to the modern world, not because of the death of Gómez, but because the demands of the oil industry had facilitated the rapid expansion and wellbeing of a new national middle class. The new professionals began to form national associations, including political parties, and to express the new consciousness in a literature with more universal themes than the *criollista* works of the early twentieth century.

The oil industry greatly influenced the development of transportation networks in Venezuela. Gómez had initiated the construction of the Trans-Andean highway to link the Andean states with the nation's capital, and there continued to be much talk of a modern rail network to provide rapid and inexpensive transportation. Yet all government and private investment in road construction focused on routes from the oil camps to ports and from the major camps to Caracas. Most of the new roads appeared along the northern axis, with Caracas becoming a bottleneck through which much transport from the east to the west of the nation had to pass. Air transport came to be the preferred manner of reaching the far-flung regions of Venezuela, and petroleum geologists were able, airborne, to prowl the entire national territory. The most famous of the early pilots was Jimmy Angel, a test pilot from Wichita, Kansas, who had been hired by the government for geological explorations. Fascinated by the stories of the legendary Auyuntapui mountain deep in the Guayana highlands, Angel in 1934 discovered the mountain, landed his plane there, and reported to Venezuelans that they had the tallest waterfall in the world. The falls were promptly dubbed Angel Falls.

Roads and airlines improved the physical communication within Venezuela, but the advent of radio and the expansion of the printed media probably did more to foment Venezuelan nationalism, especially after the death of Gómez. The Venezuelan papers had subscribed to international news services since 1909 and received foreign news by cable. Gómez's censorship meant that the literate population sometimes knew more of foreign news than of domestic happenings. After 1936, an increased number of photographs in Venezuelan papers attracted more readers and increased circulation. *El Universal* published the first literary supplement in 1937, and in 1941 it initiated a sports chronicle by Abelardo Raidi. Medina's liberalization allowed a new paper, *Ultimas Noticias*, founded by Kotepa Delgado and Pedro Beroes, to devote more space to news of the *barrios* and labor syndicates. Henrique Otero Vizcarrondo and his son, Miguel Otero Silva, incorporated these journalistic innovations when they founded *El Nacional* in 1943. Raidi came from the rival paper to head up the sports section; Francisco "*El Gordo*" Pérez took over the photography department. Color was used to highlight titles and in photographs. The paper had its own foreign correspondents and began to sponsor an annual prize for short stories. After 1936, numerous ephemeral newspapers and newsletters appeared but none had the expertise or the financial backing to be able to mount a strong challenge on a national level against *El Universal*, *Ultimas Noticias*, or *El Nacional*. However, not even photographs and sports news could greatly increase newspaper circulation in a nation which in 1936 could only claim that 39 percent of its population was literate. The more revolutionary medium was the radio, and the first transmitter was installed in Caracas in 1926. The Gómez government, suspicious of the new invention, strictly restricted the number of people who were permitted to buy a receiver. Undaunted, Venezuelans exercised their traditional *viveza* to make clandestine sets so that they could hear the musical programs, government news, and comedies which were broadcast from early afternoon until 10.30 p.m.

The real era of Venezuelan radio dawned in December 1930 when William Phelps inaugurated *Broadcasting Caracas*. A merchant who specialized in electrical appliances and who also had the Ford and Lincoln automobile concession, Phelps saw the merits of radio advertising to sell his products. Once Gómez had given up trying to control the sale of radio sets, the way was clear to sell Frigidaires from Mérida to Carúpano. The station also had some ambitions to raise the cultural level of the population, and transmitted numerous concerts, news programs, special programs for women, José Nucete Sardi's narratives of the history of Venezuela, and daily children's programs which featured Venezuelan folkloric heroes like Tío Tigre, Tío Conejo, *La bruja Cumbamba* (Witch Cumbamba), and *La comadreja* (The Weasel). On Sunday nights, there were remote transmissions of the Martial Band from Plaza Bolívar, under the direction of Pedro Elías Gutiérrez. Gutiérrez was the composer of Venezuela's unofficial national anthem *Alma llanera* (Soul of the Llanos, 1916), and had been a popular musical figure around Caracas since early in the century. Dramatic soap operas also included national scenes and figures; *El misterio de los ojos escarlata* (The Mystery of the Red Eyes) took its listeners to all regions of Venezuela as the story unfolded day by day. *La comedia Santa Teresa*, sponsored by Santa Teresa Rum, became so popular that listeners sent flowers to the fictitious middle-class couple when they married and toys to their newborn child. Indignant fans called the station when the baby "Cocoliso" was born and cried in response to the nurse's slap; they demanded to know how the radio performers had made the baby cry. Before the Caracas city prefect stepped in to punish such child abuse, the station explained that they were trying out some sound effect records that they had received from RCA Victor.[15]

With López Contreras, radio attained an even greater role in the national life. He became the first President to speak on radio after the riots of 1936, and he announced his plans for political reform. As Henry Allen notes, "It was to be Venezuela's introduction to the radio voice as a political instrument."[16] Under López, the Minister of National Education also began to supply rural schools with radios and to recognize their educational possibilities. Still another milestone came in 1943, when *Radio Continente* began to transmit its own radio news, gathered and written by its own reporters. The station also developed its own editorials, literary notes, sports news, and syndicate news rather than using the newspaper version. By 1946, Venezuela had more radios *per capita* (.0269) than Mexico (.0258) did — an index both of the growing wealth of the nation and of the influence of the media.

The new transportation and communications establishments, in addition to the expansion of government services and education after Gómez's death, spawned a new group of middle-class workers. These followed the example of the lawyers, doctors, dentists, pharmacists, and engineers who had formed professional associations early in the twentieth century. The *Federación Venezolana de Maestros* (Venezuelan Teachers' Federation) was formed in 1937; the *Asociación Nacional de Empleados* (National Association of Employees) in the mid-1930s; the *Asociación Venezolana de Periodismo* (Venezuelan Journalists' Association) in 1941 and the *Sindicato Nacional de Trabajadores de la Prensa* (National Syndicate of Press Workers) in 1943. The first national convention of *Cámaras y Asociaciones de Comercio y Producción* (Chambers and Associations of Commerce and Production) in 1944 became the forerunner of *Fedecámaras*. Urban, white-collar, and national (although usually concentrated in Caracas), these groups began to play a prominent role in national political life.

When López reinstituted censorship in 1936, the *Asociación de Escritores Venezolanos* (Association of Venezuelan Writers) led the move to declare a press strike. The *Federación de Estudiantes Venezolanos* (Association of Venezuelan Students) called for an accompanying student strike; and the *Asociación Nacional de Empleados* also pressed the government to rescind the censorship. The first Venezuelan Congress of Journalists in October 1943 invited President Medina to speak to them. He reaffirmed his commitment to freedom of the press and of thought and pledged that there would be no censorship under his government. At the meeting, the journalists supplemented their recommendations on salaries and social security with an exhortation to institute diplomatic relations with the Soviet Union. In 1939, some representatives of local chambers of commerce had been asked to review a projected code of commerce which the government was considering; they objected to some clauses and began to take the first steps toward forming a national organization. Medical associations wanted a say in the new social security legislation, and the *Federación Venezolana de*

Maestros aggressively opposed Church-controlled education. In a society like Venezuela's in the 1930s and 1940s, these professional associations appeared to have more influence upon the government than did *campesino* or labor syndicates. Although white-collar critics of the government suffered prison and exile, they were not subjected to the same degree of repression as were the laboring groups.

The government monitored labor unions more carefully than it did the middle-class groups. No strong, independent unions had had a chance to develop. The early strikes in the petroleum camps in 1925 were rather amorphous and unorganized, with no clear leaders and no clear goals. Venezuela had had neither an anarchist tradition nor an extensive industrial complex which might have provided bargaining experience and working-class consciousness. The government decreed contracts, organized unions, and wrote laws.

Conditions improved after 1936, when the López government investigated labor abuses and pressed the oil companies to provide more services. The 1926 labor law drew the protest of the oil companies. Yet in the first serious general strike in the petroleum fields in December 1936 to January 1937, President López Contreras showed his colors and decreed an end to the strike without considering a number of the strikers' demands. The government retained, and used, the right to cancel the organization of labor syndicates. In 1939, there were 246 syndicates with 69,139 members; in 1940, the number of syndicates dropped to 155 and the number of members to 36,326.[17] The fear of Communism tainted relations with the labor syndicates as it did not in the case of the middle-class groups. In 1937, forty-seven labor leaders and pro-labor politicians were accused of Communistic activities and exiled, while others were imprisoned. International Worker's Day had been celebrated on May 1 for the first time in Venezuela in 1936, but after 1938 the celebration was moved to July 24, Simón Bolívar's birthday. Labor leaders continued to press for the internationally recognized May 1 anniversary without success, even under the more liberal President Medina Angarita.

Like López Contreras, Medina Angarita acted with ambivalence toward autonomous labor organization. In 1944, that ambivalence assisted *Acción Democrática* leaders to gain control of the labor movement. The Second Workers' Congress had called together labor delegates to form a national labor confederation in March 1944. At that time, leadership of the unions was divided between the Communist Party and the newly-formed *Acción Democrática* party. AD proposed that leadership in the executive committee should be evenly divided between Communists and its own supporters. The Communists, aware that their followers were in the majority, refused, and the AD delegates withdrew from the confederation. President Medina and his cabinet then decided that the labor congress had violated the constitution by openly supporting a political party, and the President suspended the congress; legal recognition of all unions which were represented by delegates who stayed at the meeting was cancelled. By default, *Acción Democrática* became the only viable political party which retained strength in the labor movement. Thus Venezuelan labor syndicates, born and shaped under the paternalistic and repressive eye of Gómez, entered the modern era almost as adjuncts of political parties, especially *Acción Democrática*.

López and Medina found it even easier to control the peasant syndicates. Rural problems were acute. The Agricultural Census of 1937 revealed that 4.4 percent of rural property-owners held 78 percent of the land surveyed, and 95.6 percent of the owners shared the remaining 22 percent. Nearly 90 percent of the rural people classified as peasants worked on the land of others.[18] The concentration of land ownership had become much more intense during the Gómez regime, so that the situation of the *minifundistas* was worse in 1937 than it had been earlier in the century. Renters, sharecroppers, and squatters were probably not much better off than the wage laborers who were so completely dominated by the *hacendados*. Control was maintained by the traditional methods, supplemented with liberal use of Gómez's new national army to keep down peasant unrest. Organization was much more difficult in the countryside, and the Communist leaders in the 1930s and 1940s concentrated on the more easily reached oil and urban workers, many of whom had the additional advantage of working for foreign companies. *Acción Democrática* leaders saw the possibilities of rural organization in a nation still classified in 1941 as 68.7 percent rural. Membership in legally recognized peasant syndicates rose from three syndicates with 482 members in 1936 to seventy-seven syndicates with 6,279 members in 1945.[19]

In addition to professional associations, laborers, and *campesinos*, three other more heterogeneous groups increased their national influence and visibility: military officers, the Church and women. Younger military officers who had attended the military academy and had studied abroad, as was increasingly common after 1936, developed a greater *esprit de corps*; they came to believe that they had a national mission as a group to encourage the economic development and modernization of their nation. López Contreras and Medina Angarita paid them some attention, but the older *gomecista* generals continued to frustrate their ambitions to influence government policy.

The Church had been greatly weakened in the nineteenth century by some of the anti-clerical measures of Guzmán Blanco. Under Gómez, however, a rebuilding began. Over half the dioceses and all the vicariates of the Church were founded after 1900. In 1945, the Catholic *liceos* dominated nearly half of the total enrolment in secondary education. Coinciding with the 1933 Congress in Rome which stressed the necessity to help the poor and to fight Communism, some Catholic youth groups took more interest in politics. The influence of Padre Manuel Aguirre permeated the thinking of many of the Catholic youth in Caracas. In the 1920s a teacher at the *Colegio San Ignacio*, Aguirre left Venezuela to reside and study in Europe between 1929 and 1937. He returned to Venezuela in 1937, a Jesuit priest, and organized study groups on Christian social thought. After 1938, his ideas became better known through the magazine he founded, SIC (*Seminario Interdiocesano Caracas* — Caracas Interdiocesan Seminary). One young student who had already taken a strong interest in politics became Padre Aguirre's chief protégé: Rafael Caldera.[20]

Some women's groups began to form in the 1930s to press for women's suffrage. The most prominent were the *Agrupación Cultural Femenina* (Feminine Cultural Group), *Acción Femenina* (Feminine Action), and the *Asociación Venezolana de Mujeres* (Venezuelan Women's Association), consisting mostly of middle-class or professional women. An association of working women had appeared in 1929 in Caracas, "the Venezuelan Association of Christian Working Women;" the group sought to improve wages, hours and vacations for women and to promote mutual assistance in finding housing and in providing information on health and hygiene.[21] The *Agrupación Cultural Femenina* received the most attention, however, on account of the forceful and talented women associated with it and for some of its political actions. Founded in 1935 just before Gómez's death, the *Asociación* sponsored discussion groups and organized some syndicates with working women. They supported the 1936 petroleum strike by inviting the children of striking workers into their homes. They also organized night schools for working women and pressed for women's suffrage. The outstanding leaders who continued to be prominent in Venezuelan politics and letters were Ana Esther Gouverneur, Ana Luisa Llovera, Luisa del Valle Silva, Ana Senior de Delgado, Carmen Clemente Travieso, and Mercedes Fermín.

Fermín, a schoolteacher, had first been associated with the *Asociación de Maestros Primarios* before she became active in the *Agrupación Cultural Femenina*. As a teacher, she was concerned about women's lack of literacy and apolitical attitudes. She hoped that women who scorned political parties might be lured into a greater activism through the *Agrupación*. In a 1979 interview, she explained how she came to join ORVE (*Organización Venezolana*), *Acción Democrática's* precursor:

"I can't say that I preferred one party to another because I liked the ideology or because I had thought over the program. That would be splitting hairs. I only knew that I could not identify with the *Partido Republicano Progresista* (PRP) which claimed to be a workers' party when I wasn't a worker. On the other hand, ORVE was a movement which wanted to incorporate all citizens; it was what I could consider a front of classes, with a broad platform, where there was room for intellectuals, manual workers, students, employees. There was room for me."[22]

The women had more influence in pressing their issues through ORVE, and later *Acción Democrática*, than they did working alone. In 1942, a group of women presented to the Congress a document asking for the right to vote. President Medina did subsequently allow women to vote in municipal elections, but general women's suffrage did not come until it was decreed by the *Acción Democrática* President Rómulo Betancourt in 1947. Fermín's career illustrates the way that middle-class professionals were becoming more politicized in various national associations and then turning to overtly political action in *Acción Democrática* as the government relaxed its strictures against political parties.

The National Situation in a New National Literature

Greater freedom for newspapers and the spread of radios helped this political coalescence. So too did the burst of creative activity by novelists, painters, and poets. The years 1922–45 may have been the most fecund period of national literature for Venezuela. The intellectuals of that period were passionately concerned about Venezuelan history and problems, but had also read and absorbed European philosophies and techniques. In spite of the Gómez repression, new journals provided an outlet for creative writing: *Actualidades*, *Fantoches* (Puppets), *Cultura Venezolana* (Venezuelan Culture), *Elité*, the *Revista Nacional de Cultura* (National Cultural Review) and *El Morrocoy Azul* (The Blue Turtle). These journals by and large gave more attention to national writers and concerns than had the classic *El Cojo Ilustrado* (The Illustrated Cripple, 1890–1915). They were truly national in being owned, directed, and written for by Venezuelans in a way that was to be less true of journals after the Second World War: the era of the international mass media would draw foreign publishing chains into

Venezuela, altering the style and substance of much subsequent Venezuelan writing.

In contrast to much of the North American and European writing of the 1930s, Venezuelan novels and short stories expressed a guarded optimism about the national future. Venezuelans had remained rather isolated from the two great tragedies of World War I and the Depression. Petroleum revenues and the *movimiento* prompted by the oil-fueled development contributed to a new confidence. The student and military revolts of 1928 and 1929, although failures, also encouraged the young to believe that the weight of history lay with those who intended to change and modernize the system. It is perhaps most illuminating to compare the pessimism of Rómulo Gallegos in *Reinaldo Solar* (1920) with the optimism of *Doña Barbara* (1929). In the latter the "civilized" Santos Luzardo conquers the "barbaric" Doña Barbara and brings law, order, and progress to the Venezuelan *llanos*. The book conveys both a strong affection for the landscape and people of the *llanos* and a revulsion from the brutality and lawlessness that have charactertized the region. In contrast with Reinaldo Solar, who associated with various groups composed largely of people of his own class, Santos Luzardo wins his struggle because he enlists the support and sympathy of the working-class *llaneros*.

Concern and respect for the working classes also come through in Ramón Díaz Sánchez's *Mene* (1936) and Miguel Otero Silva's *Fiebre* (1939). *Mene*, perhaps the first real petroleum novel written in Venezuela, depicts the suffering of the petroleum workers exposed to racism, arrogance, and exploitation by the company managers. *Mene* could hardly be called optimistic, since the company blocked all efforts of the workers to organize, and even the middle-class Venezuelans felt humiliated by their relations with the foreigners. J.T. Jiménez Arráiz wrote of the book:

For the generations close to mine and for my generation, *Mene* was a true story of life in the petroleum camps. It was a shout of alarm given by a good writer, blessed with a good capacity for investigation and a great human sense of life. Many men of those generations — among them the author — knew personally the deeds related in this book; I would say that they lived them.[23]

If *Mene* revealed the vulnerability of Venezuelans who did not unite, Miguel Otero Silva's *Fiebre* chronicles the 1928 student revolt and its ties with the working class. Otero Silva's workers are initially suspicious of the students, who can more easily be released from jail and return to the family business or go abroad for a time. The book implicitly points up the differences between the 1908, 1918, and

1928 rebels. In 1928 the beginning of an alliance was forged between the young military officers, the students, and the workers — groups which had remained separate in the earlier uprisings. The reader is confident that the new ties will eventually lead to success, just as Santos Luzardo's alliance with the *llaneros* did. Other books of the 1930s similarly portray the concerns and frustrations of the working classes without either romanticizing them or highlighting an antagonistic class conflict. Guillermo Meneses, for example, in *La balandra Isabel llegó esta tarde* (The sloop *Isabel* arrived this afternoon, 1934), depicts the lives of working-class people in La Guaira sympathetically but without overtly ideological categories.

Though not a book of the working classes, Teresa de la Parra's *Ifigenia* (1924) may be seen nonetheless as a plea to allow women to be released from their isolation. A "diary of a young lady who wrote because she was bored," the novel explored the apathy and passivity of *caraqueño* women and the way they were restricted by social conventions. De la Parra had lived in Europe, as had her protagonist, and when she returned she railed against the dullness and confinement of women in Caracas.

Arturo Uslar Pietri challenged the prevalent attitude that social and political change would bring forth a better world. In *Las lanzas coloradas* (The Coloured Lances, 1930), he treated the seemingly safer topic of the nineteenth-century Independence Wars. The book is a classic of Venezuelan literature, beautifully written. However, it is a novel without heroes, where men and women act upon their baser impulses and where little that is rational or noble results from their actions. Uslar's book causes the reader to question whether independence was worth the bloody cataclysm that earned it. Nor does the reader experience much sympathy for the mulattos and *castas* who wage war against their former employers and against each other.

Uslar's work may not have fed the passion for reform, but its vivid depiction of Venezuelan history and landscapes contributed to the new nationalism. Some works, such as the poet Andrés Eloy Blanco's *Canto al España* (Song to Spain), referred to a wider and positive americanism, but many shared at least a veiled criticism of foreigners, especially United States citizens. Even in *Doña Barbara*, the foreign Mr Danger allied with Doña Barbara and left the *llanos* after her defeat. The managers of the oil company in Díaz Sánchez's *Mene* had few redeeming characteristics and generally treated their Venezuelan employees and associates badly.

Painters also expressed the new national confidence. Three of the most promising painters of the *Círculo de Bellas Artes* experienced their most productive years between 1920 and 1945. They brought the exploration of light and Venezuelan landscape to a new standard of excellence. Manuel Cabré came to be known as the painter of the Avila, the mountain which separates Caracas from the sea. Rafael Monasterios executed landscapes, some of the most compelling being Andean scenes. The greatest of them, Armando Reverón produced breathtaking canvases of La Guaira, Macuto, and the seacoast. The generations of artists who followed them, like the writers, scattered into numerous different styles and genres. Generally they showed less unanimous concern with the relationship between national art and national identity than with their search for universal themes and styles.

The period between the wars was a rich one for Venezuelan culture. Then, after 1936, much of the national creativity became expressed increasingly in politics rather than in art. Many of the outstanding members of the generation of 1928 devoted their lives to political writing, journalism, and political organization. There were exceptions, of course, such as Juan Liscano, Miguel Otero Silva, and the more senior Arturo Uslar Pietri, although each of these men also played political roles at times. Rómulo Gallegos became the outstanding example of an artist diverted to politics. He published *Doña Barbara* in Spain in 1929. On his return to Venezuela, he discovered that even the dictator Gómez loved the book and named him senator from Aragua, in recognition of his work. Rumors flew that Gallegos was about to be named President of the Congress or Minister of Education. The novelist fled from Venezuela in 1931 to avoid the choice of having to collaborate with Gómez or oppose him. He returned again in 1936, and held the position of Minister of Education before becoming a Congressional Deputy (1937–40), president of the municipal council of Caracas (1941), and symbolic presidential candidate in 1941. As a founder of *Acción Democrática* and its chief activist, he was elected President of the nation in 1947. None of his novels or writing which appeared after the mid-1930s measured up to his earlier works. The most talented Venezuelan writers who began to publish in the 1930s and who continued into the 1960s and later were those like Arturo Uslar Pietri, Mariano Picón Salas, and Miguel Otero Silva, who chose not to enter the political fray wholeheartedly.

The Development of Modern Political Parties

Writers could hardly be blamed for leaving their pens to participate in the rebirth of political parties in Venezuela. These parties and the form they took were greatly influenced by Gómez's long reign, the official hostility toward Communism, and the social and economic changes that petroleum was producing in the nation. The emergence of organized middle groups, labor organizations, urbanization, and powerful foreign investors all contributed to the tactics which the new *políticos* would find most successful. Given the scattered peasantry and the greater vulnerability of labor syndicates to government repression, it was almost inevitable that a successful party had to appeal to the urban middle classes. Petroleum workers and the urban masses could be strong allies or formidable enemies and had to be courted. It was a challenging and exciting time for the young political organizers.

Many studies of Venezuelan politics emphasize the continuity of political leaders like Rómulo Betancourt, Jóvito Villaba, Raúl Leoni and Gonzálo Barrios from the student revolt of 1928, through the leftist, multiclass groups of 1936-7, to *Acción Democrática*. In fact, the "generation of 1928" splintered into many groups ranging from the Communists to those who admired the evolutionary style of López and Medina, and to those who remained aloof from political activity for much of the rest of their lives. Ideologies, and men competed for the following which would ensure them the control of the government. None of the competititors cared to compromise, and all wanted the right to dictate the terms by which politics would be conducted for the foreseeable future.

All the groups agreed to some extent that it was necessary to control foreign investment, to punish *gomecistas*, to reform the political system, to promote economic development and modernization, to guarantee civil liberties and human rights, and to invest in the human resources of Venezuela. They differed bitterly on whether there should be ties to international Communism (Comintern), on whether it was possible or advisable to collaborate with López or Medina, on whether the political structures should be based on economic classes, and on whether the Catholic Church should retain a privileged position in education. From 1936 to 1941, the moderate *lopecistas* won the struggle by the relatively progressive February program (see p. 75, above) and by outlawing and dissolving competing groups. From 1941 to 1945, AD gradually achieved domination by cleverly exploiting opportunities and by avoiding divisions that other groups suffered.

The Communist Party had the advantage of time in the struggle. Venezuelan Ricardo Martínez had been exiled from the country in the 1920s and had joined the Communist Party of the United States; he had influenced labor groups to criticize Gómez. Gustavo Machado had worked with the Communist Party of Cuba, had helped form the *Partido Revolucionario Venezolano* in Mexico, and had also worked with Augusto Sandino in Nicaragua. The first real organization of the Communist Party in Venezuela came in 1931, aided by the visit of Joseph Kornfeder, a US citizen and representative of the Communist International. The party necessarily had to act through clandestine cells, suffered from arrests and the exile of members, but received a classification as a "sympathetic" party from the Communist International, which it retained until 1935 when it was accorded full status. The party in Venezuela, judged by its platforms and programs, was more narrow, dogmatic, and ideological than had been the PRV in Mexico. The founders called for a workers' party, for the Soviet Union as a model, and for other platform issues which smacked much of Comintern rigidity such as was typical at the time. In 1936, the group reorganized as the *Partido Republicano Progresista* (PRP), which did not overtly classify itself as Communist; in 1937, it returned to clandestine status as a Communist party, and after 1941 some branches at least were allowed to act openly again on the political scene.

The other significant group of leftists was the group made up by Betancourt, Raúl Leoni, Valmore Rodríguez and others, who issued the Barranquilla Plan and termed themselves the *Agrupación Revolucionaria de Izquierda* (Revolutionary Leftist Group — ARDI) in 1931. Although Betancourt, like Machado and Martínez, had worked with the Communist Party — in his case in Costa Rica — he had broken with the orthodox position. The ARDI plan had a stronger American flavor to it and predicted victory for the progressive forces of Venezuela, just as the progressives had defeated Porfirio Díaz in Mexico. The emphasis was on a tight analysis of the Venezuelan situation rather than on international ideology. Although much stress was laid on benefits for workers and *campesinos*, the tone was more populist and less dogmatic than that of the Communists. Betancourt and ARDI called for civil liberties, a literacy campaign, and a fight against the civic vices from which Venezuela suffered. Like the *apristas* of Peru, ARDI had a minimum and a maximum program, but they emphasized the relatively mild political reforms.

In March 1936, the two major leftist groups came together with the *Federación de Estudiantes de Venezuela* (FEV) headed by Jóvito Villaba, to form the ORVE (*Organización Venezolana*). ORVE preceded the wider opposition coalition of the *Bloque de Abril*. In October the same year, the *Partido Democrático Nacional* (PDN) unified all the opposition groups into a short-lived party. Although the various coalitions criticized López and coincided with Popular Front enthusiasm, tensions existed from the beginning. Betancourt's followers struggled with the Communists over the issue of the relationship to international Communism. The FEV had experienced a significant division in May 1936, when young Rafael Caldera led a group of Catholic students out of a meeting which was debating the secularization of education and other anticlerical issues. Caldera's group espoused social reform measures, but deplored Communism and atheism and attacks on the Church. They also continued to support the government of General Franco in Spain, which set them apart from the FEV and most of the leftists who championed the Republic. Caldera and his group formed a Catholic student group called the *Unión Nacional Estudiantil* (UNE). Subsequently two Catholic political associations came to life, the *Acción Electoral* (1938) and the *Acción Nacional* (1942). Catholics proved as susceptible to division as the left, however, and divided over the issue of whether to support Medina Angarita and his choice of a successor in 1945 or whether to back General López Contreras' bid to return to power. Caldera had argued that the AN should not take a position, but he probably favored Medina. After the division, Caldera returned to university teaching until COPEI was founded in 1946. The Catholic political groups could hardly be considered full-fledged political actors at this point, since their program appeared to consist primarily of opposing AD or PCV initiatives.[24]

Disagreements within the PDV became moot in 1937 when López Contreras refused to legalize the party. In clandestine action, the Communists and Betancourt's followers grew further apart. The Communists lost sympathy in Venezuela with their advocacy of neutrality in World War II during the period of the Hitler-Stalin Pact. *Acción Democrática* also had another advantage over the Communists during the period of illegality. Two outstanding and highly respected intellectuals continued in legal opposition to López: Rómulo Gallegos and Andrés Eloy Blanco. Both had close ties with the people who would form *Acción Democrática*, and provided a symbolic and visible opposition which attracted voters and attention.

The return to legality, with the authorization of *Acción Democrática* as a party in 1941, marked the final stage of AD's success. Tactically the AD leaders made all the right moves. They pressed to organize the *campesinos*, although not on a class basis. The improved road system facilitated their efforts to construct a national organization. Although Medina showed himself to be flexible and liberal, *Acción Democrática* maintained a rigid opposition to him, arguing that real reform could not come from an old *gomecista*. Their opposition afforded them greater visibility in Congress; also, AD leaders were skilled at organizing mass meetings and moving the crowds with rhetoric. Many middle-class professional people who wanted to participate in political decision–making found the AD multiclass program appealing. To carry home the point that they were not firebrands, they aggressively disavowed Communism and attacked the Communists. Their weakest point, until 1944, was that the Communists had proved more skilled and enthusiastic in penetrating the labor movement. Their final brilliant coup, perhaps not premeditated, came when they walked out of the Labor Congress in 1944 just before Medina dissolved all the participating unions. AD then remained in control of most of the existing labor syndicates.

By 1945, *Acción Democrática* had prevailed over the other nascent political groups, including the official party of Medina, the *Partido Democrático Venezolano* (PDV). Even so, their ultimate success in capturing political control of the nation depended on two developments over which they had no control. The division between Medina and López Contreras in 1945 threw both the conservatives and the Communists who had collaborated with Medina into disarray. More importantly, the *Unión Patriótica Militar* (Patriotic Military Union — UPM) of young military officers had become impatient with the slow pace of development under López and Medina. They were ready to insist on their chance to direct the nation, but so much had they been affected by the political liberalization of the decade that they sought a civilian political party with which to ally themselves. AD fulfilled the requirements of a moderate, nationalistic, non-Communist group which enjoyed a fair amount of support. One might speculate that if in 1945 the UPM had taken the path it took in 1948 of organizing an apolitical government run by an apolitical military clique, the young AD politicians would not have recovered from yet another period of clandestine struggle or exile. AD might well owe its dominance of Venezuelan politics during the next quarter of a century to the accident of having been chosen to legitimize a military coup.

NOTES

1. Arturo Uslar Pietri, *De una a otra Venezuela* (Caracas: Monte Avila, 1972), p. 18.
2. Edwin Lieuwen, *Petroleum in Venezuela: A History* (Berkeley: University of California Press, 1954), pp. 44–60.
3. Quoted in Vernon C. Donnelly, "Juan Vicente Gómez and the Venezuelan Worker, 1919–1929" (Ph.D. diss., University of Maryland, 1975), p. 139.
4. Ibid., p. 168.
5. Ibid.

6. Memorandum No. 29, *Boletín del Archivo Histórico de Miraflores* 70 (Jan.-Feb. 1972): 341-2.
7. Ibid.
8. Lieuwen, pp. 34-7.
9. Ibid., p. 92.
10. Freddy Vivas Gallardo, *Venezuela en la sociedad de las naciones 1920-1939: descripción y análisis de una actuación diplomática* (Caracas: Universidad Central de Venezuela, 1981), pp. 208-15.
11. John Duncan Powell, *Political Mobilization of the Venezuelan Peasant* (Cambridge, Mass.: Harvard University Press, 1971), p. 25.
12. Miguel Izard, *Series estadísticas para la historia de Venezuela* (Mérida: Universidad de Los Andes, 1970), p. 169.
13. Donnelly, pp. 101-2.
14. José N. Arguello to Juan Vincente Gómez, 19 June 1924, *Boletín del Archivo Histórico de Miraflores* 77 (Jan.-Feb. 1974): 230-1.
15. Alfredo Cortina, *Breve historia de la radio en Venezuela* (Caracas: Dirección General de Cultura de la GDF y Fundarte, 1978).
16. Henry V. Allen, *Venezuela, a Democracy* (New York: Doubleday, 1941), p. 24.
17. Powell, p. 63.
18. Ibid., p. 23.
19. Ibid., p. 61.
20. Donald L. Herman, *Christian Democracy in Venezuela* (Chapel Hill: University of North Carolina Press, 1980), pp. 18-19.
21. Donnelly, p. 63.
22. Fania Petzoldt and Jacinta Bevilacqua, *Nostotras también nos jugamos la vida* (Caracas: Editorial Ateneo, 1979), p. 71.
23. J.T. Jiménez Arráiz, "Ramón Díaz Sánchez," in *Rámon Díaz Sánchez, Mene* (Buenos Aires: Editorial Universitaria de Buenos Aires, 1966), p. 7.
24. Herman, pp. 14-17.

4

THE TRIENIO AND THE NEW NATIONAL IDEAL, 1945–1958

"Come with me. Let's talk of the present. No more talk of yesterday; yesterday is the calm of the altar; our ancestors will surely thank us for speaking less of them and doing more for their idea."[1]

Andrés Eloy Blanco

The year 1945 was a watershed in Venezuelan political history. When Isaías Medina Angarita, perhaps the most popular Venezuelan President since Simón Bolívar, chose his successor, political schisms were caused. Old *gomecistas* rallied around López Contreras to protest the open political activity of the civilian politicians, especially the Communists. Moderate civilians like Rómulo Betancourt and his *Acción Democrática* accepted Medina's first nominee, Diógenes Escalante, because they believed that he would promote direct, universal suffrage. However, Escalante became ill, and *Acción Democrática* did not support Medina's second choice, the Minister of Agriculture, Angel Biaggini. Other civilian factions acceded to Medina's will from fear of López on the right and *Acción Democrática* or the Communists on the left. The key group in this melange proved to be the conspiratorial group of young military officers, the *Unión Patriótica Militar* (UPM). They were impatient with the pace of modernization and professionalization in the armed forces and with the impediments to their careers that the old *gomecista* generals still represented. They shared also some of the civilian desire for more rapid modernization and economic development of their nation. By the Fall of 1945, they had decided to take matters into their hands and remove Medina from power before he could guarantee the continuation of the *gomecista/medinista* system, or before López Contreras would turn the clock back even further.

The military conspirators, led by Marcos Pérez Jiménez, Carlos Delgado Chalbaud, and Luis Felipe Llovera Páez, looked for a civilian political party to share power with them and to legitimize their *golpe*. The Communists were obviously unacceptable. The only other civilian party which boasted both some degree of organization and consistent opposition to Medina's policies was *Acción Democrática*. Betancourt's party at first rejected the overtures of the officers and hoped for the Escalante compromise. When that hope failed, they agreed to participate in the military conspiracy. They entered the political scene as principal actors then just as Francisco Madero had done. They deplored *golpismo* and *de facto* governments, but participated in a military movement which brought them to power.

Surprisingly, Medina's government put up virtually no fight. The conspiracy had been discovered on 17 October, and Marcos Pérez Jiménez was arrested. The arrest provided the signal for the rebellion to break out. Unlike Gómez in 1918 and 1928 or López in 1936, Medina lacked the will or the conviction to fight, and the government fell. The startled and generally unprepared young conspirators scrambled to establish a provisional government and to arrange for the first elections based on universal, direct suffrage that the nation had had in the twentieth century. Rómulo Betancourt became provisional President of the nation. Other *Acción Democrática* members and civilians made up the rest of the cabinet, with only two positions going to the military conspirators. This clearly was a revolution to bring "new men, new ideas, new procedures" to government, as Cipriano Castro had falsely claimed in 1899.

The three years that followed revealed that *Acción Democrática* and the young officers of the UPM shared many attitudes and goals for their nation. They comprised a generation who had known no other government than the *gomecistas*, or any real partisan activity until the last few years, and who could still remember the poverty and desolation of their nation before the oil revenues began to sift through the treasury into the hands of the elite and the expanding middle class. They accepted the strongly centralized state of the *gomecistas*, but espoused a more interventionist, activist state which would assume responsibility for economic and social development. They saw the need for national planning in order best to maximize the benefits which came from the oil bonanza. They hoped to diversify the economy and to provide a communications and transportation infrastructure which might facilitate national industrial development and provide more benefits for the abandoned countryside. They were nationalistic, but accepted the role that foreign investors would continue to play in the national economy for years to come. Similarly, they might have been critical of US influence in Venezuela, but they could ill-afford to antagonize their major trading partner and protector. The military officers and the civilian politicians also shared a fierce anti-communism and a belief that the national destinies would be best directed and controlled by the emerging middle classes.

Yet agreement on these major issues could not permanently hold together a coalition which had such separate bases of power and legitimacy. *Acción Democrática*'s determination, both pragmatic and philosophic, to deepen and expand its political control of the country increasingly alienated the military officers. Five major issues came into conflict. First, *Acción Democrática* wanted to organize the workers and peasants. The civilians gambled that they would be able to control these newly organized sectors, which would broaden their legitimacy. The military, on the other hand, feared that politicization by sector or class would invite disorders like those of 1936. Allegations that AD leaders occasionally used intimidation or fraud to squeeze out other competing civilian organizers did not reassure the officers. Secondly, *Acción Democrática* clearly mistrusted their military allies and wanted to relegate them to a subordinate, apolitical role. The UPM, with its newfound *esprit de corps* and desire for a role in national development, resented and resisted AD high-handedness. Thirdly, *Acción Democrática* initiated a foreign policy based on ideology and confrontation which was the most aggressive that Venezuela had known since the days of Cipriano Castro. The armed forces preferred the now traditional neutrality and perhaps took umbrage at some of the slurs upon their companions-in-arms in other nations. Fourthly, *Acción Democrática* had made agrarian reform and land distribution a major priority, while the officers feared the political ramifications and preferred a greater stress on large-scale agricultural development. Finally, although both military officers and civilians wanted a greater state intervention in the economy, they differed on the extent to which the state should affect the distribution of the national wealth and power. The officers were as eager as *Acción Democrática* to see a healthy, well-fed, well-educated, and well-trained population, but they feared the disorder which could accompany rapid social change.

The young conspirators all had some leanings toward Hispanic corporatism, although the civilians sought a veneer of democracy similar to the Mexican model. The officers looked to the south, chiefly to Peru, for their model. Both civilians and the armed forces were also aware of the implicit limits imposed by the United States' uneasiness over instability or radicalism. From their models, their middle-class attitudes, and their limitations, both the officers and the civilians feared a true pluralistic democracy in which autonomous groups and individuals competed for power and favors. They further rejected parties organized along class lines. Politics and political direction would be multiclass or *déclassé* in nature whether organized by sectors within a political party (AD) or whether organized nationally with no intervening interest sectors.

The similar outlooks and shared values of this generation of leaders dominated national politics until at least the late 1970s. The political labels which divide them into democrats and dictators obscure some of their agreement. Betancourt believed that political parties could in the long run promote fuller political participation, stability, and national consensus. Pérez Jiménez saw only the confrontations and divisions which accompanied partisan politics and feared that the nation would revert to the nineteenth-century civil wars with a loss of stability and national consensus. True sons of the positivists, Betancourt and Pérez Jiménez wanted order and progress. Betancourt, more politically experienced and with more faith in his compatriots and himself, believed that he could ride the "unloosed tiger" better than Francisco I. Madero of Mexico. Pérez Jiménez, naive in politics and wary of the unknown, predicted the rise of demagogues and revolutionaries who would bring not development but anarchy.

The Trienio, 1945-1948

Politics and economic policy logically fell into two discrete periods between 1945 and 1948 when *Acción Democrática* controlled the government—subsequently termed the *trienio* — and the period after 1948 when the military officers stressed their priorities. *Acción Democrática*'s most outstanding accomplishment was the political organization from 1941 and mobilization of the majority of the population for the first time. Rómulo Betancourt acted as provisional President and ruled largely by decree from October 1945 until the election of Rómulo Gallegos in December 1947. The National Constituent Congress of December 1946 confirmed and validated most of the decrees. *Acción Democrática* sympathizer and poet, Andrés Eloy Blanco, presided over the Congress, which was dominated by the party. The new constitution was signed on Venezuela's Independence Day, July 5, 1947.

On March 15, 1946, Betancourt issued two decrees which laid the groundwork for the elections to follow. The government would uphold citizens' guarantees and civil rights, and extended suffrage to all citizens over the age of eighteen, male and female, literate and illiterate. *Acción Democrática* thus took on the task of mobilizing not only the hitherto unorganized workers and peasants, but also women, and youths between the ages of eighteen and twenty-one. The AD leaders proved more than equal to the task, working from their head start over the existing Communist party, and the other new parties. Rafael Caldera and his colleagues founded the *Comité de Organización Política Electoral Independiente* (Committee of Independent Political Electoral Organization — COPEI) in 1946, and Jóvito Villaba and many former *medinistas* formed the *Unión Repúblicana Democrática* (URD) in the same year. The other parties generally neglected the nation beyond Caracas when they set to organizing. The exception proved to be the COPEI group in Táchira and the Andes, where many conservatives and *gomecistas* turned to the Christian Democrats rather than to the feared *adecos*. The URD party proved unable to cash in on the general popularity of Medina. The Communists had still not overcome the loss of influence in the labor organizations that they suffered after the Labor Congress of 1944. With a class-based ideology and also with their support of Medina, they faced some credibility problems in trying to construct a multi-class alliance like the *adecos*, and their own natural constituency had been damaged. Four elections were held in Venezuela between October 1946 and May 1948, and *Acción Democrática* won each of them by a large majority over the other political groups. Yet, ominously, their percentage of victory shrank a little with each election, and the most obvious beneficiary of a conservative backlash was the COPEI party.

	AD	*COPEI*	*URD*	*PCV*	*Misc.*
27 Oct. 1946 (Const. Assembly)	78.8%	13.2%	3.8%	3.6%	0.6%
14 Dec. 1947 (Congress)	70.8	20.5	4.3	3.7	0.7
14 Dec. 1947 (President)	74.4	22.4		3.2	
9 May 1948 (Municipal Elections)	70.1	21.1	3.9	3.4	0.5[2]

The larger AD vote for President in 1947 than for Congress suggests that the popularity of Rómulo Gallegos was greater than that of the party in general. Betancourt speculated that the people may have become exhausted with so much intense political activity during the three years.[3] The total vote in 1946 was 1,395,200, but in the municipal elections of 1948 it was only 693,154. The total vote in the December 1947 Presidential elections (1,170,470) was also less than that of 1946.

The electoral slippage did not cause *Acción Democrática* to be ejected from office, but it might have encouraged military conspirators. In a nation which had not enjoyed free political debate and competition and had not seen partisan activity since the 1890s, it was hardly surprising that a heated discussion of the issues produced disagreement. Press freedom and the forums provided by the Constituent Assembly and the freely elected Congress, with representation of minority parties, allowed other parties to attack *Acción Democrática* and its programs. Allegations, not always based on fact, flew wildly. Political rivalries, which lasted to the 1980s, often traced their origin to the *trienio* and the partisan actions of *Acción Democrática*. As example of the latter, three future presidential candidates and a guerrilla in the 1960s recalled early conflicts with AD activists. José Vicente Rangel remembered *Acción Democrática* members sabotaging one of Jóvito Villaba's political rallies in 1946.[4] Arturo Uslar Pietri resented the confiscation by *Acción Democrática* of Bs 245,000 because he had collaborated with the Medina and López government.[5] Rafael Caldera resigned his position in the provisional government because AD loyalists had interferred with COPEI meetings in Táchira.[6] Guerrilla Douglas Bravo claimed that his father had been assassinated by a police patrol in 1947, with the connivance of some AD members.[7] In short, the dominant politicians of the third quarter of the twentieth century had been formed both by their memories of the Gómez regime and by their perceptions of AD during the *trienio*.

The *adecos* were not only fiercely partisan and determined; they were also indefatigable workers and organizers. From 1941 their motto was "not a single district nor single municipality without a party organization." Once in power, they did not relax. Party membership climbed from 75,000–80,000 in 1941 to nearly half a million by 1948.[8] Organization of the peasants was especially remarkable. *Adeco* Ramón Quijada led the Peasant Federation, and AD dominated the leadership of most of the peasant syndicates. The AD moderate agrarian reform, which provided for leasing of lands of farmers, logically became the source of power and influence for the local peasant leaders and, also logically, peasants affiliated with AD could expect more favorable treatment from the AD government than those affiliated with other political parties. The local leaders also controlled the distribution of agricultural credit.

Other workers also organized. Over 500 syndicates were formed, and the national *Confederación de Trabajadores de Venezuela* accepted both urban unions and peasant syndicates. Middle-class associations, especially school teachers in state schools, also became strong followers of *Acción Democrática*. Expansion of education and of careers in public health and other services provided more opportunities for women workers and gave *Acción Democrática* a chance to organize and mobilize the new female electorate.

Increased state intervention in all aspects of national life provided more jobs and followers for the party. Gómez had founded the first state autonomous institutes in 1928: the *Banco Obrero* and the *Banco Agrícola y Pecuario*. López and Medina established eight more between 1937 and 1945, including the *Banco Central de Venezuela*, *Linea Aereopostal Venezolano*, the *Instituto Venezolano del Seguro Social* and the *Instituto Nacional de Obras*

Sanitarias. The *Acción Democrática* governments initiated seven more in 1946 and 1947, and the dictatorship brought forth twenty-two between 1948 and 1958. These institutes decentralized some of the functions of government and channeled the oil money to a variety of different groups and individuals. Incidentally, they also became effective channels of political patronage.[9]

Acción Democrática won 137 of the 160 seats to the Constituent Assembly. The second party, COPEI, had only nineteen seats. *Acción Democrática*, led by the poet Andrés Eloy Blanco, virtually dictated the terms of the constitution. The political charter guaranteed political liberties and rights, but the real novelty for Venezuela were Articles 53–57 which committed the nation to social welfare measures, and Articles 61–63 which established labor rights and guarantees. Universal direct suffrage would choose the President and the two houses of Congress. A President could not succeed himself. The states had little real meaning, although each state was represented by two senators. The Supreme Court could review the constitutionality of congressional law. A much debated clause allowed the President to order the preventive detention of anyone who was presumed to be conspiring against the government.

The AD trienio program has been seen as a sharp break with the Venezuelan past. Yet many of the objectives of the *adecos* had deep roots in the Venezuelan experiences of the nineteenth century, if not the more recent *gomecista* past. The Federal revolution of the 1860s had advocated anti-clericalism and secular education. State and regional development were banners that *El Mocho* Hernández had waved, and the national government had shown an interest in economic development at least since the founding of the Ministry of Development in 1863. Joaquín Crespo had initiated trials for administrative peculation, although he later abandoned them. *Acción Democrática*'s criticism of European colonies in the Caribbean, the effort to form economic and political blocs within the hemisphere, and the nationalistic insistence that Venezuela should set the rules for foreign investment harked back both to Guzmán Blanco and to Cipriano Castro. At least since 1899, Venezuelan Presidents had lived with the knowledge that they could not ignore the presence, power, and desires of the United States. Nor could the country provide the amount of investment necessary for the exploitation of the mineral wealth and for infrastructural or industrial development.

Some of the AD programs had roots in the national past, but the situation in 1945 called for innovative direction of the nation. The government was now strongly centralized and greatly expanded, and the populace largely accepted an abandonment of *laissez-faire*.

Land was probably more concentrated than it had been at any time in the past, at least partly as a result of the greed of Gómez and the oil concessions. At the same time, agriculture languished. The government depended increasingly on the revenues from the oil industry for income; new demands for services and development meant that government revenues had constantly to increase. Venezuela in 1945 experienced greater economic inequality than at any time in its history, despite the increasing prosperity and visibility of the urban middle groups. Many more people lived in cities in 1945, and the cities, especially Caracas, controlled the distribution of power and revenues throughout the nation. The national armed forces were intended to supervise economic and political development rather than to serve some personalistic *caudillo*. Two world wars and the looming Cold War, as well as the increasing importance of petroleum, inevitably propelled Venezuela on to the world stage, and nearly as inevitably into the geopolitical sphere of the United States.

Acción Democrática policy during the *trienio* may be divided into three categories: economic — including oil policy — international, and social. The effectiveness of the economic initiatives strongly influenced the party's ability to implement other measures. *Acción Democrática* did not alter the 1943 petroleum law. The oil companies, especially Creole, encouraged a flexible relationship since they wanted to avoid expropriation, labor conflicts, and extreme nationalism. Minister of Development Juan Pablo Pérez Alfonzo, who had criticized the 1943 law as too mild, proved not to be such a terrible foe after all. AD's major objectives were to increase the government's share of the profits from the industry, to encourage more refining inside the country, and to give a break to the Venezuelan consumer. On December 1, 1945, the government forced a reduction in the price of petroleum sold in Venezuela. It also decreed in the same month an extraordinary tax on company profits and announced a commitment to the 50–50 principle: i.e. the companies should not under any circumstances receive greater profits than those received by the Venezuelan government. Pérez Alfonzo pointed out that even with the excess profits tax, the companies paid less income tax in Venezuela than they did in the United States.

Labor Minister Raúl Leoni intervened in contract negotiations between oil workers' unions and the companies. His intervention secured higher wages for the workers, but allowed the companies.to resist the workers' demands for more influence in the industry and for greater worker security and benefits. The three-year collective contract signed in February 1948 contained wage and overtime increases, three weeks' annual paid vacation, frozen commissary prices, higher housing allowances, and other benefits. Not all workers, especially the Communist ones, were happy at the idea of a three-year contract; they may have realized that real wages had risen by 39 percent in 1946 and 1947, but dropped by 6 percent in the first six months of 1948. The AD government did all in its power to prevent strikes in vital industries; in June 1948, when a Communist–controlled union called a strike of the maritime workers who worked on the oil tankers, President Gallegos ordered them back to work. He cited Article 231 of the labor law proscribing strikes which would adversely affect the national economy.[10] The Communist unions chose not to challenge the government action, but the lesson was clear that AD intended to control union activity. The oil companies could live with this policy of "social peace," although they were not ecstatic about the higher wages or the possibility that the government might condone the unions' demands for greater voice in the industry.

The AD government laid the basis for a more nationalistic oil policy in other ways. Pérez Alfonzo was concerned about conservation and wanted to exploit the natural gas, which had been allowed to escape into the atmosphere. Three companies agreed to build natural gas plants, but the weak commercial market in Venezuela meant that about 85 percent of the natural gas was still lost. The AD government also announced that no more petroleum concessions would be given out on such disadvantageous terms as existing ones. Finally, the government asserted that it would exercise its privilege of accepting royalties in petroleum. By so doing, the groundwork was laid for a national petroleum enterprise, and at the same time the government could independently determine the petroleum price level on the market. It turned out that Venezuela could market its crude oil at prices higher than those received by the international companies. To prevent Venezuela from continuing to test the world market, Standard and Shell in 1947 agreed to buy the government's royalty crude oil for higher prices than their announced market prices. Unfortunately for Venezuela, by 1948 Soviet and Middle Eastern production had risen, and prices dropped. The possibility of securing higher prices and more information on the oil companies' pricing practices was lost for the moment. The companies' monopoly on pricing and marketing information would remain unchallenged until producing nations worked together after 1958. The Korean conflict and the Suez crisis in 1956 allowed the Venezuelans to reap good benefits from the oil, but without much effort on their part. In sum, the *trienio* opened the door for tougher bargaining with the companies, but accomplished relatively little in real terms.[11]

Venezuelan policymakers had long argued that the oil companies had a responsibility to assist Venezuelan development. In June, 1947, Nelson Rockefeller of Creole/Standard Oil and the Venezuelan government began negotiations to set up a joint company financed by the government and the oil companies with the object of promoting various social and economic projects. The Venezuelan Basic Economy Corporation (VBEC) provided a vehicle for the companies to reinvest a portion of their profits in Venezuela. VBEC chose to spend more on the promotion of commerce, tourism, and rural nutrition than on industrial infrastructure.

The *Corporación Venezolana de Fomento* (Venezuelan Development Corporation — CVF) tried to direct the national revenues into more productive areas. Plans abounded for electrical generating plants, irrigation facilities, and the construction of roads, airfields, and ports. The creation of the Gran-Colombian Merchant Fleet with Colombia and Ecuador fed national pride and challenged the high freight rates of the other Caribbean shipping companies. The CVF provided credit and technical advice for small industries, especially those related to consumer goods, such as fishing fleets, food processors, fertilizer producers, textiles, shoes, and cement.

Foreign policy was more active and expansive than it had been since the days of Cipriano Castro. The AD leaders wanted to professionalize the Foreign Ministry and the diplomatic service. In 1926, there had been 139 employees of the Foreign Ministry, including consuls, diplomats, and Caracas staff; by 1939, the figure had only risen to 149, reflecting the slight importance placed on diplomacy. Although some of the most famous of Venezuelan intellectuals customarily served stints as ambassador, the general level of training and experience of the foreign service establishment was not high. In 1946, the government passed a new statute to encourage professionalization and at the same time to offer improved benefits for foreign service officers and employees. Unfortunately the 1948 *golpe* reinforced the long tradition of replacing career professionals with political cronies or intellectuals who wanted to live abroad.

Acción Democrática had taken an active foreign policy stance, especially in the Caribbean. Betancourt implemented the policy which became known as the "Betancourt Doctrine," an effort to form strong alliances between the democratic nations of the Americas and to freeze out *de facto* dictatorships. This aggressive thesis brought hostility from Anastasio Somoza of Nicaragua and Rafael Trujillo of the Dominican Republic. Betancourt also held back from relations with Perón's Argentina until elections were held and with Franco's Spain, terming them both fascist dictatorships. Caracas enthusiastically participated in the formation of the United Nations and the Organization of American States, although the OAS was the preferred organization for settling hemispheric disputes. Relations with the United States generally were good. In July 1948, President Rómulo Gallegos and his wife visited the United States for a twelve-day stay. Yet in April 1948, Betancourt, as the head of the Venezuelan delegation to the Inter-American Conference at Bogotá, condemned the remnants of colonialism in the Western Hemisphere, with some specific references to Puerto Rico and British Guiana.

In addition to conflicts with the oil companies and with foreign governments, Betancourt met fierce resistance at home when he tried to effect some of his most cherished social programs. The campaigns for state control of education, agrarian reform, and punishment of those who had enriched themselves from posts in the public administration alienated powerful and vocal groups within Venezuela: the Catholic Church, the large landowners, and nearly all who had held office in the Gómez, López, or Medina governments.

The education reforms produced the loudest outcry. On May 30, 1946, *Acción Democrática* issued Decree No. 321 to regulate both public and private schools more strictly. Spokespersons for the private, Catholic schools believed that the decree threatened their autonomy and their philosophy of education. In sum, Catholic educators believed that the family and the Church held the first responsibility for education; that private education and private training of teachers were basic rights; that religious education should be available for all students during the daily schedule; and that the state should have no authority over private education.[12] The issue became so highly charged that Betancourt was willing to rescind the decree, but his colleague, Luis Beltrán Prieto Figueroa, among others, insisted on enforcing it. Student strikes and unrest caused political problems for the government and resulted in many students losing the school year of 1947. The Organic Law of Education, passed in 1948, nullified most of the provisions of decree 321, but the public and parliamentary debate over the issue continued until the *Acción Democrática* government was overthrown.

The conflict had several unhappy consequences. High school students in private high schools, who had been aloof from politics before, became more involved in the political debate. The bitterness that had originated in the break in the FEV in 1936 between the Catholic and anticlerical students became more intense, giving more impetus to the evolution of a Catholic political party. The distrust and suspicion that each side bore the other continued to provoke acrimony, in spite of Betancourt's willingness to compromise. At stake was not only the Church's independence in education and examination policy, but also the dominance of the education establishment of teachers and bureaucrats turned out by the *Instituto Pedagógico*. Like the peasants and workers, these teachers largely fell into the *Acción Democrática* camp. They believed that their jobs and salaries depended on the expansion of state education.

Agrarian reform raised less of a hue and cry than the education measures had done, perhaps because of the unprofitable condition of agriculture. Moreover, much of the land that was distributed to peasants was state land which had been taken over at the death of Gómez, either his own extensive landholdings or the land which had fallen into the hands of the *Banco Agrícola y Pecuario* because of defaulted mortgages. The agrarian reform program created the Land Commission in the Technical Institute for Immigration and Colonization; the old Latin American dream of luring hard-working European immigrants to work the land continued, although the dream had no more success in Venezuela than it had in most other Latin American nations in earlier times. The Land Commission also distributed land to the organized peasantry. Here again, AD received the political benefits of insisting that only organized *campesinos* could apply to receive land, and AD-affiliated syndicates received priority. In the first four months of the AD government, over 12,991 hectares were distributed to thirty syndicates with a total membership of 5,700. Like many such programs, the problem then changed from *latifundia* to *minifundia*, since the average peasant received only 2.2 hectares of land to work.[13] In May 1946, a Credit Department was created and within a year, the institution had spent 8 million of the initial Bs 10 million in funding. Local peasant syndicate leaders could be effective organizers for AD when they controlled the distribution of credit.

There are various estimates of the total amount of land distributed during the *trienio*. A conservative estimate found that 90,000 hectares had been given out to some 55,000 people, and a liberal estimate reckoned that 165,000 hectares had gone to 80,000 people.[14] The reform might be compared to the early years of the Mexican agrarian reform. As with Mexico, the edge went to organized peasants and those who could be expected to deliver some loyalty to the political party in power. The program probably caused fewer problems than the Mexican one, since Venezuela was more lightly populated and had more land to be distributed near the capital. Most of Venezuela's modernizing elite had probably already shifted investments to urban land, finance, services, and light industry. Much of the land was already in government hands, so few people were losers.

The Venezuelan military government after 1948 quickly returned much of the distributed land to the original owners. Gómez's land went to his heirs and other claimants to the estate; land held by the *Banco Agrícola y Pecuario* and the Ministry of Agriculture was sold to private investors and speculators, on generous terms. Many government officials acquired a taste for weekend *haciendas*. Some figures suggest, however, that there was a modest increase in the number of middle-sized agricultural holdings between 1950 and 1960. The total number of farms rose from 248,734 to 315,215, and the average hectares per farm dropped from 90 in 1950 to 83 in 1960.[15] This seems to suggest that the combination of the AD agrarian reform and the redistribution that came through the military junta did achieve a slight change in the structure of land owning and land holding in Venezuela. The number of farms and the average size of the holdings do not, of course, provide any information on how many of these farms were productive units.

Betancourt's third controversial measure during the *trienio* was the institution in 1946 of Tribunals of Administrative Responsibility. The Tribunals gathered the names of 125 people who had collaborated with Gómez, López, and Medina. After an examination of their wealth and its probable sources, the Tribunals decreed confiscation of the wealth which was presumed to have come from peculation or from the trafficking of influence in the government. Those accused and condemned naturally resented the action, and some civil libertarians objected to the partisan and retroactive character of the measures. As with the protests about the education decree, Betancourt relented and allowed a new committee to re-examine the findings of the Tribunals. Some people had their property returned to them, but the political damage had been done. Betancourt's government passed the Law against Illicit Enrichment in an effort to institutionalize the judicial proceedings to be taken against bureaucrats who enriched themselves at the nation's expense. Each government official had to swear out a declaration of property on taking office and again on leaving it. A permanent commission would examine the declarations and investigate presumed abuses.

Some of the *Acción Democrática* measures caused disaffection from the regime, even when the real interests of the disaffected were only marginally affected. Efforts to undo the damage done by the education law and the peculation trials came to nothing. Many Venezuelans had become so convinced of AD partisanship that they could not recognize genuine efforts at conciliation or to control the excesses of the radicals. Most telling of all was the suspicion of the military officers, especially Pérez Jiménez and other architects of the *golpe* of 1945; they perceived more disunity and disorder than probably existed, and they feared the growing strength of the party. Moreover, President Rómulo Gallegos, after February 1948, was probably more highly regarded and trusted than Betancourt, but was less experienced and less willing to defer to military demands. Betancourt, for example, counseled Gallegos in November 1948 to meet some of the demands of the conspirators in order to gain time at least to mobilize some opposition. Gallegos replied that he was a legally elected President, and did not intend to negotiate with the armed forces. He showed either an excess of confidence or a loss of nerve also when he refused to arrest Minister of Defense Carlos Delgado Chalbaud who presumably could have halted the conspiracy, even if he was not fully involved in it. Too late and ill prepared, Betancourt called on petroleum workers to strike on November 23. That move only prompted Delgado and the conspirators to arrest the AD ministers and Gallegos. By November 24, the coup was accomplished. Delgado Chalbaud assumed control and became the President of a military junta.

The Dictatorship, 1948–1958

Politics and political activity now came to a halt for a decade. Delgado served as President from 1948 to 1950, when a botched kidnapping attempt resulted in his death. His kidnapper, Rafael Simón Urbina, was killed the same day, allegedly in an escape attempt. Popular opinion pointed to Pérez Jiménez as the obvious beneficiary of the death of Delgado, if not its instigator. A new junta ruled from 1950 until elections were held in 1952 for a new Constituent Assembly, which appointed a constitutional President to serve until 1958. The 1952 elections were a farce, since *Acción Democrática* and the PCV had been outlawed; URD and COPEI continued to function, and URD candidate Jóvito Villaba apparently won the election of 1952, until the government halted the public announcement of returns. The election then handily went to the junta's "party," the *Frente Electoral Independiente* (FEI), and Pérez Jiménez became President. Many URD and COPEI leaders went into exile and abandoned the hope that they would be permitted to play a major role in a return to democracy, without the participation of AD. Enforced largely by Laureano Vallenilla Lanz, the son of the positivist author of *Cesarismo Democrático* and Minister of the Interior, strict press censorship and imprisonment of political dissidents turned Venezuela again into the harmonious country of Gómez's days. A national police force founded during the *trienio*, the *Seguridad Nacional* led by Pedro Estrada, eliminated opposition. Labor syndicates and peasant unions were abolished because of their domination by AD or by PCV leaders; new unions were allowed, if they adhered to the nonpartisan strictures of the government. Thus, all the sources of political competition — the chief parties, the unions, the peasant syndicates, the free press — were cancelled. Politics were considered divisive, wasteful and useless — no different from the nineteenth-century civil wars. Pérez Jiménez and his advisers did not recognize the depth of support for the more recent partisan activity nor did they understand that it would be more difficult to crush the newly confident groups. The election of 1952 should have been a warning, but Pérez and his colleagues tried an even more obvious fraud in 1957 when the promised elections again became an issue. They constructed a plebiscite in which people could vote whether or not they wished Pérez Jiménez to continue to govern. He won, of course, but the insult of the plebiscite became one of the precipitating factors which forged a new clandestine coalition of civilian groups, military officers, and urban masses to force Pérez's resignation and departure from the country. Thus ended the misguided effort to go back to the political vacuum of the Gómez period.

Although Pérez wanted a political vacuum, his concept of an activist government which would encourage economic development bore little relation to the timid state of the Gómez days. His "New National Ideal" called for a complete transformation of the communications and transportation infrastructure of the nation, for the development of an iron and steel complex in Guayana, for rapid and showy urban construction especially in Caracas, and for major defense expenditures.

The government entered the business, not only of providing basic social services, but of sponsoring recreational opportunities. Los Caracas became a model workers' beach community along the coast not far from La Guaira. The *Círculo Militar* contained swimming pools, restaurants, hotel facilities for the armed forces. The *Instituto Nacional de Deportes* initiated in 1949 a national concern to develop various team sports in Venezuela; a major program of construction of sports fields and stadiums began, and Venezuela began to field more national teams in international contests. Venezuela participated in the 1948 Olympics, but the most exciting competitions for Venezuelans were probably the Caribbean League baseball championships and the Pan American games. Pérez also showed his enthusiasm for auto racing by establishing the *Gran Premio* of Venezuela around Lake Valencia. Dog races became a brief fad. The government tried to achieve some international recognition through athletic events and teams, although the results were, at best, mixed. The Ministry of Labor sponsored the travels and performances of Yolanda Moreno and a group of Venezuelan folkloric dancers. Quite popular in Venezuela, they also traveled abroad in emulation of the famous *Ballet Folklorico de Mexico*. Some complained, with justification, that many Venezuelans still lacked basic needs of nutrition, health, and education; government money might better be expended on those than on the showy programs designed to win international attention.

Generally, Pérez's international posture recalled Gómez's passive one. Preference for democratic governments ended, and Pérez reestablished relations with Franco's Spain. Although he maintained relations with most nations in the Americas, he was closest to similar regimes such as Perón's in Argentina and Odría's in Peru. Some military spokesmen, such as junta member Luis Felipe Llovera Páez, became enamored of geopolitics, and Venezuela sought to establish firm boundaries and to defend them. In 1956 Caracas unilaterally extended the territorial sea from three miles to twelve, engendering potential conflicts with neighboring countries, especially the Dutch and English islands and territories which claimed a three-mile limit. Various conflicts caused the government to withdraw from the AD-sponsored Gran-Colombian fleet, but a Venezuelan merchant marine received more support in an effort to reduce the country's dependence on foreign shippers. The government continued to support the Inter-American system, and took great pride in hosting the 1954 Inter-American Conference. Military missions, the Inter-American defense board, and the Rio Treaty also strengthened ties with the United States. The Caracas government generally approved of the US campaign against Communism, especially in Guatemala. Pérez made a bid for hemispheric leadership at the Panama conference in 1956 when he suggested a hemispheric program for economic development; he pledged a portion of the Venezuelan budget for such a project and invited other American nations to do the same. The United States had not yet seen the advantages of such a project and ignored the initiative. Pérez later withdrew the offer.

International economic relations assumed more importance as Venezuela became more dependent on oil income and as the postwar world became more economically interdependent. Industrialists and some nationalists in Venezuela clamored for a revision of the US-Venezuelan commercial treaty of 1939 in order to provide some protection for nascent Venezuelan industries. The new treaty of 1952, however, gave nothing to the Venezuelan industrialists, although it gladdened the hearts of the commercial sector and of the US subsidiaries which continued to enjoy freedom of action in

Venezuela. The hospitality to foreign companies forced some Venezuelan enterprises either to go out of business or to be absorbed by the multinationals.

Even more controversial than the favoritism to foreign firms or the commercial treaty was Pérez's sale of new petroleum concessions in 1955–6; his government was in need of more revenues to finance the sumptuous public works projects he had begun. The Suez Crisis, the Iranian oil nationalization and the Korean war all spurred the demand for Venezuelan petroleum, but by 1956 the demand had lessened and prices were lower. The US government, pushed by independent producers in the US, began to consider quotas on the importation of foreign oil. Venezuelan economic missions, the oil companies operating in the country, and the Venezuelan-American Chamber of Commerce lobbied the US Congress forcefully to prevent such a blow to Venezuelan national revenues and indirectly to the Venezuelan government which depended on those revenues.

Pérez's use of the national income of the 1950s continues to be debated. There is no doubt that the traditional custom of kickbacks and illicit enrichment came to be current again and that there was much waste in many of the government contracts. Some grand works of infrastructure were undertaken and completed: the dredging of the Maracaibo bar facilitated oil shipments from the Lake; highways and urban freeways reached to most parts of Venezuela; ports were improved; grand hotels were built to lure tourists and to provide accommodation for the rash of entrepreneurs who flocked to Venezuela; great irrigation projects, refineries, and urban construction like the Simón Bolívar Center in Caracas completed the picture.

Government expenditures give an indication of where the majority of the funds were going (see the accompanying table[16]). In 1950 and in 1957, the Ministry of Public Works spent about one third of total government expenditures, making it the most important ministry. The Ministry of Education in 1950 consumed only about 6 percent of the total budget and in 1957, spent only 5 percent of the budget. The Ministry of Public Works became the principal source of channeling government revenues to other sectors of the economy in the 1950s. In the 1948–58 period, of the sixteen principal contracting firms engaged in Public Works, only four lacked well-known links with the government. Government workers, and Pérez Jiménez himself, shared in the lucrative subcontracting business. EVICSA, founded for the sole purpose of receiving government contracts, divided up the profits with Pérez Jiménez. The rapid urban construction also saw a new boom in speculation on urban land and a rapid rise in the banking and mortgage businesses. Pérez and his ministers benefited by the government purchase of land for freeways and other public works; one option which an intermediary of Pérez's purchased for Bs 30 per square meter was subsequently sold to the government for Bs 120 per square meter, with the intermediaries presumably pocketing the difference. Reflecting the construction boom, the Venezuelan construction-related industries like cement also grew rapidly during the decade and contributed to the most rapid increase in the index of industrialization that Venezuela had yet seen.

	1940	1945	1950	1955
	%	%	%	%
Interior Relations	26.0	19.1	17.4	13.0
Foreign Relations	1.6	1.7	0.9	0.8
Treasury	7.9	13.1	6.2	12.0
Defense	10.0	7.9	9.0	8.9
Development	2.7	3.9	6.6	5.1
Public Works	22.2	32.1	35.7	32.3
Education	6.5	6.4	6.2	5.4
Health and Social Assistance	4.9	4.6	6.5	5.8
Agriculture and Livestock	12.8	6.9	5.7	5.0
Labor		3.6	0.8	0.9
Communications		0.7	5.0	5.0
Justice				2.7
Mines and Hydrocarbons				3.1

The growth of output in manufacturing was impressive, although it must be remembered that it had begun from a virtual standstill. The contribution of the nonpetroleum GDP rose from Bs 5,462,000 in 1948 to 13,854,000 in 1957.[17] Venezuela became slightly less dependent on petroleum exports; whereas in 1948 the share of petroleum in the total export earnings was 97 percent, by 1957 it had dropped to 93.4 percent.[18] Although manufacturing production increased, the tertiary sector, with an 8.7 percent annual average rate of growth, was the outstanding performer. Commerce contributed Bs 1,726,000 to the GDP in 1950 and 3,933,000 in 1957; other services increased during the same time period from 3,301,000 to 5,365,000.[19]

Labor's share of the national income dipped somewhat in the 1950s, although never back to the 1936 level. In 1936, the share was 46 percent of the national income, in 1949 it was 61 percent, but it fell to 52 percent in 1957 and 54 percent in 1958.[20] Some of the slippage no doubt was due to the type of industrialization that had developed in Venezuela. The newer industries were capital-intensive and modern, often subsidiaries of foreign firms, and this sort of expansion in industrial capacity brought no attendant expansion in the labor force. For example, the proportion of the labor force which was employed in manufacturing remained the same from 1950 to 1965, although that sector increased its participation in the gross national production from 10.2 percent to 17.9 percent.[21]

Postwar Society and Culture

The period 1945 to 1958 saw more changes in Venezuelan society than in the economic structure. Petroleum revenues continued, of course, to promote various changes. The pace of urbanization increased, and Caracas achieved a more marked economic, demographic, and political primacy. Its population grew from 203,342 in 1936 to 495,064 in 1950, and 786,863 in 1961. In 1946, 405,000 persons in Venezuela lived in cities with a population of 100,000 or over, by 1958 that figure had risen to 1,697,000. Smaller towns also attracted their share of rural migration; the number of persons living in towns with a population over 10,000 was 1,036,000 in 1946 and rose to 3,396,000 in 1958. The fastest-growing cities between 1950 and 1961 were Caracas, Valencia, Maracay, Puerto La Cruz/ Barcelona, Ciudad Guayana, Maturín, Cabimas, Ciudad Bolívar, Lagunillas, El Tigre/El Tigrito, Los Teques, and Barinas.[22] In 1941, 24.72 percent of the population were classified as urban; in 1950, the percentage had risen to 42.03 and by 1961, it was 57.79 percent. Between 1950 and 1961, the rate of growth of the population as a whole was 3.88 percent. The population rose from 3,850,771 in 1941 to 5,034,838 in 1950, to 7,523,999 in 1961.

The population growth in general reflected both a higher influx of European immigrants after World War II and a higher birth rate and lower death rate among Venezuelans. The improved health facilities could largely be attributed to the AD efforts to eradicate some of the debilitating diseases that had struck the nation; malaria, for example, practically disappeared in 1946–7 under the program supervised by Dr Arnoldo Gabaldón. Venezuelan life expectancy rose from thirty-eight years in 1936 to 43.2 years in 1941, to 53.9 years in 1950 and 60.9 years in 1961. The birth rate did not fluctuate much during the period, but the mortality rate fell from 25–30 per 1,000 population in 1936 to 7.4 per 1,000 in 1961.

Foreign immigration rose from 49,928 in 1941, or 1.3 percent of the total population, to 206,767 or 4.1 percent of the population in 1950, and 526,188 or 7 percent of the population in 1961. Between 1940 and 1961 a change occurred in the make-up of the foreign population. In 1941, the Colombians represented 34 percent of the entire foreign population, and Spaniards were 13.9 percent of the foreign born. In 1950, the Colombians still led with 22 percent, followed by Italians with 21.1 percent and Spaniards with 13.9 percent. In 1961, the Spaniards led with 30.8 percent, Italians followed with 22.5 percent, and Colombians came third with 18.9 percent.[23] Many of the Europeans left after the fall of the dictatorship. The economic and political situation was less secure after 1958, and fewer new European immigrants arrived. By the late 1960s, Colombians had regained first place among the foreign-born.

The US population by the end of the 1960s only reached about 13,000, although some unofficial estimates set it as high as 35,000. Nonetheless, the US community had an influence out of proportion to its numbers. First, their association with the oil companies and with the new multinationals coming into Venezuela gave them an economic and technical importance, as did the dominant position of the US in Venezuelan trade. Secondly, in the 1950s, the US citizens moved more into the Venezuelan cities and communities rather than remaining isolated in the oil camp enclaves. Thirdly, the expansion of radio, television, and movies in the more prosperous cities all reflected US patterns of consumption and taste. Fourthly, the urbanization and expansion of the tertiary sector of the Venezuelan economy naturally brought more Venezuelans into contact with foreigners than had the traditional agricultural structure. The indigenous Venezuelan culture and intellectual life which had begun to reawaken and to flourish in the 1930s gave way somewhat to the onslaught of the US-dominated mass media.

The impact of the mass media can hardly be underestimated. The urban population turned out in record numbers to see movies, most of them made in the United States. In 1949, 17,623,349 moviegoers expended a total of Bs 23,812,451; by 1956, the number of spectators had leapt to 42,259,965, spending Bs 72,230,435. These figures meant that annual attendance per person in Venezuela rose from 3.6 movies in 1949 to over seven in 1956. Of the films shown, 65 percent came from the United States; the small rural theaters were the major exception, since they used only 16-millimeter film, most of which came from Argentina and Mexico. Venezuela's own film industry had a promising revival in the early 1950s, through Bolívar Films under the leadership of poet, writer, and humorist Aquiles Nazoa. Argentine filmmakers and stars contributed to the co-productions. The most famous were *El demonio es un angel* (The Devil is an Angel) and *La balandra Isabel llegó esta tarde*, the latter based on a novella by Venezuelan writer, Guillermo Meneses. Another Venezuelan film of the epoch, *Venezuela también canta* (Venezuela Also Sings), nearly caused a major international incident with Colombia because it contained an unflattering portrayal of a Colombian character.

More people bought radios, and the total number of sets increased from 116,000 in 1946 to 992,000 in 1958. Television came on the scene in 1952. Critics and viewers worried lest Venezuelan youth would be corrupted by the low cultural level of the wrestling matches so frequently shown. Television apparently did not boost national culture, as the radio had done in the 1930s. Commercial advertising firms did, of course, realize the advantages of selling products through the new medium. The government tried to protect jobs for Venezuelan performers by passing a law in 1954 prohibiting foreign movies from being shown on Venezuelan televison. Live shows multiplied, chiefly comedy and variety acts, but the media came to be dominated by the Cubans who had flocked to Venezuela as the entertainment industry expanded. Not a large colony in Venezuela, the Cubans nonetheless arrived with superior experience acquired in the nightclubs of Havana in the post-war period.

Increasing literacy also helped increase the circulation of magazines. The literacy rate in Venezuela had grown from 35.67 percent in 1936 to 40.88 percent in 1941, 51.24 percent in 1950 and 65.21 percent in 1961. Urban rates, of course, were higher than rural, and the literacy rate for females between the ages of 10 and 19 was higher than for males of the same age in 1950, 1961, and 1971.[24] One might speculate that teenaged boys lost more time from school when the schools were closed due to unrest; the girls probably continued to attend the Catholic private schools. Six of the most popular magazines of the 1950s were edited in the US: *Temas*, *Selecciones* (*Readers' Digest*), *Life*, *Visión*, *Time*, and *Newsweek*. The Venezuelan Press Association and Venezuelan Chamber of Magazine Editors demanded that the government either ban or tax the foreign magazines, which were frequently cheaper than the Venezuelan ones. Venezuelan writers also objected to the fact that stories often either had no Venezuelan content or carried unflattering portraits of the country. Newspaper circulation *per capita* fell between 1946 and 1953, but then began to rise again in the last years of the dictatorship.

If increasing literacy, radios, and movie attendance indicated a greater prosperity in the 1950s, there were also indicators that the wealth was not evenly shared. A United Nations study on income distribution revealed that half of the Venezuelan population received only 14.3 percent of total national income, while the other half received the other 85.7 percent — the greatest disparity in Latin America. These figures, taken from a Venezuelan survey made in 1962, suggest that the growth of the 1950s affected the modern parts of the Venezuelan economy directly but had little effect on the more traditional sector. An optimist might point to the allegedly stabilizing effect of the relatively affluent middle group, the 45 percent of the population which fell above the median but below the upper most 5 percent. A pessimist would note that the trend begun in the 1950s would be difficult to reverse: that the most productive sectors of the economy — oil and manufacturing — provided fewer jobs than did the less lucrative service and agricultural sectors. The economic inequality could be measured in the differences between city and rural areas, between the petroleum and non-petroleum (or iron) regions, and, of course, between men and women.

Extreme poverty and the disparities brought about by the oil development had done little to improve the unstable family patterns of Venezuelans. The percentage of married couples increased from 24.4 percent in 1941 to 34 percent in 1961.[25] As more people left agricultural employment, women also entered the workforce in appreciable numbers. The percentage of women in the economically active population fell from 11.62 percent to 10.98 percent between 1950 and 1961 before it began to rise again. Yet the structure of women's work became more varied in the ten-year period. In 1950 over 76 percent of all working women were engaged in traditional areas: services, sports, entertainment, as artisans and factory workers, and in agriculture. In 1961 services and factory workers provided less employment, and more women worked in offices or as technicians. In absolute numbers, women office workers rose from 8,742 in 1950 to 24,068 in 1961. A profession which no doubt did not show up in the statistics was prostitution. In 1951, according to one estimate, there were between 3,000 and 4,000 brothels in Caracas alone, not counting the cabarets and nightclubs. In 1966, a survey of prostitutes in the Caracas area revealed that fully 54.77 percent of them claimed to have turned to prostitution because of economic necessity.

Women were often the sole support of their children. Estimates of abandoned children are difficult to verify, but even the conservative published figures revealed a serious social problem. In the early 1950s, estimates ranged from 100,000 to over half a million children without homes. The *Consejo del Niño* in 1951 could care for only 30,000 of them. With thousands of Venezuelan children roaming the streets, it was interesting to note the reaction among Venezuelans to the European war orphans for whom Dr José Herrera Uslar sought homes in 1950. Venezuelans practically fought each other to adopt one of the (usually) blond, blue-eyed children. A popular Venezuelan cartoon figure, Lalo, commented: "If the project of Pepito Herrera, of importing European children, succeeds, don't you think that national production will be affected . . . ?''

Women's traditionally sheltered roles, for the middle and upper classes, as portrayed in Teresa de la Parra's *Ifigenia* had changed considerably by the end of the 1950s. The press, especially the English-language *Caracas Journal* (later the *Daily Journal*), often complained of the difficulty in finding good servants. Women from the provinces tended to prefer less demanding or more lucrative jobs than domestic service. One of the upper-class matrons, Margot Boulton de Bottome, praised the new clean and efficient *supermercados* like the ones erected by Nelson Rockefeller's organization. There, she said, she increasingly saw other women of her acquaintance rather than the servant women doing the shopping. Señora de Bottome became an energetic role model for the more affluent Venezuelan woman; active in founding and running the *Centro Venezolano-Americano*, she also founded a women's organization — *Intercambio* — which sought to provide opportunities for women to speak in public and gain social skills. She had also been one of the first women elected to office and served on the City Council of Caracas in 1948, even becoming mayor briefly in the absence of that chief official. Middle- and working-class women might have identified more with some of the editorials and articles in the new magazine, *Páginas* (Pages), which appeared in 1948. The magazine frequently expressed bitterness and exasperation over the faults of Venezuelan men as husbands and counseled women on the precarious position of divorced women.

Younger women had more opportunity to leave the shelter of the home. Women's basketball received some notice from the press — and from conservative Church officials who believed that the women's appearance in public wearing short pants offended moral standards. Beauty pageants kindled an enthusiastic response, especially after Susana Dujuim won the Miss Universe contest in 1956. Some Venezuelans expressed pride at the recognition which came to their nation, while others bemoaned this commercialization of feminine beauty.

One illustrative case of how far roles had changed was that of Ligia Parra Jahn, a middle-class officer worker. She met a man at the office, and soon considered herself engaged to him. The man began dating another woman. Parra Jahn believed her honor offended and she shot and killed her lover. During much of her trial, it was debated whether it was proper for her to take justice into her own hands and kill her lover. She in fact received a relatively mild prison sentence, but it was commonly contended that if a male relative of hers had committed the same crime, he would never have had to serve a single day in prison.

If Teresa de la Parra's *Ifigenia* epitomized the frustration of a proper young woman who was bored in the 1920s, Antonia Palacios captured the spirit of a modern girl in the 1950s. Her *Ana Isabel, una niña decente* (Ana Isabel, a respectable young girl, 1949) portrays the resentment of a girl on the edge of adolescence who is told that she can no longer run freely through the plazas and play with the boys. She must conduct herself like a "decent girl":

Her body, her woman's body contained by bars! Her body which would have to remain very still, a prisoner, in the Alcántaras' house! She could no longer run through the plaza, nor climb to the roof, nor clamber to the top branches of the mango tree![26]

Although Ana Isabel's distress at the end of her active and egalitarian childhood is great, the reader doubts that Ana Isabel will ever be imprisoned in the same oppressive cage that held Ifigenia.

In addition to affecting the lives and roles of women, the rapid growth and easy prosperity of the 1950s encouraged the habits of an ostentatious living and consuming style for the urban middle sectors. Christian Dior and Yves Saint-Laurent opened boutiques in Caracas in the 1950s. Venezuela earned the reputation for being one of the world's greatest consumers of imported Scotch whisky and champagne. Automobile registration leaped from 46,000 in 1946 to 206,000 in 1955, thirty-six cars for each 1,000 persons.[27] A *Caracas Journal* writer counted more Cadillacs than Fords in the San Bernardino section of Caracas in 1951. Bars, nightclubs, and restaurants filled the elegant Sabana Grande section of Caracas. Santa Claus and Christmas trees (imported) supplemented or replaced the traditional *creches*; in 1951, the Three Kings sped up to the *Clínica de Nuestra Señora de Guadalupe* in a car decorated with Pepsi Cola tops. An editorial in *La Religión* in July, 1957, condemned the materialism:

Our modern society abounds in luxury, from many points of view. Luxury in dress, in vehicles, in too many comforts in the home, in the dances of so-called high society, where thousands and even millions of bolívares are wasted, which would be better put to use on charitable works for the many needy persons in our midst.[28]

The easy comforts of urban life coupled with the censorship practices by the government did not provide an atmosphere which encouraged an active intellectual life. Student protests in the newly-opened *Universidad Central de Venezuela* led to prompt closure by Pérez Jiménez in retaliation. Corporations and the Catholic Church collaborated to found what would become one of the most prestigious private universities in the country, *Universidad Católica*

Andrés Bello, but there was little continuity in university life in the 1950s. The improvement of journalism which had come in the early 1940s and flourished under the freedom of the *trienio* came to an end. *El Nacional*, along with lesser papers, was closed by the administration for days at a time for alleged violations of the censorship rules. Venezuelan writers complained that the influx of foreign magazines, movies, and television programs limited their outlets even more and accustomed the population to prefer the literary patterns or styles of the English-speaking US audience.

Short story writing appeared to flourish during the period, aided somewhat by *El Nacional*'s annual contest to choose the best ones. No single author appeared to fill the void left by Rómulo Gallegos, who wrote little after his turning to politics and exile in Mexico. The most prominent essayists and novelists were Arturo Uslar Pietri and Mariano Picón Salas, writers who had made a reputation in the 1930s and early 1940s. Guillermo Meneses, Antonia Palacios, Julian Padrón, Ramón Díaz Sánchez were also active. Themes of race, poverty, and psychological conflicts came to the fore in short stories and in novels. Real experimentation in form would not appear until the post-dictatorial period, marked by the publication of *Los pequeños seres* (Little People, 1959) by Salvador Garmendia. A new generation then emerged for the 1960s and 1970s.

The Revolution of 1958

If conflicts and tensions appeared in some of the novels and short stories of the decade, little overt conflict was expressed in public. The *Seguridad Nacional* and the army and Vallenilla Lanz as Minister of the Interior appeared to have the nation under control. *Acción Democrática* and the Communist Party had carried on an active clandestine struggle until the time of the 1952 elections, but subsequently had posed little threat to the regime. URD and COPEI had not been active. Students appeared relatively quiescent, many studying abroad or at the private universities. The relative prosperity had also lulled many, even the workers and peasants whose unions had been dissolved.

Signs of disaffection, however, began to appear from May 1957. Monseñor Rafael Arias published a pastoral letter which implicitly criticized the Pérez Jiménez regime for its lack of social consciousness. The newspaper *La Religión* began to carry on a running battle against *El Heraldo's* strong support of the regime and its materialistic philosophy. The challenge was especially courageous because it was an open secret that the Minister of the Interior, Laureano Vallenilla Lanz, wrote the editorials for *El Heraldo* under the pseudonymous initials "R.H." Then gradually a number of minor irritations took on more importance to various groups. Pérez Jiménez, coming to the end of his constitutional term, decided on a plebiscite in which the people could vote for or against him. Numerous Venezuelans were offended at such an obvious piece of electoral chicanery. Businessmen and contractors with state contracts worried about the government's slowing rate of payments. The circle of decision-makers and beneficiaries of the oil wealth seemed to be getting smaller and more arrogant. The custom of decreeing that public works projects would be completed by December 2 for a grand inauguration annoyed engineers, architects, and contractors and meant that workers experienced unemployment after the December 2 deadline. The visible presence of Portuguese, Spanish, and Italian immigrants in the construction crews continued to aggravate Venezuelan workers, who were often unemployed or underemployed. Most serious of all was the dissatisfaction among military men with Pérez Jiménez's highhandedness and his reliance on the *Seguridad Nacional*, even to supervise military officers. At different times officers were jailed, forced into retirement, promoted or refused promotion at the whim of Pérez and his civilian advisors. Officers grew conscious of the disaffection of other segments of the society. Some of the high command divided between those who wanted to force Pérez out and replace him with another military man and those who wanted to overthrow the regime altogether. The latter planned a conspiratorial movement for January 1, 1958. Although the movement was poorly executed and failed, it encouraged the civilian elements, who had not been aware of the hostility toward Pérez within the armed forces. The two events coming so close together — the plebiscite and the January conspiracy — prompted various professional groups and intellectuals to circulate manifestos protesting the abuses committed by the Pérez Jiménez government. A *Junta Patriótica* (Patriotic Junta), clandestinely formed in June 1957, had gradually united all of the civilian forces which opposed the government. By January, with the encouragement offered by the military revolt, all the opposition forces were ready to act.

Just as in 1928 and 1936, the urban masses of Caracas also added their weight to the revolt that began on January 21, when a general strike had been called by the *Junta Patriótica*. There was intense fighting on January 21 and 22, and Pérez Jiménez finally fled in the early hours of January 23. Admiral Wolfgang Larrazábal headed a governing junta which pledged to restore liberties and prepare for elections.

Thus, in the 1945 to 1958 period, two groups struggled for power in Venezuela. The Pérez Jiménez government could hardly be called a return to the *gomecista* tradition, but it did proscribe any popular organization and participation in the government. *Acción Democrática* allowed the organized workers, peasants, middle groups to have some participation in the decision makirlg and to derive some benefit from the government. The rather egalitarian tradition of Venezuelans, the admiration for *viveza*, for the rabbit who could outwit the stronger and more powerful tiger flavored the changing society which had been shaped by the oil revenues. There was money to construct a social services establishment which would both help to improve the quality of life for many and would provide a means of channeling government resources to the middle groups of bureaucrats, professionals, and military officers. Although many rejected the extreme partisanship of the *adecos* of the 1940s, they found less attractive the arbitrariness and authoritarianism of the *perezjimenistas*. The arrogance of the *perezjimenistas* had proved to be more abhorrent than that of the *adecos*.

NOTES

1. Andrés Eloy Blanco, *Poemas continentales* (Caracas: Ediciones del Congreso de la República, 1973), p. 5.

2. John Martz, *Acción Democrática: Evolution of a Modern Political Party in Venezuela* (Princeton: Princeton University Press, 1966), p. 75.

3. Rómulo Betancourt, *Venezuela: política y petróleo.* 3rd edn (Caracas: Editorial Senderos, 1969), p. 265.

4. Alfredo Peña, *Conversaciones con José Vicente Rangel* (Caracas: Editorial Ateneo de Caracas, 1978), p. 19.

5. Alfredo Peña, *Conversaciones con Uslar Pietri* (Caracas: Editorial Ateneo de Caracas, 1978), pp. 49–55.

6. Donald L. Herman, *Christian Democracy in Venezuela* (Chapel Hill: University of North Carolina Press, 1980), p. 22.

7. Alfredo Peña, *Conversaciones con Douglas Bravo* (Caracas: Editorial Ateneo de Caracas, 1978), p. 18.

8. Martz, pp. 77–8.

9. Allan-Randolph Brewer-Carías, *Cambio político y reforma del estado en Venezuela* (Madrid: Editorial Tecnos, 1975), pp. 368–88.

10. Steve Ellner, *Los partidos políticos y su disputa por el control del movimiento sindical en Venezuela, 1936–1948* (Caracas: Universidad Católica Andrés Bello, 1980), p. 135.

11. Franklin Tugwell, *The Politics of Oil in Venezuela* (Stanford: Stanford University Press, 1975), pp. 44–7.

12. Daniel H. Levine, *Conflict and Political Change in Venezuela* (Princeton: Princeton University Press, 1973), p. 69.

13. John Duncan Powell, *Political Mobilization of the Venezuelan Peasant* (Cambridge, Mass.: Harvard University Press, 1971), p. 71.

14. Ibid., p. 77.

15. Louis E. Heaton, *The Agricultural Development of Venezuela* (New York: Praeger Publishers, 1969), p. 106.

16. Banco Central de Venezuela, *La economía venezolana en los últimos treinta y cinco anos* (Caracas: Banco Central de Venezuela, 1978), p. 275.

17. Jorge Salazar-Carrillo, *Oil in the Economic Development of Venezuela* (New York: Praeger Publishers, 1976), pp. 118–19.

18. Ibid., p. 97.

19. Ibid., pp. 122–3.

20. Ibid., p. 195.

21. United Nations Economic Commission for Latin America, *La distribución del ingreso en America Latina* (New York: United Nations, 1970), p. 53.

22. Chi-Yi Chen and Michel Picouet, *Dinámica de la población: caso de Venezuela* (Caracas: Edición UCAB-ORSTOM, 1979), p. 42.

23. Ibid., p. 31.

24. Ibid., p. 447.

25. Ibid., p. 91.

26. Antonia Palacios, *Ana Isabel una niña decente* (Caracas: Monte Avila, 1972), p. 126.

27. *Hispanic American Report* 8 (Nov. 1955): 471.

28. *La Religión*, 24 July 1957.

5

ROMULO BETANCOURT AND THE NEW VENEZUELA, 1958-1963

" — Betancourt is the most capable, most patriotic, most valiant, most honorable and most progressive politician we have ever had!
— Lies! Betancourt is a partisan, a miserable administrator, an agent of imperialism, a malicious and deplorable leader for the country!"[1]

Miguel Otero Silva

Pérez Jiménez's departure opened up the political competition again. In theory, several political options existed: rule by a military junta which would leave the Pérez Jiménez system intact, a leftist revolutionary regime such as Fidel Castro's became, or a return to the basically centrist, reformist partisan democracy of the 1945-8 period. When all groups called for a continuation of the unity of the days of January 1958, the extreme possibilities faded as viable alternatives, and the choices narrowed to a non-partisan unity government or a coalition of the multiclass parties. Gradually during the year, *Acción Democrática*'s determined reorganization of the party at all levels enabled Rómulo Betancourt and his followers to dominate the political scene. That domination and Betancourt's skill shaped Venezuelan political choices and structures for the next quarter of a century. Much like the Mexican revolution, Venezuela's "democratic revolution" became institutionalized in a way which precluded radical social and economic change, but provided stability.

Since the Plan of Barranquilla of 1931, Betancourt and his cohorts had advocated a multiclass party. The experience of the *trienio* and the dictatorship had further taught them that *Acción Democrática* could not rule alone without the other centrist groups. In 1958, the party confronted the tasks of negotiating the rules of the game for sharing power, of refining and implementing their party platform, and of isolating any groups which challenged their ideology or tactics.

In choosing allies, *Acción Democrática* gave the greatest weight to those groups most easily organized and most likely to accept the new rules: other parties like COPEI and URD, organized labor, and organized peasants. Recognized as legitimate, and powerful, pressure groups which could influence political decisions but not share power were *Fedecámaras*, the armed forces, and the Church. Students, the PCV, and unorganized masses had no official channels to exercise power directly or to affect policy indirectly. The greatest benefits from the petroleum wealth went to middle groups, including rural peasants and organized labor, military officers, and industrialists. The scattered rural peasantry and the unskilled urban workers received little of substance from the new government. Betancourt used a number of tactics to implement the *Acción Democrática* program and to remain in power. He constantly negotiated with and rewarded all the sanctioned groups. *Acción Democrática* leaders tirelessly integrated organized peasants and labor groups into the party network while they attacked and isolated the Communists and AD youth who challenged the leadership of the generation of 1928. Finally, Betancourt employed an aggressive foreign policy which increased his international stature and contributed to the success of his centrist and nationalistic politics at home.

Within six years (1958–63), Venezuela had successfully made the transition from dictatorship to democracy. Betancourt's leadership had skillfully directed most political conflict into institutional channels. He used the loyalty of the armed forces to defeat the violent attacks which came from the groups outside the democractic system. Petroleum wealth reached more hands than before, and all political parties accepted the goal of improving the benefits of the working and middle groups. Venezuela's more active foreign policy increased regional tensions, but drew the nation further on to the international political stage.

Several indirect results of Betancourt's administration planted seeds of future problems. The government's increased responsibility for economic development and social welfare augmented the centralization of power in Caracas. Genuine local participation in decision-making decreased, a trend since the days of Guzmán Blanco. The preference given to political discipline and structure over administrative reform contributed to a highly politicized, sometimes inefficient, delivery of services to the Venezuelan people. The pragmatic decision to strengthen and work only through organized groups and parties left Venezuela with the same dilemma which Mexico faces: how to direct benefits to the rapidly growing population of rural unskilled workers. Finally, we have not yet seen the consequences in Venezuelan politics of forcing an entire generation of young radicals out of the system. The clandestine movements against Pérez Jiménez and the guerrilla experience molded the generation of 1958 much as the fight against Juan Vicente Gómez had affected Betancourt's generation. The political confrontations of the 1980s are likely to pit the former guerrillas against the more prosaic technocrats or partisans who remained with the AD and COPEI old guard. The 1963 election confirmed Betancourt's decisions in the short run, but the real plebiscite may not come until the 1990s.

The Transitional Year

The year of unity began on January 23, 1958. The military, the Church, the economic élite, the middle groups, and the masses had all acted in concert to force Pérez Jiménez, Pedro Estrada, and Vallenilla Lanz to flee. All agreed that elections should be held quickly. Wolfgang Larrazábal's junta set an election date for December 1958. The junta also decided to conduct the election under the 1953 Constitution so that a democratically elected President could supervise any constitutional revisions. Enjoying the political harmony, Venezuelans hoped for a single Presidential candidate on whom all could agree. But the search for a unity candidate strained the national consensus. Venezuelans quite naturally disagreed on national priorities for the future and on who could be trusted to set these priorities. The deepening economic recession, the devastating drought, and the visit of US Vice President Nixon to Caracas provided a troubled background for the political debate.

During the year, the economic élite's influence slipped a little. Critics termed the first junta the "Oligarchs' Cabinet" and were suspicious of the active political participation of the wealthy entrepreneurs. Indeed, the junta quickly, and perhaps unwisely, pleased the businessmen by paying off the $1.4 billion short-term unfunded debt which Pérez Jiménez had left behind from his inflated public works projects. Larrazábal's relations with the élite also soured as his own ambitions rose, and on May 18, Eugenio Mendoza and Blas Lamberti resigned from the cabinet. Representatives of the oligarchy monitored the transitional politics carefully, but remained in the background for the rest of the year.

Several military officers made a bid for power. Two of those most closely associated with Pérez Jiménez lasted only one day in the junta. Colonel Hugo Trejo had been one of the conspirators who had spearheaded the military movement against Pérez Jiménez, but he wanted a larger role to play, although he ostensibly supported the democratic transition government. Larrazábal and Minister of Defense General Jesús María Castro León checked Trejo's influence by appointing him ambassador to Costa Rica. Trejo's absence encouraged Castro León, who on 22 July demanded the suppression of *Acción Democrática* and the Communist Party, press censorship, delay of elections for three years, and the formation of a new junta more to the liking of the conservative wing of the Armed Forces. Larrazábal resisted, and most of the armed forces remained loyal, as did Eugenio Mendoza, who refused the presidency which Castro had offered him. Thousands of students and workers took to the streets in protest against the conspiracy. In the face of such widespread opposition, Castro León backed down and went into exile. Larrazábal began to reorganize the ármed forces, replacing the *perezjimenista* general staff with a joint Chiefs of Staff. Another conservative revolt, this time headed by Lt.-Col. Juan de Díos Moncada Vidal and Lt.-Col. José Hely Mendoza, broke out in September. Workers and students again supported the government and called for a general strike. At the conclusion of the movement and at *Acción Democrática* urging, Larrazábal took stronger measures to punish the conspirators and warned that the costs of rebellion were going up. The unified front of civilians and the majority of the armed forces effectively thwarted the *golpistas* who believed that Venezuela had rejected the person of Pérez Jiménez, but not the option of military rule.

The left, represented in 1958 by the *Partido Comunista de Venezuela* (PCV), participated freely in politics. Its influence with students, some professional groups, labor and urban *barrios* dwellers built on the prestige it had acquired in the struggle against Pérez Jiménez. Party membership rose from 1,000 in 1957 to 9,000 in 1958, and reached 40,000 in 1962.[2] But most of its strength was in the cities. It provided and led numerous street demonstrations such as those against the military *golpes* and the May 1958 protests against Richard Nixon. In spite of their urban and labor influence, the PCV leaders could not consolidate their gains quickly enough to demand a more prominent role in the government.

Rómulo Betancourt worked in 1958 to isolate the Communist leaders. If he tempered his partisan aggressiveness toward the centrist parties, he refused to consider sharing power with the left. In January 1948 in New York, Betancourt had met with leaders from URD and COPEI to discuss cooperation after the fall of the dictatorship. Betancourt argued that inclusion of the Communists in the pact could only damage the stability of the agreement without adding much strength. During 1958, Betancourt and other AD leaders continued to espouse a unity of centrist forces, while they worked feverishly to rebuild their own party network in labor and *campesino* organizations. They took particular care to visit rural areas and small towns, the heart of their strength during the *trienio*. When it became clear that no candidate was acceptable to all, the two major parties nominated their own leaders: Rómulo Betancourt for *Acción Democrática* and Rafael Caldera for COPEI. The URD turned from its founder Jóvito Villaba to support the popular Wolfgang Larrazábal, as did the PCV which saw the Admiral's candidacy as the most likely means of defeating Betancourt.

The centrist parties all experienced some generational and ideological conflicts, as younger members balked at the stodginess of the founding generation and at the exclusion of the left from the unity pact. At AD's national convention in August, a restive middle level of leaders identified with Jesús Paz Galarraga and Raúl Ramos Giménez while the youngest and most radical — veterans of the underground movement against Pérez Jiménez — followed Domingo Alberto Rangel and Simón Sáez Mérida. In 1958, the divisions were smoothed over, but they were soon to come into the open again.

Not only were generational and ideological differences shelved for the moment within the parties, but AD, COPEI, and URD reaffirmed their intention to cooperate. Meeting in October at Rafael Caldera's home "Punto Fijo" leaders of the three major parties signed a pact in which they agreed to abide by election results, uphold the Constitution, and to share cabinet positions. Representatives of labor, *Fedecámaras*, and the student movement were included in the gentlemen's agreement subsequently known as the "Pact of Punto Fijo," but the Communists were not invited.

Rómulo Betancourt first benefited from the pact when he won the December 5 election with 49 percent (1,284,092) of the popular vote. Larrazábal was second with 35 percent (903,479) and Caldera came third with 16 percent (423,262). The only ominous signs for AD were that they won by a smaller percentage than in 1947, and they came a poor fourth in the capital city of Caracas.

Popular history according to *Acción Democrática* frequently stresses the continuity of objectives and programs between the *trienio* and the Betancourt government of 1959–63. Yet it is well to recognize the substantive contribution of the Larrazábal year. Most important of course was Larrazábal's unwavering dedication to early elections and his resistance to efforts to postpone or cancel them. His government began the process of weakening and isolating opponents of democratic government within the military, the oligarchy, and the left. He oversaw the reorganization of the armed forces and required the members of the *Comisión Investigadora contra el Enriquecimiento Ilícito* (Investigating Commission against Illicit Enrichment — CIEI) to compile records on the corruption of the members of the previous government. There was special enthusiasm for making the case against Pérez Jiménez and his police chief, Pedro Estrada. Unemployed workers in Caracas were aided by the Emergency Plan, which created jobs and subsidies and by the suspension of rent payments in government housing. Costly and perhaps ill-conceived and politically motivated, these programs at least demonstrated that the junta was as willing to provide reparations for the poor as it was for the rich. Larrazábal ordered the formation of the *Comisión de Administración Pública* (Public Administration Commission — CAP), whose responsibility was to recommend administrative reform. In December, Larrazábal issued two significant decrees. One established the *Oficina de Coordinación y Planificación* (*Cordiplan*), which was charged with long-term economic planning. The other in effect increased the taxes paid by the major oil companies so that the nation received close to 65 percent of company profits.

With the exception of the Emergency Plan and rent moratorium, Betancourt continued all these measures when he took office on February 13, 1959. The year of unity had not produced an uncontested presidential election, but it had indicated that there were broad areas of consensus, as well as potentially troublesome points of conflict.

Acción Democrática: Politics and Coalitions

Betancourt's inaugural address set forth his goals. He intended to preside over a coalition government which would attack the fiscal, educational, social, and developmental problems of Venezuela. Betancourt declared that he would exclude only the Communists from positions in his government; they had no place in a democratic government, and their international postures could only harm Venezuelan interests.

The government initially included three cabinet positions for URD, two for AD, two for COPEI, and five for independents. The three major parties also shared leadership positions in Congress and in the states, whose governors the President appointed. Betancourt frequently consulted leaders of the other parties, and he often visited military barracks to maintain open lines of communication with the armed forces. Yet he had not altogether lost the contentiousness that had alienated others in the *trienio*. URD leaders such as José Vicente Rangel began to criticize Betancourt's strident response to urban demonstrations and terrorism. Betancourt responded early in 1960 by demanding that Rangel cease editing the newspaper *La Razón* and that URD either collaborate fully with him or leave the government. Jóvito Villaba allowed the coalition to limp along for a few more months. Betancourt's attacks on Fidel Castro's Cuba became the issue which finally drove URD into opposition in November 1960. The more conservative COPEI party, on the other hand, enthusiastically endorsed the President's campaign against the left. It gained directly from URD's defection, when it received additional cabinet positions. Their support became crucial to

Betancourt as the tempo of opposition stepped up in Congress and in the streets.

The AD leadership was troubled by cleavages within the party. Betancourt and the founding generation insisted on the party discipline and on the centrist program they had espoused since the 1930s. In March 1960, Domingo Alberto Rangel and Américo Martín criticized the reformist position in general and specifically AD's moderation in negotiating a contract between the oil workers' union and foreign companies. Rangel and Martín refused to accept the discipline imposed by the AD leadership, resigned from the party, and in May organized a new party which soon went by the name of *Movimiento de Izquierda Revolucionaria* (Movement of the Revolutionary Left — MIR). The second division of *Acción Democrática* came in January 1962, as the faction known as ARS failed in its efforts to control the party apparatus and challenge the old guard's leadership. Betancourt's allies called in the rank and file of the party, among whom they enjoyed high standing, and defeated Raúl Ramos Giménez and his followers. At issue in part had been Ramos Giménez's presidential ambitions for 1963, which were threatened by Betancourt's rumored deal with Caldera. Ramos Giménez quitted the party, along with peasant leader Ramón Quijada and numerous other middle-level leaders. The division threatened AD's electoral strength in the presidential election to come and immediately destroyed the AD/COPEI majority in the Chamber of Deputies, although AD still controlled the Senate.

Betancourt gambled that the loss of the party's left wing would not irreparably damage *Acción Democrática*. In the long run, the party would have to attract new young talent if it was to survive, but Betancourt's immediate solution was to draw closer to Rafael Caldera's COPEI. Betancourt and Caldera both chose to recruit a new generation of youth rather than surrender their parties to the men who had matured in the clandestine struggle against Pérez Jiménez.

The Congress which was elected in December 1958 had the responsibility for writing a new Constitution, which was promulgated in February 1961. The document confirmed governmental responsibility for social welfare of its citizens, provided for proportional minority representation in Congress, and prohibited the President from immediately succeeding himself. In spite of the limitation on succession, the Constitution only minimally circumscribed Presidential authority by congressional or judicial powers. Congress elected the Supreme Court judges, and the President appointed the state governors. Congressional deputies and senators would not represent states or regions, but parties. In practice, the proportional representation system contributed to a fragmentation of opposition groups which could obstruct policy, but rarely allow it to be initiated. Under Betancourt, the government coalition majority in Congress slipped from 94 percent in 1959 to 41 percent in 1963. Even purges and arrests of the leftist senators and deputies did not strengthen the majority coalition.

As might be expected, the President received authority to suspend all guarantees of personal and civil liberties. Betancourt's use of that power during his presidency evoked considerable criticism. In his campaign against the left, he censored or closed newspapers, closed the University, ordered the arrest of political opponents, had parties declared illegal and their members arrested, and refused permission for groups to assemble or demonstrate. The new national police force — *Dirección General de Policía* or *Digepol* — which replaced the *Seguridad Nacional* was accused of irregular arrests and mistreatment of political prisoners. Betancourt overrode all objections and insisted that a democratic President should have all means at his disposal to counter undemocratic enemies. All things considered, Betancourt and his police force should probably not be charged with inordinate abuse of power; however, it is at least arguable that his willingness to use force gave the left the pretext to escalate their own violent tactics.

Acción Democrática, and to a smaller extent COPEI, collaborated in organizing and dominating the labor and peasant unions and the *barrios* of urban poor. They developed experienced and loyal union and community leaders, provided them with patronage and services from the state, and forced out the radical or the recalcitrant. Leftist leaders proved unable to counter the government initiatives, or to foment a comparable organization and discipline, and became increasingly isolated and frustrated.

The underemployed and unemployed masses in the Caracas *barrios* proved the most difficult to channel into the political structure. Pérez Jiménez's prohibition of political organizations had been most successful in the capital city. Moreover, Larrazábal's Emergency Plan had won over the *barrios* in 1958. To eliminate PCV and URD influence and to check the stream of rural migrants to the city, Betancourt took an unpopular gamble in August 1959. He abolished the Emergency Plan, which had provided a means for the left to build up a clientele. AD lost even more support in the *barrios* when the young *miristas* left the party, for they had spearheaded AD's political organization in the *barrios*. From 1959 to 1962, the government parties continued their double strategy: eliminate the left and channel all patronage through AD and COPEI loyalists. Only AD or COPEI leaders in the *barrios* could secure water, garbage collection, electricity or other urban services for the newer *barrios* which appeared on the hills around Caracas. The obligatory permits for the squatter communities in their cardboard houses came more rapidly if the spokespersons for the community were members of AD or COPEI. When the leftists turned in frustration to terrorism, they alienated many *barrios* residents who saw friends in the police and army felled by bullets and bombs. After the leftist hold had weakened, the government returned to the *barrios* in 1962 with the *Movimiento Pro-Desarrollo de la Comunidad*. AD directed the assistance given by the community development movement through the Federal District Governor's office.[3]

Nudging organized labor and peasant federations into the party fold proved easier. Many union leaders had retained their AD sympathies in spite of the dictator's persecution. At the first congress of the *Confederación de Trabajadores de Venezuela* (Venezuelan Workers' Confederation — CTV) in 1959, AD claimed 54 percent of the delegates. COPEI had 10 percent, the PCV 22 percent, URD 11 percent, and independents 4 percent. The government parties agreed that they would compete within a given union for leadership rather than form rival party unions. Yet the majority coalition of AD and COPEI established the rules and forced the PCV-URD-MIR militants out of the CTV in November 1961. The left then formed a rival confederation, the *Central Unica de Trabajadores de Venezuela* (CUTV). As an "unofficial" federation, the CUTV found its strikes declared illegal, its leaders arrested, and its political allies in Congress subject to arrest and expulsion. Logically, unions which were responsive to AD and COPEI labor bureaux met more success with their strikes and demands for collective contracts. COPEI tried to develop a rival Christian trade union movement, but although this effort led to the formation of the *Comité de Sindicatos Autónomos* (CODESA) in 1964, the federation remained weak.

Peasant federations benefited from the political patronage system through the agrarian reform bill, agricultural credit, rural education, and other services. Most of the benefits went to residents of small rural settlements in the north-central region of the country or those who were willing to resettle. Peasant leaders affiliated with AD and COPEI became the channels for rural benefits. The First Peasant Congress of June 1959 elected AD leader Ramón Quijada as its president, confirming AD's dominance in that organization. Many of the federation leaders, especially at the national level, could hardly be classified as peasants; they had received their leadership training in other unions or in the party itself. AD's moderate agrarian reform program provoked divisions within the peasant movement. Ramón Quijada joined some of the the leftists who urged a more rapid distribution of land to the landless. Betancourt and the AD leadership then purged Quijada and his faction from the agrarian section of the CTV. Quijada fought the move, but his peasant affiliates no longer received the government subsidy from the Ministry of Labor after the split in 1961. Quijada subsequently joined the ARS dissidents who withdrew from AD to follow Ramos Giménez in 1962.

In sum, AD successfully pulled key sectors into the new democratic political system. COPEI agreed to cooperate and to keep their conflicts within institutional bounds. Betancourt simultaneously secured the dominance of his centrist philosophy in his own party. Then in Congress, the *barrios*, the organized labor movement, and the peasant federations, he and the COPEI leadership carefully channeled benefits and services through their own loyalists and isolated the leftist leaders as we have seen. The minority PCV-MIR-URD leaders could not respond through the official channels, which were partly blocked to them, and they turned to violence. Terrorism and guerrilla warfare brought in the keystone to Betancourt's system: the armed forces, with whom Betancourt struck an implicit bargain. He allowed them a greater role in national security and in the direction of military affairs, but he denied them a voice in political matters. Since a national security policy encómpassed responsibility for defense and development of the sparsely populated frontiers, the line between civilian and security matters eventually became somewhat blurred.

A number of policies, or events, strengthened Betancourt's hand with the armed forces and helped him to convince the officers that they should play the role he had planned for them. First, the reorganization of the armed forces, which began in 1958, increased the influence of the navy and the air force; the army no longer had such a clear dominance as before. Betancourt raised officers' salaries and benefits to a level comparable to that of their counterparts in the United States; the Ministry of Defense provided generous credit plans to assist officers in the purchase of homes. The military academies became more selective and the curriculum more nearly comparable to that of the national universities. The benefits and training improved the officers' living standards and gradually raised the prestige of a military career from its low point at the end of the *perezjimenista* period. Finally, the loyal armed forces developed both confidence and a sense of mission as they defeated the series of revolts against the democratic government. The war against the leftist guerrillas offered valuable combat experience with an enemy that Betancourt characterized as external or foreign.

After the 1958 revolts, the nation enjoyed a brief respite from armed conflict. Then, in April 1960, the redoubtable Jesús María Castro León invaded Táchira from Colombia. He accused the government of corruption, lack of authority, and Communist influence. The revolt was quickly put down, and Castro León was sent to San Carlos Prison, where he died in 1967. Another unsuccessful conservative military uprising occurred in February 1961. Lt.-Col. Juan de Díos Moncada Vidal, who had accompanied Castro León in 1958 and 1960, had an ideological change of heart after the 1960 failure. He became a guerrilla commander for the *Fuerzas Armadas de Liberación Nacional* (FALN), reconciling his apparent ideolological inconsistency by explaining that he had always been a revolutionary who abhorred both Betancourt and the oligarchy; as he saw it, the Castro León movements and the Communist FALN sought the same ends. Moncada Vidal was captured and jailed in December 1963.

A conspiracy of leftists and military officers in 1962 resulted in the most serious and costly armed movement against the Betancourt government. In May 1962, the Marine Infantry Batallion of Carúpano rebelled with a leftist program. After the movement was quelled, with fairly high casualities, Betancourt suspended constitutional guarantees and prohibited the MIR and PCV from all activities. A second bloody revolt came at the naval base in Puerto Cabello in June 1962, and it too proclaimed leftist, nationalist objectives. These attempts marked the effective beginning of FALN activities and a division within the left between those who advocated a military movement to remove Betancourt from power and those who argued for a long *campesino* war in the style of Cuba. Betancourt responded forcefully to the armed violence and the international tensions of the Cuban missile crisis in October. In that month for the first time, he called a meeting of the Supreme Council of National Defense to divide the country into four military zones. He ordered more equipment and support for the armed forces and reiterated his "shoot first and ask questions later" policy toward subversives. Betancourt strengthened his national security doctine when he linked the Cuban/Soviet threat with the internal subversion in Venezuela. The pressure mounted in 1963, as the FALN combined urban terrorism with rural guerrilla activity to try to prevent the election of December 1963 from taking place. Although some military officers like Moncada Vidal joined the FALN, Betancourt had apparently won the loyalty of the majority of the officers.

In effect, Betancourt laid a trap for the left. By excluding them from his carefully constructed political and institutional channels, he left them no choice but to remain impotent or to seize the bait of the Cuban model of revolution. By reinterpreting the Venezuelan events of 1958 in the light of the Cuban developments in 1961–2, the MIR and the PCV hoped to forge a revolutionary coalition of students, peasants, and urban masses. Instead, the quixotic turn to violence lost the respectability the Communists had earned during the dictatorship and the foothold they had in the labor and peasant unions. Betancourt consolidated his position and convinced the right that *Acción Democrática* was now a moderate and responsible party.

Acción Democrática did not integrate business organizations or the Church so directly into the formal political channels. Betancourt did succeed in neutralizing them as opponents and winning their grudging acceptance; the coalition with COPEI reassured the ecclesiastical officials that the strident anti-clericalism of the *trienio* would not be repeated. Betancourt's government doubled the state subsidy to the Church by comparison with the Pérez Jiménez figures.[4] AD leaders urged the anticlerical teachers' union, the Venezuelan Federation of Teachers and the Venezuelan College of Professors, to cooperate with the Church. In 1964, after Betancourt left office, the Venezuelan government signed a *modus vivendi* with the Vatican, which granted the Church greater freedom from state control than it had enjoyed since the days of Guzmán Blanco.

The business community clearly wanted a greater participation in the economic and political decisions at national level. Betancourt had either to politicize the business associations or to seek their advice without allowing them to dominate the decision-making process. The nature of *Fedecámaras*, founded in 1944, encouraged a less formal association between business and the government. It included commercial, industrial, and agricultural affiliates, and its interests obviously conflicted with those of the government on specific issues, such as agrarian reform, import substitution policy, and the proposed revision of the commercial treaty with the United States. *Fedecámaras* leaders wanted to remain a national, all-inclusive association, so they tried to conciliate the rival interests. Consequently, more effort was given to defending and enlarging the private sector in general than to lobbying for measures of specific interest to one sector. Affiliated chambers and local bodies did of course act on their own to influence policies of interest to them. *Fedecámaras* also tried to avoid schisms by not allowing its internal elections to become politicized as those of the labor unions had been.[5]

Fedecámaras power may have been greatest during the Betancourt years, when Betancourt tried to woo the economic leaders. AD sympathizer Alejandro Hernández was its president from 1958 to 1960 and continued to exercise considerable influence throughout the life of the Betancourt government. From 1961 to 1963, a struggle raged within the association to define its role as critic or ally of the government. Hernández proposed a relatively uncritical alliance in exchange for government support. His opponents argued that the association must remain politically independent in order criticize the government and put pressure on it when necessary. By the end of Betancourt's term, the independent faction had won. Alejandro Hernández withdrew from *Fedecámaras* and became a leader in *Pro-Venezuela*, an association of industrialists formed in 1958 to promote import substitution policies. *Acción Democrática* leaders viewed *Pro-Venezuela* as the more nationalistic economic association and criticized *Fedecámaras* for its alliance with multinational companies. Even with the conflicts, business interests achieved a greater voice under Betancourt than they had ever enjoyed before.

The Acción Democrática Program

Acción Democrática's efforts to dominate the political structure of the nation were of course not an end, but a means to achieve the party's objectives. Betancourt struggled to overcome the economic problems and to implement a program based on long-range planning, national control of resources, and social justice.

The AD platform laid out five principal aims: political freedom and civil liberties; state planning for balanced economic growth; improvement of health, education, and welfare; national control of economic resources and the economy in general; and promotion of strong, independent institutions. Neither the objectives nor the means to achieve them were revolutionary, except in contrast to the dictatorships that the nation had previously endured.

The economic recession sharply limited Betancourt's ability to implement the AD programs. The worst years were 1958–61, and the decline contrasted sharply with the booming 1950s when national income had increased at a rate of 10 percent a year in real terms. Pérez Jiménez's monumental public works and Larrazábal's lavish spending left the nation with its largest budget deficit in history: Bs. 900 million. The drop in posted oil prices by 27 cents a barrel resulted in a loss of $105 million a year to the Venezuelan government. Petroleum income as a percentage of government income dropped from 57 percent in 1959 to 52.7 percent in 1963.[6] To compound the difficulty, capital flight became acute, and foreign investment tapered off. The unemployment rate during Betancourt's term averaged 12 percent a year.

Three different finance ministers tried to improve the situation. They contracted foreign loans, cut government appropriations, twice cut government salaries by 10 percent, and imposed exchange controls. Finance Minister José Antonio Mayobre proposed a devaluation of the *bolívar*, but the measure was so unpopular with COPEI and URD that it was not implemented. Mayobre resigned in late 1960. The deflationary measures helped the outward flow of capital somewhat, but expansionist construction projects initiated in August, 1961, boosted the economy. Relations with Venezuela's principal trading partner, the United States, remained delicate. Venezuela passed higher tariffs to implement the import substitution policy, and the United States imposed mandatory import restrictions on foreign oil in the Spring of 1959. Indeed, any objective assessment of Betancourt's government must take into account the obstacles raised by the unique economic situation and the political violence.

Against all odds, Betancourt's presidency made real strides towards achieving more national control over petroleum production and marketing. He and his Minister of Mines, Juan Pablo Pérez Alfonzo, believed that immediate nationalization of petroleum could be disastrous for the Venezuelan economy; the country needed a transition period to train a generation of managers and engineers to direct the production and marketing of the national resource. And in a democracy, Pérez Alfonzo believed, the public too should become knowledgeable about petroleum policy. He patiently outlined the issues and the AD decisions at numerous press conferences.

The major oil companies responded to *Acción Democrática* moderation with panic and subtle forms of pressure. The luxury of an international oil glut allowed them to transfer new investments to the Middle East and African fields. Venezuelan oil, they explained, was no longer profitable. They gambled that their lower rate of investment in Venezuela, the lower world prices, and the drop in employment in the Venezuelan petroleum industry (28 percent between 1960 and 1967) would weaken the mild AD economic nationalism. Venezuelan petroleum did cost more to extract than that of the Middle East, but the proximity of the United States market somewhat offset the disadvantage. Moreover, the oil companies themselves could affect the production cost by offsetting high-cost fields with low-cost fields; in Venezuela, they chose an especially expensive combination of fields.[7] The companies joined *Fedecámaras* in 1959 and persuaded their business allies that economic development depended on favorable treatment of the international oil companies. The strong petroleum lobby within

Fedecámaras aroused *Acción Democrática* suspicions of that association.

The immediate crisis passed, but Venezuela's relative position as an oil-exporting nation was slipping. To maintain maximum revenues as long as possible, Venezuela sought information on pricing and marketing, found allies among other producing nations, and increased control over decisions which involved petroleum policy. The December 1958 tax law had raised the nation's share of oil profits to approximately 65 percent, a percentage that Betancourt found acceptable for the moment. Pérez Alfonzo established the coordinating Commission for the Conservation and Commerce of Hydrocarbons to monitor the companies' actions in general and the controversial discounting of posted prices in particular. In 1960, the Commission found that the Superior Oil Company and the Sun Group had granted excessive discounts. The companies refused to change their contracts, and the government ordered their wells closed and all production halted. The companies finally gave in, but the major companies were not intimidated. They believed — correctly, as it seemed — that the government could not afford the loss of revenues which would result from closing down a major producer.[8] The Commission did not apply sanctions again during the Betancourt government.

Pérez Alfonzo's grandest vision proved to be the Organization of Petroleum Exporting Countries (OPEC). Such an association would have been impossible in the 1940s because the Arab and African states were not then major exporters. The 1960s looked more promising. Pérez Alfonzo attended the First Arab Petroleum Congress in Cairo in 1959 to lobby for an international producers' association. The Arab nations greeted the proposal lukewarmly, until the sharp drop in oil prices in August 1960. In September of that year in Baghdad, five nations formed OPEC: Iran, Iraq, Kuwait, Saudi Arabia, and Venezuela. By 1973, there were twelve voting members. The Middle Eastern nations wanted to raise revenues and showed little interest in controlling the industry. OPEC fell short of Pérez Alfonzo's hopes for it in its first decade, but it did at least provide a framework for consultation and exchange of information.

Pérez Alfonzo met with even less success in persuading the United States to alter its import quotas. Alfonzo protested the US Government's mandatory restrictions on Venezuelan oil and he proposed a preference system for Western Hemisphere suppliers to the US market. By this system, the quotas would be assigned to foreign governments, not to the companies. The companies and Washington rejected such a major change in the marketing system, and Venezuela had to accept the limits imposed by the nation which purchased the largest share of Venezuelan oil.

Caracas could take pride in the nationalistic announcement that foreign companies would receive no new concessions and that Venezuela would found its own national petroleum company. The *Corporación Venezolana del Petróleo* (CVP) came into existence in 1960, marking the state's first direct participation in the oil industry. The CVP, an autonomous institute attached to the Ministry of Mines, had wide authority to explore, exploit, refine, transport, and market oil as well as to acquire shares in other companies. Pérez Alfonzo wanted the CVP to negotiate service contracts with foreign companies for the exploitation of its own concessions. The companies naturally resisted competing with their own operations, and the Venezuelan government chose not to increase direct production while the world oversupply existed. The CVP provided a training ground for Venezuela, but little more during its first decade of existence.

Betancourt's moderate oil policy in sum produced a number of indirect advances and laid the basis for the future of the national industry. It did not immediately alter the structure of the industry or the relations between the companies and the nation.

The Ministry of Mines, like many other ministries, established its own goals and priorities. Betancourt was concerned, however, for the integral long-range planning for the economy. *Cordiplan*, established by the junta in 1958, became the central planning agency under the leadership of Dr Manuel Pérez Guerrero, a respected economist and former United Nations official. Betancourt invited the economic elite, technocrats, and some foreign consultants to participate in Venezuelan economic planning. The first four-year plan covered the period from July 1960 to June 1964. Its annual revisions became more detailed year by year, but did not appear actually to affect the direction and priorities of the economy. The lacklustre beginning of institutionalized planning probably reflected conflicting priorities as much as inexperience and the difficult political situation.

The *Corporación Venezolana de Fomento* (Venezuelan Development Corporation — CVF) and autonomous institutes under its authority bore the primary responsibility for promoting industry. The CVF welcomed private, foreign, or mixed investments and encouraged industrial poles of development far from the metropolis of Caracas. The incorporation of the newly-planned city of Santo Tomás de Guayana in 1961 and the attention paid to the state *Corporación Venezolana de Guayana* (CVG) signalled the determination to spread out the industrial growth with special emphasis on the resource-rich Guayana region. Private investors benefited from the CVF's policy which allowed them to put up as little as 20–25 percent of the working capital for a new industrial enterprise, while the CVF furnished the remainder. Foreign corporations found equal favor. Reynolds Metal entered into a 50–50 agreement with the CVG to start up an aluminum plant in Guayana.

The development strategy had some weaknesses. For example, decision-making for the CVG and other state corporations remained in Caracas. Lisa Redfield Peattie recounts the frustration of inhabitants of a *barrio* in Ciudad Guayana in 1964 when the CVG installed a sewer outlet where it would pollute the river water used for bathing and laundry. They did not know where or to whom to complain in Ciudad Guayana or in faraway Caracas.[9] In practice, the objective of centralized planning competed with that of encouraging community participation and self-help.

Another flaw concerned the import substitution policies. Paradoxically, more US companies were attracted to Venezuelan investments because of the tariff barriers; US and other foreign investors chose to move their operations to Venezuela, rather than lose the lucrative consumer market fueled by the petroleum wealth. The companies by and large used local credit to construct capital-intensive industries which would import raw materials and intermediate products for assembly or finishing in Venezuela. In 1960, US firms set up canning, foodstuffs, clothing, auto tires, paint, cigarettes, glass, aluminum, and auto assembly plants. The development succeeded in the short run in replacing some of the consumer goods imports, but the second step to self-sufficiency became more difficult because the foreign companies had little interest in eliminating the importation of the raw materials and semifinished products. Moreover, the relatively high tariffs which sometimes protected Venezuelan monopolies of some products, contributed to the concentration of capital, and pinched the Venezuelan consumer. According to *mirista* Domingo Alberto Rangel, in 1963 one Venezuelan firm dominated 50 percent of beer production, one controlled 60 percent of cement production; one company produced half of all the sugar processed by the private sector; and one company accounted for over 50 percent of the manufacture of liquors apart from beer.[10]

A few Venezuelan entrepreneurs built up investments with little risk capital of their own. They depended on the government for their economic success, and the government and its autonomous institutes depended on them to manage the investments. Labor and agriculture did not secure as strong a position with the government and the autonomous institutes, political rhetoric notwithstanding.

Some of the AD social reforms were limited by the goal of rapid industrialization which required the support of the entrepreneurial class. Betancourt may have had no realistic alternative in 1959 but to placate the economic elite and foreign investors. He did, however, take the Mexican path of conducting a rhetorical revolution, implementing sufficient social reforms to give the revolutionary rhetoric some credibility, and quietly wooing the business community.

Betancourt's agrarian reform promised to improve productivity and income in the agricultural sector of the economy. Land distribution to the landless received a high priority, but the President insisted that distribution should be gradual, planned, and accompanied by all legal formalities. Peasant leader Ramón Quijada and leftist spokesmen called for more rapid distribution. Betancourt acted quickly against any peasants who seized land without authorization, accusing them of Communism; by 1961 he had forced Quijada and the left out of the agrarian movement. The President's moderation settled 118,737 families on plots, a figure which fell short of goals but lessened the political tension in the countryside. Leftist guerrillas later made little headway in rural Venezuela. The agrarian reform program could also be termed a political success because it alienated few of the landed elite. Nearly half of the land distributed (2.6 million hectares in 1959–65) was public land, and much of the private land came from exiled *perézjimenistas* or from uncontested purchases.[11]

Venezuela's agricultural production increased between 1959 and 1963 as did the total area given to farming. In 1961, only 28.7 percent of the national territory was devoted to farms, and only 6.4 percent of the total farm land was planted in crops.[12] Nearly a quarter of the total public funds expended on agriculture went to the construction and maintenance of irrigation facilities. Public funds also provided other support services such as community water supply, rural housing, loans, technical assistance, and agriculture education.

There were results. The *per capita* income and the income per person employed in agriculture increased by 20 percent between 1961 and 1965, a rate of growth greater than that of any other economic sector. Still, in 1965, the agricultural sector received only 7.7 percent of national income, amounting to a *per capita* sum of Bs 686 ($152) a year, compared with Bs 2,694 ($599) for the nation as a whole.[13] Population growth limited the real economic progress somewhat. In Venezuela, 32.3 percent of the population depended on agriculture in 1961, and that percentage dropped to 30.3 percent by 1965. Yet the absolute number of persons in the sector rose from 2,458,665 in 1961 to 2,639,711 in 1965.

Administrative incompetence sometimes damaged the effectiveness of the program. Less than 10 percent of the land transferred was actually ready to be worked by family groups. Legal problems abounded, and by 1966, few of the families who had received land had also received legal titles. The *Instituto Agrario Nacional* (IAN) favored agricultural settlements in productive zones near roads so that the recipients could receive services and could produce results at once; thus the benefits of the agrarian reform were not evenly distributed throughout the nation. Rural schools, housing, and training naturally went more easily to peasant settlements near the north coast than to scattered rural inhabitants. The IAN allotted relatively small amounts of money for research and extension work. There is little evidence that the rise in productivity came from increased efficiency of the small units. The administrative and accounting procedures of the *Banco Agrícola y Pecuario* (BAP) proved woefully inadequate. The Bank seldom collected the loans due, so that in effect much of the money transferred to agriculture became grants rather than loans which could be reissued to other farmers.

Betancourt's government did make a real, and effective, effort to improve the quality of life of working-class and rural Venezuelans. *Acción Democrática* gave priority to education, public health, public water supplies, electricity, rural roads, housing, child care and nutrition, and recreation. The gap between the standard of living in the cities and the countryside had already narrowed considerably since the Second World War, but Betancourt's programs benefited rural and small town residents even more.

Public health improved greatly. Supervised by Dr Arnaldo Gabaldón, the Ministry of Health and Social Assistance absorbed nearly 9 percent of the total national budget. Gabaldón established scholarships for medical personnel to receive further training in Venezuela and abroad. His Directorate of Malariology and Environmental Sanitation attacked malaria by improving rural housing and water supply. Deaths from malaria dropped from 163 per 100,000 in the 1949–57 period to 96 per 100,000 in 1962. There was a twenty percent increase in the number of hospital beds in government hospitals by 1962. More small health centers were erected in the interior. Live births in hospitals rose, more children received vaccination, and a free school lunch program helped to improve nutrition. The *Consejo Venezolano del Niño* received money from the government to assist with health care, nutrition, early childhood education, recreation, and care for homeless and delinquent children. Infant mortality dropped from 64 per 1,000 live births in the 1955–59 period to 46.5 in 1966.[14]

Better rural and urban water supplies no doubt contributed to the improvement in health. In 1959, there were 149 rural centers which had water for 726,000 persons; by 1965, 700 centers served 1.6 million people. Between 1958 and 1962, the number of urban residents with water rose from 1.8 million to 2.45 million. Another indicator of improved living conditions, the consumption of electricity, also rose: in 1958 the *per capita* consumption of electricity was only 559 kilowatt hours, while in 1963, it had risen to 831 kilowatt hours.[15]

Construction of low cost housing received priority in the country and the cities. Rural housing affected health as well, for the host of the Chagas disease lodged in the thatched roofs of rural huts. The AD government could meet less than 10 percent of the rural need during the 1959–65 period, and housing for the burgeoning urban population also lagged far behind the need. The *Banco Obrero* constructed or financed single-family dwellings or small apartments in the interior and encouraged residents of Caracas *superbloques* (large apartment complexes for low-income housing) to initiate community action projects and to use generous bank financing to purchase their apartments. Mortgage loans were supplied for ten to fifteen year periods, an innovation in financing which probably assisted more middle-income groups than the working poor.

Carlos Behrens, director of the *Instituto National de Recreación para los Trabajadores*, persuaded private companies to subsidize paid vacations for workers at the government resort of Los Caracas. The measure lowered costs at the resort because of a year-round occupancy, and encouraged the idea of family vacations for workers. The *Instituto Nacional de Deportes* (IND) turned away somewhat from the construction of monumental stadiums and provided more modest facilities in small towns whose residents were willing to supply the initiative and labor. Critics noted that a large portion of IND budgets still went for travel to prestigious international competitions. Effective training of Venezuelan athletes received a lower priority, so Venezuela garnered little glory at the international meets.

Finally, *Acción Democrática* dramatically expanded the educational network. AD leaders like Luis Beltrán Prieto Figueroa and Mercedes Fermín had long been active in the *Asociación de Maestros* as well as in *Acción Democrática*. AD's aggressive educational programs in the 1940s had brought conflicts with the Catholic Church, but in the 1960s experience and the coalition with COPEI tempered the anticlericalism. The AD government focused on radically expanding the public school system rather than on attacking the private schools. Over 3,000 public primary schools were built, and nearly 200 secondary, normal, and technical schools appeared, many in small towns in the interior. Secondary and university enrolment more than doubled, and total primary enrolment went from 916,764 to 1,370,665 between 1959 and 1963. Most of the expansion came in the public school system.

The rapid expansion required rapid training of new teachers. The government established new teachers' training institutes and in-service training programs. Betancourt claimed that Venezuelan teachers' salaries were the highest in Latin America. Teachers received assurances of job security, expanded social security benefits, and control over promotion and dismissal policies. But in spite of the assurances of job security, leftist teachers complained that they had been purged from the public schools in 1962, to be replaced with AD partisans.

Government spending through the Ministry of Education reached nearly 11 percent of the national budget, not including the money spent by the *Ministerio de Obras Públicas* (Ministry of Public Works—MOP) to build new schools. Regional universities sought to provide post-secondary education in the interior and to provide alternatives to the over-crowded and politicized *Universidad Central de Venezuela.* Technical education, the Office of Adult Education's adult literacy campaign, and the *Instituto Nacional de Cooperación Educativa* (National Institute of Educational Cooperation—INCE) reached out to the non-traditional student. INCE required employers of more than ten people to allow 5 percent of their workforce to be made up of apprentices between the ages of fourteen and eighteen. Quantitative measures of the educational achievements were impressive. Betancourt claimed that adult illiteracy dropped from 33.5 percent in 1961 to 26.5 percent in 1962. Overall literacy percentages rose from 60.8 percent to 68 percent between 1958 and 1963.

Problems still existed. *Acción Democrática* blamed many of the failings on political fervor in the schools, but the rapid increase in school enrolment produced overcrowding and a sixty to one teacher/student ratio. A higher percentage of children had to repeat a school year. The drop-out rate continued to be high. Only twenty-eight students out of every 100 who entered primary school continued to receive their primary school diplomas, according to a 1966 survey.[16] Secondary education divided into three tracks — academic, vocational and normal — and curricula remained relatively traditional. A majority of university students still opted for traditional fields of study such as law and humanities. Private *liceos* and universities continued to attract the children of the elite. Rural areas received more schools and higher educational budgets, but decision-making centered in the Ministry of Education in Caracas. Educational expansion had helped to erase the deficit of the *perezjimenista* years. Yet the very rapidity of growth meant that the democratic school system was born with a number of congenital disorders which would be difficult to cure.

Indeed, a constant theme of the 1959–63 period is the tension between goals and planning on one hand and implementation on the other hand. Betancourt frequently attacked the waste and inefficiency in public administration and promised to eliminate it. The *Comisión de Administración Pública*, established in 1958, made numerous recommendations. It suggested that a decentralization of authority would improve efficiency and limit political patronage. But Betancourt remained unenthusiastic about effecting the reforms, and individual ministers dragged their feet when it came time to restructure their ministries. In 1961, the Commission urged a merit-based civil service law, but the law was not passed until 1970. The burgeoning social services and development projects led to the creation of many new autonomous institutes, which further compromised the effort to supervise and control government programs and spending. Betancourt naturally resisted changes which conflicted with his desire to strengthen loyalty to the party and to the coalition through patronage and involvement of diverse groups in government decision-making. Moreover, as was true of teachers, there probably were not enough skilled and experienced bureaucrats to fill all the positions, even if Betancourt had wanted to give up his political clout. In any case, the $1 million annual budget of the CAP was doomed to be a conspicuous waste.

Betancourt sincerely wanted to remove graft and corruption from the public administration, but even there political priorities limited him to symbolic victories. The *Comisión Investigadora contra el Enriquecimiento Ilícito* (CIEI), revived with the fall of Pérez Jiménez, complained frequently of inadequacy of support, financing, and enthusiasm from other government bodies. Remembering the violent reaction to the peculation trials of the 1940s, Betancourt proceeded cautiously and required rigorous adherence to the letter of the law. Numerous malefactors whom "everyone" had watched grow rich from public funds escaped investigation and prosecution. The PCV in Congress called for more rapid, less ceremonious treatment of *perezjimenistas*, but it came up against AD's insistence on judicial formalities. The major exception was Pérez Jiménez himself. Betancourt's government requested the extradition of Pérez Jiménez from the United States for common crimes of murder and fraud, and in August 1963 the US government surrendered him to stand trial for peculation, or criminal malversation, before the

Venezuelan Supreme Court. The symbolic value of the Pérez Jiménez trial was great, but it did not solve the problems of an inefficient and patronage-ridden bureaucracy.

Foreign Policy

The foreign policy of the new, democratic regime broke with Venezuelan tradition. For the first time since the blockade of 1902, public reaction and support affected the conduct of foreign policy. Betancourt's aggressiveness and the relationship between domestic and foreign politics created numerous tensions, which challenged both the Ministry of Foreign Relations and the coalition government.

Ignacio Luis Arcaya of URD was Betancourt's first Foreign Minister. He reorganized the international politics section of the *Cancillería* into four divisions: America, Europe and Asia, Africa and Oceania, and the Division of Coordination and Research which oversaw the execution of foreign policy. A more rigorous policy of selection of foreign service personnel coupled with a scholarship program for the study of international law and diplomacy began a movement toward a career foreign service. The Ministry continued to be heavily politicized, however, and Arcaya resigned in August 1960. He disagreed with Betancourt's decision to sign the Declaration of San José, which characterized Fidel Castro's alliance with the Soviet Union as a threat to American solidarity. A few months later, URD left the government coalition. Since the radical *miristas* had already left AD, and COPEI's Rafael Caldera endorsed the belligerant attitude toward Castro, Betancourt now had free rein to isolate Cuba in the hemisphere as he had isolated the Venezuelan left at home.

Betancourt explained his foreign policy principles to the Second Congress of the Inter-American Association for Democracy and Freedom in April 1960. The OAS Charter was based on democratic principles and, he argued, should not allow any but democratic governments to remain as members. American nations should act together to isolate and depose all illegal governments of the left and the right in the Hemisphere. Democratic governments might also consider judicial trials and punishment of deposed dictators who had committed crimes against the citizens and resources of their nations. Betancourt's campaign against dictators continued his *trienio* policies and came to be known as the Betancourt Doctrine. Over the years, he had developed a fierce antagonism towards the Dominican Republic dictator, Rafael Trujillo. The rivalry went beyond words on June 24, 1960, when Trujillo hired an assassin to kill Betancourt. Miraculously, Betancourt survived a bomb explosion and persuaded the OAS to impose sanctions on the Dominican government. The attack increased Betancourt's popularity at home, since many admired his courage and were horrified at the assassination attempt. He also added to the case against Fidel Castro, when he accused Castro of sponsoring the terrorism and guerrilla activity in Venezuela; he broke relations with Cuba in November 1961. In January 1962, Venezuela voted for the resolution to expel Cuba from the OAS, and in November 1963 Betancourt asked the OAS to impose sanctions on Cuba in view of its intervention in Venezuelan affairs. An arms cache destined for the FALN, allegedly planted by Cubans, had been found on a Venezuelan beach. Betancourt's unflagging hostility toward Castro won friends in the United States and among Venezuelan moderates, but spurred the Venezuelan left to more protests and terrorism. Brief sanctions against the Dominican Republic and more lasting ones against Cuba were the only real victories for the Betancourt Doctrine. Betancourt vainly called on other American nations to follow Venezuela in breaking diplomatic relations with *de facto* governments in Paraguay, Haiti, Argentina, Guatemala, the Dominican Republic, and Peru. Even Betancourt's close relationship with US President John F. Kennedy cooled as Washington promptly recognized the beneficiaries of the string of *golpes* which occurred in 1962 and 1963.

Venezuela's location on the southern rim of the Caribbean, regional tensions, oil, and the increased role of the armed forces as the guarantors of national security encouraged an emergence of democratic geopolitics. AD Rubén Carpio Castillo in 1961 wrote that Venezuela could expand its influence in the Caribbean because the United States would block Cuban initiatives and the Mexican government did not have a Caribbean orientation.[17] The Cuban missile crisis of October 1962 and the guerrilla campaign heightened Venezuelan concern about sabotage and foreign attack. Caracas might rail at specific United States policies, but it accepted United States hemispheric hegemony as both inevitable and necessary for Venezuelan defense. In December 1961 John F. Kennedy became the first United States President to visit Venezuela. Venezuela's revolutionary expansiveness then turned to smaller Caribbean neighbors. Added to the tensions with the Dominican Republic and Cuba, Betancourt hoped, with regard to Guyana, both to weaken the leftist prime minister Cheddi Jagan and to push for recovery of the disputed territory through the United Nations. Venezuelan Foreign Minister Marcos Falcón Briceño presented the Venezuelan argument that the 1899 arbitration decision should be nullified because the Russian arbitration judge had made a deal to support the British position. Relations with Trinidad and Tobago also faltered after independence in 1962, when Betancourt ignored Prime Minister Eric Williams' request for the abrogation of the 30 percent tariff on goods imported from there. The AD government was not unwilling to remove the tariff, but it delayed in order to convince Venezuelan industrialists and merchants that they would not be harmed by the measure. The tariff was finally removed in December 1965. Venezuela and Trinidad also continued to dispute fishing rights in the Gulf of Paría. The conflicts foreshadowed the eventual competition for influence over the small states of the eastern Caribbean. To the west, Betancourt settled disputes over smuggling and other frontier issues by personal negotiation with his liberal counterpart in Colombia, President Alberto Lleras Camargo.

Opposition from the business community delayed Venezuela's entry into the Latin American Free Trade Association (LAFTA) until 1967–8. Betancourt had decided in 1961 to join the association, but postponed entry in deference to the wishes of the economic leaders.

The Venezuelan Left

Rómulo Betancourt is nearly unique in Latin American history. He gave no quarter either to the dictatorial right or to the revolutionary left, and yet he survived in office to hand over power to a democratically chosen successor. His tenacity virtually eliminated the old, antidemocratic right as a force in Venezuelan politics. For the moment he — and his successor Raúl Leoni — also vanquished the guerrillas, but here the victory was less complete. Paradoxically, Betancourt may have contributed to the legend of heroism which grew up around this young generation of 1958. They developed their political ideologies and tactics entirely apart from the two major parties. As outsiders with a larger than life reputation as former guerrillas, they would vie peacefully for political power in the 1980s. It is worth examining their postwar experiences and some of the reasons why they rejected the relatively flexible reformism which Betancourt represented.

Four men and one woman illustrate the development of the radical generation of 1958: José Vicente Rangel (*b.* 1929); Teodoro Petkoff (*b.* 1931); Douglas Bravo (*b.* 1933); Américo Martín (*b.* 1938); and Argelia Laya (*b.* 1926). Rangel entered politics in the URD party, broke with them in 1964 and later became closely associated with, and presidential candidate for, the *Movimiento al Socialismo* (MAS). Petkoff remained with the Communist Party of

Venezuela (PCV) until he broke with it in 1970 to found MAS. Bravo too was a member of the PCV until he was expelled in 1967 for refusing to give up the guerrilla action and to accept party control. Martín entered political life in the AD youth movement, broke with AD to found MIR in 1960, and also participated in the guerrilla campaign against the AD governments. Finally, Laya first was a member of AD, then turned to the Communist Party, and in 1970 became a founding member of MAS. She too participated in the guerrilla movement of the 1960s. Rangel, Petkoff, and Martín later became presidential candidates.

These leftists did not remember the Venezuela of pre-petroleum days, and only Laya and Rangel retained even childhood memories of dictator Juan Vicente Gómez. They grew up in the excitement of the first civic activity of the 1930s and 1940s, although they did not become politically active until the late 1940s. Free discussion of radical ideologies and the political experiments of the 1940s affected them strongly. All participated in the struggle against Pérez Jiménez. Rangel was forced into exile from 1953 to 1957, but the others worked in the clandestine movement. All but Laya were imprisoned by the SN, and her husband spent three years in jail. Bravo and Martín were tortured or beaten. They all were moved by the experience of the popular victory over the dictatorship in January 1958. In contrast to the AD view that the year 1958 was merely a prelude to the AD institutionalization of democracy, Petkoff characterizes the year 1958 as the freest in Venezuelan history. The other four would agree that it was a crucial turning-point for the nation.

Their individual experiences are also significant. Rangel's *tachirense* father held some minor offices during the Gómez regime and had to flee to Colombia after Gómez's death. The family did not join in the new political agitation. Rangel attended the relatively conservative Catholic *Liceo La Salle* in Barquisimento and then went on to study law at the university in Mérida before moving to Caracas to continue his studies at the UCV. In 1946, he joined URD, at least partly because he had been offended at some AD partisans who had broken up a political rally held by Jóvito Villaba. By 1950, he was in the National Directory of URD, a position he held until 1963. He and the other URD leaders believed they could act freely and legally after the *golpe* of 1948 and did not join the AD/PCV underground. He worked hard for Villaba in the fraudulent election of 1952 and was then forced to go into exile in Chile until 1955. He married a Chilean woman and then moved to Spain where he took a course in insurance, before returning to Venezuela in 1957. He earned Bs 3,000 a month in an insurance business in Caracas, while he formed contacts with the *Junta Patriotica*. From 1958 to 1963, he supported Villaba as an URD leader, but broke with him and the party in 1964; he disagreed with Villaba's decision to form a political coalition with AD and Arturo Uslar Pietri after the 1963 election. Rangel joined the few leftist political leaders who had not been jailed or exiled, but he did not support the leftist turn to violence in 1962. Rangel had originally disliked AD tactics and, as he drifted toward the left, he also deplored what he interpreted as AD's choice to side with the economic interests rather than the workers and masses.

Teodoro Petkoff's parents were Bulgarians who came to Venezuela during the Gómez dictatorship. His father and mother, respectively a chemical engineer and a doctor, settled near Maracaibo. As a youth, Teodoro heard discussions of Communist ideology. After entering *Liceo Andrés Bello* in Caracas, he joined the PCV in 1949 and was influential with youth groups. He joined the staff of the Communist newspaper, *Tribuna Popular*, while he began medical studies at UCV. Deciding that he could not be both a doctor and a politician, he gave up his medical studies after two years and later (1960) completed his degree in political economy. He entered the clandestine movement and rose to the Central Committee of the UCV in 1961. He advocated armed revolt to overthrow Betancourt in 1961 and in 1962 joined Douglas Bravo to establish one of the first guerrilla movements. Arrested in May 1963, he escaped from the sixth floor of the Military Hospital six months later to return to guerrilla activity. In June 1964, he was recaptured and remained in San Carlos jail until 1967, when he and several other prisoners made a spectacular escape through a tunnel.

Douglas Bravo's father was a modest merchant in the small town of Cabure in Falcón. Douglas recalled heated political discussions in his home when he was a child. His parents had the only radio in the town, and townspeople gathered to discuss the world war, with special interest in Red Army activities. He also remembered his Catalan granfather as well as numerous tales of legendary rebels and heroes of the hills of Falcón. Students from Coro and Caracas also gathered at his house when they were home on vacation. Bravo's father had fought against Gómez in the 1920s, but in the 1940s supported Medina and later joined URD. Douglas founded a Communist youth group in Cabure in 1946. He attended high school in Coro and saw his father shot in front of his high school in 1947 as a result of a local feud. Young Bravo believed that the AD police condoned the killing. Although he attended the University in Maracaibo after 1953, most of his attention turned toward politics and organizing workers. He helped spur the petroleum strike of

1950 which resulted in the outlawing of the PCV and his own brief imprisonment. He also became involved in a student strike of 1952, for which he was again arrested and tortured. While free during the 1950s, he worked in a cement factory and participated in clandestine organization of the 1958 revolt. He married another student and member of the PCV in 1953 — a marriage that lasted three years — and remarried in 1960. After Pérez Jiménez's fall, Bravo led the militant wing of the PCV to launch the guerrilla effort in 1962.

Américo Martín was born to a comfortable Caracas middle-class family. His father was a Chilean architect who came to Venezuela during the Gómez years. Both parents were AD supporters, and Martín naturally joined AD youth groups during the Pérez Jiménez period. He attended *Liceo Andrés Bello* in Caracas and studied law at the UCV. He felt close to the generation of 1958, including Petkoff and *mirista* guerrilla Moisés Moleiro and novelists Salvador Garmendia and Adriano González León, who represented a new and more political direction for Venezuelan literature in the 1960s and 1970s (see pp. 188–90, below). In 1958 he wanted to see AD restructured, revitalized and democratized and was discouraged by the skillful manipulations of Betancourt and the old guard which kept the party firmly in their hands. Martín objected to Betancourt's tough measures against popular mass demonstrations. He and Domingo Alberto Rangel wrote editorials which provoked the old guard to discipline them, thus precipitating their resignation from AD and the formation of the *Movimiento de la Izquierda Revolucionaria* (MIR). Betancourt's actions made the guerrilla conflict inevitable, Martín argues, forcing him and others to be drawn along with the tide of violence. With hindsight, he believes the MIR should have supported Wolfgang Larrazábal for President in 1963; it could not put forward its own candidate, since it was outlawed by the time of the election. Only after the election did MIR actively participate in the guerrilla activity, Martín claims, although there were forms of "self-defense" in 1962 and 1963. Martín spent a year and a half as a guerrilla and two and a half years in prison, where he began to write. He married for a second time in 1969.

Argelia Laya is the only one of the leftists whose parents were poor. Partly because of some anti-*gomecista* sympathies, her father spent three years in prison and later was hounded off his small plot of land in Higuerote in eastern Venezuela. When the family moved to Caracas, they lived in working-class neighborhoods or in *ranchos* (slums) without electricity or water, according to the economic luck of the family at the moment. One of Argelia's younger brothers died in the *ranchos*. Argelia and her brothers could not go to school until her mother won a lottery ticket for Bs 5 which enabled her to buy shoes and school clothes for the children. Two formative influences of her youth were the *Agrupación Cultural Femenina* and the Presbyterian Church. Her mother Rosario joined the ACF, and Argelia recalls celebrating the death of Juan Vicente Gómez with her mother and the women's group. Some Presbyterians lived near the Laya family and helped them out in some of their family crises. Argelia became a member of the congregation and worked actively for the church in the 1940s.

Argelia's father, Pedro, died in 1942. With the help of a family friend, Argelia attended normal school and graduated in 1945. Her first teaching job was in Maracaibo where she joined the *Federación Venezolana de Maestros* and first came in contact with *Acción Democrática*. After the 1945 revolution, Argelia returned to Caracas and became a member of AD in 1946. She organized for AD and taught civic education in the *Universidad Popular Víctor Camejo Berti* in La Guaira. Political discussions were animated, and Argelia found herself at odds with some AD organizers regarding the nature of the party and its relation to COPEI and the PCV. She became less active in the party and began to educate herself in marxist theory and ideology. Always a fighter, she participated fully with her AD colleagues in the clandestine struggle against the military dictatorship from 1948 to 1950. Disgusted with what she called the laziness and irresponsibility of some of the AD clandestine leaders after the death of Delgado Chalbaud in 1950, Laya finally left AD and joined the PCV.

After her marriage (1952) and the birth of her first two sons (1952 and 1957), Argelia continued her work with the resistance. Some of her work could be characterized as traditionally "feminine" tasks of carrying messages, sheltering those who were sought by the police, and taking food to and maintaining contact with political prisoners. She became a member of the *Comité Femenina* of the *Junta Patriótica* in 1957–8. She had also always insisted, however, on performing the same tasks that the men did in the resistance. She painted slogans on walls at night, delivered Molotov cocktails to groups of clandestine fighters in the Caracas hills in the tense days of January 1958, and she herself joined in some of the final, violent skirmishes with the police of Pérez Jiménez. Like the other leftists, Argelia Laya believed that she received her real political education during the 1950s resistance to Pérez Jiménez.

Yet her experience broadened even further as a member of the PCV in the 1960s. She traveled to China and the Soviet Union, taking a special interest in meeting with women's groups in her foreign visits. Between 1964 and 1966, she joined the guerrillas in Lara state, using the *nom de guerre* of "*La Comandante Jacinta.*"

When her children visited her there and the youngest asked her to come back to Caracas, she responded that her commitment to a revolutionary vision of the Venezuelan future meant that she had to stay with the guerrillas. She later confessed that she also dreaded a return to Caracas where her freedom would be restricted as long as she had to remain in hiding from the police. She broke with the PCV in 1970 and became a founding member of MAS.

The biographies of the four men reveal some striking similarities; Laya's experience differs somewhat because of her sex and her poverty-stricken youth. The four men are of middle-class background;

\:e exception), and studied tradi-omy. None has known any real lren of immigrants (Petkoff and lan grandfather (Bravo), and considerable time in exile — Spain. All developed a hostility \:ard. Spanish, European, and ayed a greater role in their \:ited States models. The radi-\:zuela in the 1890s entered with)s and their children. The model s may have inspired the turn to \:he Euro-socialist roots of the \:s from those of the four men, \:nost purely "*criolla*" of these \:bly derived from a youthful, sequently her contact with the \:ore sophisticated and formal cipline did not, however, oblit-\:rate her commitment to a relatively radical feminism and to community service in the poor urban neighborhoods.

In retrospect, and in self-criticism, all but Bravo consider the violence of the 1960s to have been a costly error for the left. Eventually the MIR and MAS leaders turned back to democratic socialism. They have renounced violence, but have retained their hostile interpretation of Betancourt and the AD old guard. The MAS and MIR leadership believe that Betancourt gradually and effectively shut out the truly popular leadership, as represented on the 1958 *Junta Patriótica*, and the young leaders of the early 1960s. More seriously, they charge that he favored the oligarchy of economic élites over the workers, especially the lower level of unskilled and unorganized workers. By the end of the 1960s, these young leaders had replaced the revolutionary myth of the generation of 1928 with their own more recent legend of heroism on behalf of the masses. They had been formed both by Pérez Jiménez and by Betancourt. It remains to be seen whether they can convert their legend into the reality of political power.[18]

The Election of 1963

The leftist challenge looked ominous in 1963. The election of that year became the crucial turning point that verified Betancourt's success in the short run of completing his term, of organizing political activity, and of withstanding threats from all sides.

Seven men stood for election to the presidency of Venezuela, emphasizing the splintering of the political unity of early 1958. Betancourt had proposed that the AD convention in July select a field of five or six candidates and allow COPEI to choose one of them. That proposal was too conciliatory even for the AD old guard, and the AD faithful nominated Raúl Leoni. His tenure as Minister of Labor between 1945 and 1948 won him the labor segment of the party and indicated that AD was still drawing on the credits established earlier. COPEI could not accept Leoni as a unity candidate and had had no success in convincing AD to support Caldera as such either, so finally they nominated their own Rafael Caldera. After a brief struggle with many of his party who wanted to support Wolfgang Larrazábal again, Jóvito Villaba won th URD nomination. Larrazábal also ran on a coalition ticket, but was perhaps weakened by the leftist tactic of abstention and his own aimless campaign which did not make much of an effort outside Caracas. The AD splinter group, now called *AD en Oposición*, nominated its leader Raúl Ramos Giménez, but could not manage a forceful campaign. Two other candidates claimed to be nonpartisan: Arturo Uslar Pietri, who drew the backing of the economic elite, and Germán Borregales, who made little impact.

Specific campaign issues focused more on personalities or speed and direction of reforms than they did on any major disagreements with AD policy. Uslar Pietri most effectively distinguished a different stand when he rejected partisan politics and an interventionist foreign policy, and advocated rapid economic development. At the other extreme, MIR, PCV, and the guerrillas hoped that a high abstention rate would reflect rejection of Betancourt's whole system and would open the way to a more radical socialist experiment. The campaign proceeded in spite of voters' initial apathy toward registering. AD and COPEI relied on party loyalists to turn out the voters. Uslar most effectively used a large campaign chest and sophisticated media techniques which appealed to urban dwellers. And the left increased the outbreaks of terrorism and violence.

The results were clear in broad terms. When 91.33 percent of the registered voters turned out, they rejected the leftist alternative, either because of ideology or because of their alienating tactics. Leoni won, but AD's percentage of the votes dropped by 16.3 percent from the 1958 level, while COPEI's congressional vote rose by 6 percent. The AD-COPEI coalition together won 54.5 percent of the congressional vote. The greatest surprise was Uslar Pietri's impressive 16 percent of the presidential vote, a tribute to his effective campaign and perhaps to voter weariness with the intense political agitation of the past five years. Almost all of AD's support came from rural areas, where its organization remained strong. Conversely, most of Uslar's vote lay in major cities, especially Caracas. The hostility of Caracas voters to AD had surfaced slightly in 1947, but increased in 1958 and 1963. The "Caracas question" — AD's better performance in the nation than in Caracas — plagued the party in the next two elections; it could ill afford to ignore a city which had grown from 414,802 inhabitants in 1941 to 1,501,802 in 1961 and from 10.8 percent to 19.9 percent of the national population during the same time. A strategy based on the alliance of rural peasants, industrial workers, and part of the oligarchy would not suffice for an urban, service sector economy.

The election then provided a valuable referendum for Betancourt's vision of Venezuela and his implementation of that vision. It also gave due warning that AD could not comfortably continue to dominate Venezuelan politics by drawing on tactics and ideologies formed in the 1920s and '30s. AD had to solve the problems of recruitment and formation of the young who would continue the party, of electoral organization and mobilization in an increasingly urban nation linked by mass media, and of forming an efficient and dedicated public administration. Obviously, it must still deliver enough benefits to maintain the loyalty of the middle and working class and enough impetus to economic development to lull the economic elite. It had to prove conclusively to the left that armed attacks on the government were futile, and it had to continue the campaign abroad to assure the world that a reformist democratic system would be stable, prosperous, and a worthy ally. In short, it had to prove that it had the staying power to make the transition from the politics of the 1930s to those of the 1980s.

NOTES

1. *Un hombre llamado Rómulo Betancourt* (Caracas: Catalá/Centauro Editors, 1975), p. 281.

2. Robert J. Alexander, *The Communist Party of Venezuela* (Stanford: Hoover Institution Press, 1969), p. 138.

3. Talton Ray, *The Politics of the Barrios of Venezuela* (Berkeley: University of California Press, 1969), p. 117.

4. Daniel Levine, *Conflict and Political Change in Venezuela* (Princeton: Princeton University Press, 1973), p. 44.

5. Robert D. Bond, "Business Associations and Interest Politics in Venezuela: The Fedecámaras and the Determination of National Economic Policies" (Ph.D. diss., Vanderbilt University, 1975).

6. Banco Central de Venezuela, *La economía venezolana en los últimos treinta y cinco anos* (Caracas: Banco Central de Venezuela, 1978), p. 273.

7. Franklin Tugwell, *The Politics of Oil in Venezuela* (Stanford: Stanford University Press, 1975), pp. 82–3.

8. Ibid., pp. 58–60.

9. Lisa Redfield Peattie, *The View from the Barrio* (Ann Arbor: University of Michigan Press, 1970).

10. Domingo Alberto Rangel, *El proceso del capitalismo contemporáneo en Venezuela* (Caracas: Dirección de Cultura, Universidad Central de Venezuela), p. 169.

11. Louis E. Heaton, *The Agricultural Development of Venezuela* (New York: Praeger, 1969), p. 102.

12. Ibid., pp. 97–8.

13. Ibid., pp. 64–5, 143.

14. Kenneth Ruddle and Donald Odermann (eds), *Statistical Abstract of Latin America 1971* (Los Angeles: University of California, 1972), p. 79.

15. Kenneth Ruddle and Kathleen Barrows, *Statistical Abstract of Latin America 1972* (Los Angeles: University of California Press, 1974), p. 397.

16. David Blank, *Politics in Venezuela* (Boston: Little, Brown and Co., 1973), p. 50.

17. Rubén Carpio Castillo, *Mexico, Cuba y Venezuela. Triángulo geopolítico del Caribe* (Caracas: Imprenta Nacional, 1961).

18. Information on the lives and thoughts of the five leftists has been gathered from three published interviews by Alfredo Peña: *Conversaciones con Douglas Bravo; Conversaciones con José Vicente Rangel; Conversaciones con Américo Martín*. All were published as books by Editorial Ateneo de Caracas in 1978. Additionally, the following two works were consulted: Teodoro Petkoff, *Razón y pasión del socialismo* (Caracas: n.p., 1973) and Agustín Blanco Muñoz, *La lucha armada: hablan 5 jefes* (Caracas: Facultad de Ciencias Económicas y Sociales, Universidad Central de Venezuela, 1980). The information on Argelia Laya comes from *El Nacional*, 18 July 1976, and from Fania Petzoldt and Jacinta Bevilacqua, *Nosotras también nos jugamos la vida* (Caracas: Editorial Ateneo de Caracas, 1979), 219–35.

6

POLITICAL DEMOCRACY AND STATE CAPITALISM, 1964–1973

"The powerful enterpreneurs have not even known how to set in motion a process of capitalistic development. Most of them have lived in the shadow of the State, in spite of their criticism of it, and work in a captive and protected market, benefiting in many ways from foreign investment and from the dependent character of our society."[1]

José Vicente Rangel

The decade which followed Rómulo Betancourt's presidency confirmed the durability of the political compromises represented by the Pact of Punto Fijo (see above, p.126). His AD successor, Raúl Leoni, departed only slightly from Betancourt's priorities. The 1968 election, after a third split in the ranks of *Acción Democrática*, produced a victory for COPEI. Yet President Rafael Caldera too remained within the broad political limits set by his predecessors. Leoni and Caldera still epitomized the political old guard, the Venezuelan generations of 1928 and 1936. Party harmony eroded further as younger politicians vied to take over the roles so long played by Betancourt and Caldera. In 1963, Arturo Uslar Pietri made a short-lived attempt to head a pro-business, independent political ticket, but it gradually became clear that *Acción Democrática* and COPEI had successfully claimed the political loyalties of the majority of voters. Most leftist politicians, after the guerrilla fiasco, returned to peaceful politics by 1968. A PCV division in 1970 produced a lively democratic socialist party, the *Movimiento al Socialismo* (MAS), led by some of the radical generation of 1958. Thus, under the evident political consensus, younger ambitions and ideologies prepared to challenge the control and priorities of Betancourt, Caldera and their cohorts.

Venezuela took a more active role in international affairs as the years passed. The emphasis changed gradually from Betancourt's stress on the isolating of dictators to a concerted effort to diversify trading partners and exports. The push for economic self-sufficiency led to Venezuela's participation in LAFTA and the Andean Pact and to a more active Caribbean role. Under Caldera, boundary disputes with Guayana and Colombia received less emphasis in order to encourage harmonious regional trade and check Brazilian expansion. Maritime issues received greater attention, as Caracas enthusiastically participated in the United Nations Conferences to write a comprehensive Law of the Sea Treaty.

If political and international life had few of the violent confrontations that had characterized the Betancourt presidency, economic and social development raised troublesome issues. The new economic directions of the 1960s — import substitution, agrarian reform, and greater control of the oil industry — failed in the short run to provide sustained, independent development. Government revenues still came principally from oil income, with all the instability which that fact implied. Industrialization through import substitution reached a bottleneck: the importation of finished consumer goods diminished, but importation of intermediate goods and raw materials to be processed in Venezuela increased. Even more alarming for the social objectives of the democratic reforms, the upper quarter of the population absorbed an even greater share of national income. The distributive philosophy of the AD and COPEI leaders had also hit a bottleneck: large numbers of rural residents and urban poor could not join the modern, skilled workforce required by the capital-intensive industrialization.

The self-conscious effort to develop a working democracy and the educational explosion did foment a cultural boom. AD and COPEI devoted more government funds to cultural projects than ever before, although it proved difficult to choose between mass and elite artistic expression, and to administer the funds efficiently. Free from censorship, a series of young writers from the generation of 1958 probed the universal themes of alienation and materialism in the urban environment of Caracas. Urban problems, guerrilla warfare and ideology, and the communications revolution which spread a universal North Atlantic culture generated a literature which was both national and universal. The other arts — theater, dance, music, film, painting, sculpture — also aspired to international recognition. Understandably, the new directions in art and culture and the great rush of postwar European immigrants encouraged heated discussions of the Venezuelan national identity. Much like Argentines at the turn of the century, Venezuelans longed for a clear answer to the question: Who are we?

Disappointment, frustration, and pessimism vied with confident optimism about the country's future. Clearly, fifteen years of democracy or thirty-seven of modernization did not provide an adequate basis for judgment. The generation of 1928 could take pride in how far the nation had come since the days of Gómez. The generation of 1958 impatiently pointed out how much yet remained to be done. All shared the uneasy feeling that time — like petroleum — was running out. If the social and economic bottlenecks could not be eliminated, the petroleum would not be sown; it would be wasted.

The Presidency of Raúl Leoni, 1964–1968

Raúl Leoni, born in 1906, had experienced a political existence as intense as that of Rómulo Betancourt. President of the student association in 1928, he had been jailed briefly and then gone into exile in Colombia between 1928 and 1936. He joined Román Delgado Chalbaud's invasion attempt with Betancourt in 1929, and in 1931 was one of the authors of the Plan of Barranquilla (see p. 90, above). In 1936, he had been elected a Congressional Deputy, only to see the election nullified by the Supreme Court. From 1942 he was a member of AD's executive committee, editor of the AD newspaper, and Minister of Labor during the *trienio*. Although he had paid his dues as a founding member of AD, few considered him to have the stature of Rómulo Betancourt, and the most critical characterized him as a party hack. Not as bright — by his own admission — as Gonzálo Barrios, as focused as Pérez Alfonzo or as tough as Betancourt, Leoni nonetheless was well loved by the labor wing of his party. In retrospect, his more conciliatory and less abrasive style was ideal to follow Rómulo's five years in office.

Betancourt had not been pleased with Leoni's nomination and feared that his friend could not dominate the political scene or maintain the coalition with COPEI. But despite a lack of confidence in Leoni, Betancourt left Venezuela in 1964 and eventually took up residence in Switzerland with his second wife, Renée Hartman. He stayed abroad till 1972, enabling Leoni to rule without his supervision. His aloofness from the presidency did not preclude his supervising AD party matters closely through correspondence and reports from Venezuelans who passed through Switzerland.[2]

Leoni's presidency had fewer violent challenges than had Betancourt's, but relations with COPEI and with Congress proved more difficult. In spite of his slight electoral majority (32 percent), Leoni chose not to make concessions to second running COPEI. Rafael Caldera believed that COPEI's electoral statistics proved that it was now a major party worthy of more than the three ministries that Leoni offered. Looking ahead to the 1968 election, Caldera opted to play the role of loyal opposition rather than that of a member of the coalition. By spring of 1966, COPEI volunteered closer cooperation with *Acción Democrática* in Congress, but reserved the right to criticize and differ on minor matters.

President Leoni initially turned to Jóvito Villaba of URD and Arturo Uslar Pietri of FND for a rather unsatisfactory Congressional alliance of *"amplia base."* URD remained in the coalition until 1968, but Uslar's group split with AD in 1966 over the tax reform bill. The shifting party alliances did obstruct efficient action at times, but they did not destroy the democratic system, as

Betancourt had feared. AD retained control of the Senate until the party division in 1967.

If Congress proved difficult, Leoni could take comfort from the waning guerrilla threat. In 1964, there had been sixteen guerrilla groups active in the country. By 1968, there were only three. Leoni continued Betancourt's strengthening of the army and had accepted more US training and military assistance. He also offered to commute the sentences of a number of political prisoners as a conciliatory measure. Frustrated by the seeming impossibility of a violent overthrow of the government and encouraged by Leoni's flexibility, the PCV in 1967 decided to give up the guerrilla effort and return to peaceful political combat. Leoni allowed it to propose candidates for the 1968 election under the auspices of the *Unión Para Avanzar*. The MIR and Douglas Bravo refused to give up the battle until several years later.

Leoni's government did have to face terrorism, political assassinations, and kidnapping. In response, he suspended constitutional guarantees several times, although less frequently and for less time than Betancourt had done. Leoni also followed Betancourt's lead in closing newspapers or arresting journalists or editors who wrote favorable reports of the leftist guerrilla struggle. In April 1965, the government arrested editor and newspaper owner Miguel Angel Capriles. Capriles himself had no sympathy with leftists, but the government suspected that he was endorsing a military conspiracy and, in any case, his sensationalist news stories inflated the guerrillas' reputation. Because his newspapers had encouraged the leftists and because he had received money from the Italian Communist Party and the Soviet Union. A Congressional investigation verified the charges against Capriles.

Congressmen also charged that the *Dirección General de Policía (Digepol)* systematically violated human rights and tortured political prisoners. *Digepol* had been created as the democratic government's replacement for the *Seguridad Nacional*, but even so its agents were not free from criticism. Deputy José Vincent Rangel in November 1965 cited a number of *desaparecidos* for whom *Digepol* was popularly believed responsible. Most shocking was the case of professor and PCV member, Alberto Lovera, whom *Digepol* had arrested on 18 October; it had then beaten and tortured him, and wound his body with chains before tossing it into the sea. It appeared on a beach near Barcelona a little over a week later. Subsequent Congressional investigations, press reports, Rangel's book *Expediente negro*, and some judicial hearings produced the strong impression that *Digepol* agents were responsible, but no arrests were ever made. The AD government and judicial officials obviously preferred to ride out the storm rather than publicly clean out

Digepol. To their credit, they tolerated the Congressional and press denunciations with grace. Neither Rangel nor the press suffered reprisals for their full accounts of the Lovera case. Leoni's willingness to allow such freedom strengthened the system in the long run.

Two other major domestic issues tested the mettle of Leoni and the stability of the democratic coalition: tax reform and educational reform. Inadequate public services and political patronage continued to draw criticism, and the conduct of foreign policy became a factor in domestic politics. None of the conflicts provided a clearcut victory for the government or for the opposition of the left or right. On balance, Leoni probably conceded more to the right and the economic elite than he did to the left, thus accentuating the tendency begun under Betancourt.

The outstanding battle of Leoni's term pitted the administration against the foreign oil companies and *Fedecámaras* and large segments of the domestic private sector. In the face of declining revenues, Leoni and his Minister of Mines, Manuel Pérez Guerreo, determined to extract more money from the oil companies and the private sector. In 1964–5, Pérez Guerrero allotted one-third of the domestic petroleum market to the CVP, limited the discount the oil companies could make on fuel oil sales, and imposed a retroactive tax on past oil company sales which had been made at artificially low prices. The companies tolerated the loss of the Venezuelan domestic market but rejected the legality of the sales restrictions and refused to pay any retroactive taxes. The government and the companies then entered negotiation to try to break the deadlock. In 1966, Leoni pushed further when he announced a revision of the general tax system which would increase personal and corporate income taxes. Most of the projected 7 percent increase in tax receipts would come for the special selective tax on oil company profits in excess of 15 percent of net fixed assets. Venezuelan personal and corporate taxes were among the lowest in the world, only 2.2 percent on personal income and 16.3 percent on medium-sized corporations. Comparable rates in Mexico were 8.5 percent and 44.7 percent respectively. Nonetheless, the private sector was sufficiently embattled to mount a massive public relations attack to roll back the taxes on the oil companies and on themselves. *Desarrollista* and banker Pedro Tinoco, Jr., and Arturo Uslar Pietri became the most visible opponents to the reform and spokesmen for the oil interests and *Fedecámaras*. The oil companies reduced production to the lowest rate in a decade, further squeezing government finances. For the first time, an organized press campaign prevented the passage of a Congressional bill.[3]

In the face of the formidable opposition, Leoni and Pérez Guerrero launched a "divide and conquer" tactic. In September

1966, the companies and Pérez Guerrero reached a private settlement on taxes and policy. In effect, the companies agreed to pay a set sum of retroactive taxes in exchange for the government relinquishing its efforts to intervene in day-to-day marketing decisions in the future. The companies agreed to award the government 68 percent instead of 65 percent of the profits and received incentives for reinvestment, exploration, drilling, and secondary recovery. The deal left the Venezuelan private sector defenseless; it could hardly continue arguing that the new tax proposals would destroy the oil companies on whose wellbeing the nation depended. Nor could it effectively resist the modest increments in their own tax rate. The opposition collapsed and a modified tax bill passed Congress.

Leoni won the battle, but suffered some major losses of principle. The government received the much-needed revenues, but renounced the broader goal of increasing control over oil production, pricing, and marketing. The step backward caused a division within AD and alienated former Minister of Mines Pérez Alfonzo. The political fragmentation in Congress, the private sector's self-seeking alliance with the multinational oil companies, and Pérez Alfonzo's campaign for tougher policies toward the oil companies all contributed to the politicization of national oil policy. The companies gained a momentary respite from government intervention, but casting the policy into the fray of public and Congressional debate inevitably brought the moment closer when a Venezuelan President would nationalize the industry for political reasons, regardless of the economic consequences. The 1966 brouhaha prepared the way for nationalization in yet another way. The Venezuelan private sector recognized that the oil companies had exaggerated their suffering under government taxation and were not trustworthy allies in the struggle to avoid taxes and regulations. *Fedecámaras* opposition to regulation, or even nationalization, of the oil industry weakened after 1966.

Educational reforms, often a touchy issue with the Church and with the left, also tested Leoni's government. He largely avoided conflict with the Church and COPEI over new educational laws by urging the *Federación Venezolana de Maestros* to negotiate with the Catholic educators' organization. Leoni could take pride that the Catholic and lay educators reached an agreement on most issues by 1967. Unfortunately, the AD division in 1967 left the matter in limbo before Congress, but the important truce with the Church had been reached.

Reform of the university law caused more sparks to fly. Prompted in part by the desire to check the leftist influence at the UCV, the government passed a regulation in 1964 which limited the number of times a student could repeat a college course before having to leave the University. Student strikes and violence did not halt the passage of the regulation, but it was never successfully implemented. More violence followed the government order of December 14, 1966, which sent the armed forces to occupy UCV. The government reinterpreted University autonomy in such a way that police occupation of the University grounds and adjacent roads did not constitute a violation of University autonomy. Student strikes and violence closed the University in early 1967 while the government negotiated with University authorities. The issues revealed a breach between the PCV and the MIR in the University, which may have contributed to the government's success. The PCV, following the party's tendency to return to legality, preferred negotiation and wanted to link the student unrest more closely with national politics. The MIR persisted with the isolating tactics of student strikes, refusal to take exams, and unconditional support of violent resistence. Leoni's government made the new regulations stick, and student politics calmed down again. Student elections at the University in 1968 demonstrated that the majority of the leftist students supported the PCV's stand. Chagrined, the *miristas* charged that students had become more interested in careers and *discotecas* than in the sacrifice necessary to build a revolutionary society.

The AD leadership also met obstacles when it tried to improve urban and local services. *Elecar*, a private firm, generated and distributed much of the electricity to Caracas and had been engaged during the Betancourt years in a squabble with the municipal government over rates and the provision of service to the new *barrios*. As *Elecar* negotiated to purchase the subsidiary of the American Foreign Power Company, its monopoly of urban electricity threatened to become more extensive. The AD left argued that the company should be nationalized, but the moderates held out against this, especially after the pro-business FND won some seats on the municipal council in the December 1963 election. Under Leoni, an agreement was reached in which the company would continue in private hands but agreed to electrify the *barrios* and to subsidize the municipality's electricity consumption. Similar arrangements were made with municipal councils of neighboring townships like Guarenas. AD thus backed away from alienating the private sector, although the threats of nationalization convinced the companies to accept some degree of social responsibility.[4]

Local government beyond Caracas had problems with insufficient revenues and incompetent administrators, who held their jobs through major party patronage. The *Fundación para el Desarrollo de la Comunidad y Fomento Municipal* (Foundation for Community Development and Municipal Improvement — *Fundacomun*) published a study in 1964 which pointed out that district governments had little opportunity to raise their own revenues because they had no comprehensive registries of real estate. A decade later, with assistance to take inventories of local real estate, all districts of over 20,000 inhabitants had their own registry. The ability to raise local funds in theory lessened the local district's dependency on the national subsidy and could provide more services. In 1968, a law to clarify responsibilities of district councils and to require professional qualifications of district administrators got blocked in Congress. Neither AD nor COPEI was enthusiastic about independent, professional district administrators. Politicization of local issues became more intense after 1967. AD and COPEI had cooperated to form a national lobby for local issues, the Venezuelan Association of Municipalities (AVECI). After the 1968 elections, many *adecos* moved from *Fundacomún* to AVECI. The two local community development associations, controlled by the two major parties, vied for funds and as spokesmen for local governments.

In foreign policy, Leoni followed the major principles set out by Betancourt: commitment to the Interamerican system and the United Nations, to democratic government, to protection and expansion of Venezuelan markets, and to the defense of Venezuela's territorial interests on its borders. As domestic stability returned, more emphasis could be placed on an active foreign policy. The budget of the Ministry of Foreign Relations rose from Bs 41 million in 1963 to Bs 74.7 million in 1968. Leoni continued to press for more sanctions against Fidel Castro in the OAS, and attacked or broke relations with *de facto* governments in accord with the Betancourt Doctrine. Yet by 1968 the context had changed radically by comparison with 1959. Dictatorial governments were again the rule rather than the exception in the Americas. Not only was the Betancourt Doctrine unpopular in the hemisphere, but its application occasionally conflicted with Leoni's equally fervent opposition to Communism. For example, the generals removed João Goulart from the presidency in Brazil in 1964 because of alleged Communist leanings. Leoni wavered, broke relations, and then renewed them in December 1966 after the carefully orchestrated Brazilian Congressional elections which "legalized" General Artur Costa e Silva as President of Brazil.

Economic interests were dominant in foreign policy. Venezuela joined the *Asociación Latinoamericana de Libre Comercio* (Latin American Free Trade Association — ALALC) in 1966, and Leoni began talks with other Andean nations with a view to establishing an

Andean common market. Suspicions of Brazilian economic and territorial expansionism provided an impetus for the Hispanic alliance, but agricultural and small businesses in *Fedecámaras* blocked Venezuela's participation for some years. In general terms, however, the reality and the rhetoric of economic cooperation passed muster, and Venezuela became more active in the UN group of seventy-seven developing nations.

Relations with the United States were tested in 1965 when US Marines landed in Santo Domingo, avowedly to halt a Communist-led revolt. Washington's machinations in the OAS to get the US action ratified and to create an Interamerican peace force to restore order met a cool response from Caracas. The US government also continued to ignore Venezuelan arguments for hemispheric preference in oil imports. Nonetheless, Leoni and Foreign Minister Ignacio Iribarren Borges pragmatically recognized their ties with the United States for military security, financial aid, technical assistance, and the major share of Venezuelan imports and exports. An open break with the northern neighbor would bring few benefits and much damage.

Venezuela did exercise a forceful policy toward neighboring Colombia and Guyana. After intensive negotiations on the disputed Guayana territory, Venezuela and Great Britain signed an agreement in Geneva in 1966. The agreement called for a cessation of claims, counterclaims, and border incidents while a Venezuelan/Guyanese commission secretly explored practical ways to resolve the dispute. Despite the agreement, there were numerous border skirmishes, especially in the Amakur area where Venezuela announced a $9.5 million development project. In 1968, Venezuela violated the spirit of the Geneva agreement by claiming the territorial seas and continental shelf of the disputed territory. Venezuelan spokesmen asserted that the claim was intended to check the oil concessions which Guyana had conceded in the zone; Guyana Prime Minister Forbes Burnham, on the other hand, denounced the Venezuelan claim as illegal. Relations between the two nations settled down again somewhat after Venezuela's December 1968 elections.

Relations with Colombia also became more tense. In 1966, Colombia awarded exploration concessions in the Gulf of Venezuela area to several oil companies. Venezuela became worried, participated in a series of bilateral talks, and asserted Venezuelan exclusive sovereignty over the Gulf of Venezuela and its shelves. The dispute over the approximately 60 percent of territorial sea which Colombia claimed in the Gulf added to Venezuelan concern over other border issues such as smuggling and illegal immigration into the country.

Venezuela's regional outlook increasingly became dominated by oil and water. Colombia claimed only three miles of territorial sea until 1970 and most of the former colonies of Great Britain had inherited that maritime nation's three-mile limit. However, off-shore oil technology had improved and accordingly had raised hopes of spectacular oil finds along some of the continental shelves. Venezuela, conscious of shrinking reserves and the cost of an ambitious economic and social development program, could not concede any potential sources of new oil; moreover, the nationalistic stress on defending borders from encroaching neighbors proved a popular political issue and one which pushed ideological differences into the background. The armed forces, proud of their new national security mission in fighting the guerrillas, treated seriously any threats to Venezuela's geopolitical space. Territorial issues too reflected the more confident nationalism and the constant economic concern which set the style of Venezuela's democratic foreign policy.

National elections began to take on the tone of a quinquennial carnival. During Leoni's presidency, political unity broke down further as generational, ideological, and personal divisions occurred in AD, COPEI, and URD; a coalition of independent *desarrollistas* backed Miguel Angel Burelli Rivas, and a group of resuscitated *perezjimenistas* campaigned under the *Cruzada Cívica Nacionalista* (CCN). Shifting coalitions, party divisions, and the voters' responses made 1968 an electoral turning point.

The Election of 1968

Only AD and COPEI over the years have developed the party organization, ideology, and loyalty which have allowed them to survive divisions. AD, as we have seen, had its third and most damaging division in 1967. The popular old guard figure, Luis Beltrán Prieto Figueroa, led a large number of partisans out of the party to form *Movimiento Electoral del Pueblo* (People's Electoral Movement—MEP) in 1967. Despite a friendship that dated from the 1930s, Betancourt thought Prieto too radical and his ally Jesús Angel Paz Galarraga corrupt, and so from Berne he encouraged his loyalists to manipulate the party nomination process to deny Prieto the nomination and secure it for Gonzálo Barrios, also of the generation of 1928. Betancourt's protégé who had been Minister of the Interior during his presidency, Carlos Andrés Pérez, became Secretary-General of the party. When Prieto, hurt and disappointed at the betrayal, then bolted, Pérez energetically set out to reorganize and modernize the party so that the effects of the division would be minimized. Neither Pérez nor the frenetic reforms could prevent the electoral loss in 1968, but Barrios still attracted more voters than Rául Leoni had done in 1963. AD, aided by Pérez's work and by Betancourt's return to the country in 1972, determined to recapture the presidency in 1973.

COPEI too had generation and ideological divisions, but managed to avoid an open split. The party had put the ten years of democracy to good use. The Christian Democrats had gained respect and organization, and had moved away from some of the more doctrinaire positions of the 1930s and 1940s. Venezuelans perceived COPEI as more conservative than AD, but a close examination of the two parties in the post-1958 era reveals no major ideological or programmatic differences. Both parties and their dominant leaders rested squarely in the center of the Venezuelan political spectrum. Election results showed that a majority of the voters also preferred the moderate, pragmatic path and rejected ideologues of both right and left. Major ideological differences in COPEI did surface in 1965, but the impact was not as great as the AD/MIR split in 1960. The *Juventud Revolucionaria Copeyana* (Revolutionary Copeyano Youth — JRC), created by Luis Herrera Campíns and others in 1947, looked for inspiration to the leftist Christian Democratic faction led by Radomiro Tomic in Chile. The JRC argued that the party should show more concern for the masses and social justice and less enthusiasm for capitalism, protection of property, and anti-Communist rhetoric. The objectives of Christian Democracy should be a communitarian or a socialistic society. Caldera and his allies cleverly did not muzzle or expel the dissidents, although a few did leave the party. The desire for victory dulled both ideological differences and party discipline. A few demurred that he was a three-time loser, but most COPEI members recognized that Rafael Caldera stood the best chance of winning the 1968 election. Caldera's campaign was ideal for a small party that needed party unity and a large number of independent voters. He struck a deal with *desarrollista* Pedro Tinoco, Jr., promised amnesty and pacification to the leftist guerrillas, visited poor *barrios* and chatted with wealthy matrons in *"cafe con Caldera"* afternoons, and used frequent television appearances with skill. His narrow majority (27 percent) testified to his skillful campaigning and to a reaction against AD *continuismo*.

Jóvito Villaba of URD had been a force in politics for as long as Betancourt and longer than Caldera. Yet his idiosyncratic and personalistic leadership could not build a party with the stability of AD or COPEI. The party had opportunistically endorsed Wolfgang Larrazábal in 1958, and then, at Villaba's insistence, returned to him in 1963 while Larrazábal ran on the *Fuerza Democrática*

Popular (FDP) ticket. URD had no clear ideological focus and Villaba caused a number of bitter divisions. In 1964, José Vicente Rangel and José Herrera Oropeza departed with much of the left wing of the party in protest at Villaba's Congressional coalition with Leoni. In 1966, Alirio Ugarte Pelayo, attractive to the old *medinistas* and followers of Uslar, seemed about to seize the URD presidential nomination. Villaba, who wanted the nomination again, had Ugarte Pelayo suspended, whereupon Ugarte announced that he was forming a new party and on May 16, 1966, invited newsmen to his home for an announcement. They arrived to find him dead in his study, having committed suicide at age forty-four. Villaba subsequently supported the coalition, which nominated Miguel Angel Burelli Rivas for the presidency in 1968. The "Victory Front" coalition ran from right to left with the followers of Arturo Uslar Pietri (FND), Wolfgang Larrazábal (FDP), and Villaba (URD). United by little more than an ardent dislike for AD and electoral mathematics which showed that the combined totals of the three parties for 1963 would have won, the Front came in a poor third. Newspaper editor and political gadfly Miguel Angel Capriles and *desarrollista* Pedro Tinoco had originally joined the coalition, but ultimately left to join Caldera.

Two minor parties represented the simultaneous return to legal politics of the Communists and Pérez Jiménez. Still suffering from the shattered organization and loss of public sympathy wrought by the guerrilla campaign, the *Unión Para Avanzar* (the legally recognised front for the PCV) won only 2.8 percent of the national legislative vote. The CCN, however, came up with 11.1 percent of the national vote and 26.6 percent of the Caracas vote, and elected Pérez Jiménez to the Senate. The former dictator's trial for peculation had just ended in August 1968, with the Supreme Court finding him guilty of minor financial crimes. However, he had spent more time in detention than his sentence called for, and he was immediately released. He then left Venezuela for exile in Spain. The vote for Pérez probably expressed some sympathy for his ten year ordeal which in some eyes had converted him into a nationalistic martyr. In the wake of the violence and economic problems of the 1960s, the Pérez vote may also have represented a nostalgia for the mythological stability and prosperity of the 1950s. If Pérez's vote was an embarrassment to the two major democratic parties, they had the last laugh when they nullified his election to the Senate on the technicality that he had not registered to vote.

The first really modern political campaign of the twentieth century showed that Venezuelan democracy was mature enough to allow a peaceful transfer of power from one party to another.

Unfortunately, Caldera was to find his small majority a difficult burden to bear as he set out to implement what he liked to call *"el cambio"* — change.

Rafael Caldera's Presidency, 1969–1973

Rafael Caldera belies the accepted wisdom that college professors are ineffective in politics. A leader of Venezuela's Christian Democratic forces since his university days in 1933, he moved, like Latin Christian Democracy in general, to place a higher priority on social justice than on rigid anti-Communism. Unlike Betancourt, Caldera had had no problems in accepting the López government, the Medina government, the 1945 revolutionary government of which he was briefly a member, the Pérez Jiménez dictatorship, and the liberal democracy which followed Pérez Jiménez's downfall. His only brush with the authorities came in 1957 when Luis Herrera Campíns proposed that he oppose Pérez Jiménez in the 1957 plebiscite; the dictator's suspicions were aroused, and he briefly jailed Caldera before sending him into exile. During the few months he then spent in New York, Caldera met with Villaba and Betancourt to draw up the outlines of the Punto Fijo agreement. His 1968 coalition was even broader still, when he accepted the support of Pedro Tinoco, Miguel Angel Capriles, former Communists, and former *perezjimenistas*. His more conservative background allowed him to make more concessions to the left than AD was able to do. He continued to broaden his appeal to the masses through weekly television chats. The sense of credibility inspired by his rather scholarly demeanor compensated for his lack of personal warmth in a nation which still held *doctores* in great reverence.

In between his hapless bids for the presidency in 1947, 1958, and 1963, Caldera devoted his life to the leadership of COPEI, to his wife and children, and to university teaching. With degrees in law and political science, he had been a productive scholar since his study of the life and work of Andrés Bello was published in 1935. Labor law became one of his specialties.

Caldera included no AD members in his political and administrative team. The new President wanted to set his own style and mark on his office. Unfortunately, as had happened to Leoni before him, the Congressional faction was too small to allow COPEI to govern alone. For two years, Caldera struggled to form Congressional majorities with the MEP, the FDP, and occasionally the CCN. AD, unhappy in the role of opposition, obstructed many of the government's proposals and initiated an unprecedented number of programs itself. In 1970, both major parties acknowledged frustration and agreed upon limited cooperation in Congress. AD apparently sought COPEI cooperation in order to weaken Luis Beltrán Prieto Figueroa's splinter party, the MEP. In 1970, AD made concessions to COPEI within the labor movement in order to prevent the MEP from gaining more influence with labor.

A strong, indirect influence on Caldera's cabinet and policy was the Catholic secret society, *Opus Dei*, which had been founded in Spain in 1929. A Spanish priest, Odón Moles Villaseñor, introduced it into Venezuela as a conservative, pro-business counterweight to the more liberal Jesuits. The emphasis toward technical solutions, major infrastructural projects, and heavy industry received more attention from Caldera than the JRC urge toward greater social investment. Several of Caldera's team were associated with *Opus Dei*: General Martín García Villasmil, Minister of Defense; Haydeé Castillo, Minister of Development; Hugo Perez La Salvia, Minister of Petroleum and Hydrocarbons; Arístides Calvani, Minister of Foreign Affairs; Enrique Pérez Olivares, Minister of Education; and Luis Alberto Machado and Eduardo Fernández in the Secretariat of the Presidency. The *Opus Dei* influence probably reinforced existing preferences for economic development more than it determined priorities. Like the international Christian Democratic movement, however, *Opus Dei* provided a link to important streams of Catholic political thought in the Atlantic world.[5]

Caldera's *"cambio"* represented some slight differences in style and rhetoric, but little of substance, from the AD governments which had preceded him. The most impressive change was to lie in Arístides Calvani's direction of foreign policy. Calvani announced that COPEI's foreign policy would work toward goals of international social justice, ideological pluralism, non-intervention, and economic independence. To achieve these ends, Caldera renounced the Betancourt Doctrine and established relations with *de facto* governments in Panama, Argentina, Peru, and Bolivia. In the early 1960s, Caldera had threatened to leave Betancourt's coalition if Venezuela established relations with the Soviet Union, but he initiated relations with Hungary in 1969 and with the Soviets in 1970. Trade relations with China were begun, and professional, cultural, and athletic contacts with Cuba increased. Calvani signed a bilateral anti-hijacking pact with Cuba and pressed the OAS to remove the sanctions which had been imposed on that country. The tolerance for different regimes contributed to a lessening of regional tensions, eased relations with the left within Venezuela, and — most important — opened up new trade avenues.

Calvani and Caldera disappointed the business community when they continued to press the AD initiatives toward joining an Andean common market. *Fedecámaras* spokesmen still believed that the Andean agreement would discourage investment, cause problems with the US trade agreement, place Venezuela at a disadvantage because of higher labor costs, and import inflation because of the new tariff structure. Undaunted by the opposition, Caldera denounced the trade treaty with the United States in 1971, although the reciprocal trade agreement which replaced it did not seriously alter US exports to Venezuela. Then in February 1973 Venezuela joined the Andean Pact, after laboriously ironing out many of the specific problems. Caldera reasoned that the Hispanic nations had to unite in order to keep the Brazilian economic and political expansion within bounds.

Elaboration of a more comprehensive Caribbean policy also sought to blunt Brazil's influence and to encourage economic and social development which would discourage the spread of Communism. Venezuela joined the Caribbean Development Bank and made significant contributions to it. Venezuelan private and public investment in the region increased. Caracas provided half the financing for a \$300 million oil refinery in Puerto Limón, Costa Rica. A new perception of a Caribbean interest as well as themes of international social justice prompted Venezuela to take a leading role in the new United Nations Law of the Sea conferences to "preserve the common heritage of mankind" and to delimit new maritime boundaries. Venezuela actively supported the regional Santo Domingo Conference in 1972 which defined a maritime economic zone — the patrimoninal sea — which would fall between the 12-mile territorial sea and an outer boundary of 200 miles.

In keeping with the effort to extend regional ties, Caldera's government tried to settle the outstanding border disputes. The Protocol of Port of Spain in 1970 dictated a ten-year moratorium on the dispute with Guyana. The moratorium improved Venezuela's profile in the English-speaking Caribbean, where sympathies had been with Guyana. As long as the dispute remained unresolved, Guyana still could not become a full member of the OAS or receive loans from the Caribbean Development Bank. As for talks with Colombia over the Gulf of Venezuela, Caldera tried to depoliticize them by removing all negotiations to Rome, but other issues such as smuggling and the increasing numbers of illegal Colombian residents in Venezuela fueled a higher level of hostility toward the Hispanic neighbor. Caldera tried to smoothe over the border problems, but frontier policy had become such a volatile issue with the armed forces and the public that the Minister of Foreign Relations was forced to devote more attention to them. The Ministry reorganized its Frontier Desk in 1969 and in 1970 created a National Border Council to plan, coordinate, and implement border policy. Reflecting some geopolitical theories, the government sought not only to project a Venezuelan presence toward neighboring states, but also to develop the sparsely settled frontier regions and integrate them more fully into the nation.

Venezuela's gradual drift toward closer ties with developing nations accompanied slightly cooler relations with the United States. US President Richard Nixon, perhaps harboring a grudge as the result of his close escape in 1958, delayed in sending an ambassador to Caracas. He named John G. Hurd, a Texas oilman who was on record as favoring restrictions on US oil imports, and Caracas protested. Hurd declined the nomination. When Nelson Rockefeller traveled to Latin America in 1969 on his whirlwind fact-finding mission, Caldera asked him not to come to Caracas. Student protest had broken out again, and Caldera feared for Rockefeller's safety. Caldera himself tried to smooth relations when he chastised Venezuelan students for their criticism of the US invasion of Cambodia just before his trip to the United States in May 1970. Venezuela's continuing pleas for hemispheric preference in United States oil imports became a moot point at the end of Caldera's term in 1973, as the Middle East crisis shut off the Arab oil flow to the United States.

At home, Caldera's pacification program and the left's decision to abandon the guerrilla struggle (with a few exceptions like Douglas Bravo) brought a new harmony to the nation. Human rights violations lessened, although the armed forces interest in border issues contributed to a developing national security concern which took a serious view of unauthorized criticism of the government or its policies.

Caldera's government freed political prisoners, allowed exiles like Américo Martín and Teodoro Petkoff to return, and legalized the PCV in 1969 and the MIR in 1973. Additionally, Caldera replaced the much-criticized *Digepol* with a new national police force, the *Dirección de Servicios de Inteligencia y Prevención del Estado* (DISIP). The government vowed to pursue common criminals instead of political dissidents. *Operación Vanguardia*, an energetic police offensive, began in early 1970. The initiative at first won the approval of the middle classes, but it eventually drew criticism for excesses and was abandoned. Caldera also tried a more positive approach toward the elimination of crime by promising a stepped-up low-income housing program and improvement of services and opportunities in the urban *barrios*. Borrowing from the Chilean Christian Democratic program, the Venezuelan *Promoción*

Popular suffered from inadequate financing and AD opposition. AD, of course, jealously guarded its own political patronage channels in the *barrios*.

Caldera's government met no major military conspiracies, but Caldera worried about the political influence of AD among the existing senior officer corps. He passed over the senior General Pablo Antonio Flores to appoint General Martín García Villasmil as Minister of Defense. In August 1969, Caldera ordered the arrest of three officers who had publicly criticized government policy. Flores in turn objected to Caldera's action and sought the backing of other officers. Without further ado, Caldera had the general arrested and tried for conspiracy. Found guilty, Flores received a sentence of two years in prison. Minister of Defense García Villasmil won no prizes for discretion either. In 1969, he inspired a Congressional demand for clarification when he announced that the armed forces could intervene to restore order without civilian authorization. After he retired in 1973, General García stoked his political ambitions with public statements on the decadence of political parties. He deplored the lack of political rights of officers on active duty. His presidential candidacy in 1973 failed to attract the hypothetical majority of voters who were believed to want a militarized, non-political system, and he faded from the limelight. Some officers apparently longed for a larger political role, but the majority seemed content with their rising professional status and benefits.

Ironically, as military threats diminished, some Church spokesmen confronted the government more openly. Influenced by the leftist influence that surfaced at the Medellin conference in 1969, some of the foreign priests in Venezuela publicized the misery in the urban *barrios*. A Belgian priest, Padre Francisco Wuytack, in 1970 led a small demonstration to the National Congress to protest unemployment and poverty. He had not asked for official permission to stage the demonstration, and the Minister of Interior, Lorenzo Fernández, expelled him from the country. The Church hierarchy endorsed the action against a foreigner who had consistently broken national laws, but younger priests and students supported Padre Wuytack's work and denounced the harshness of the government's action. Conservative Catholics like Alfredo Baldó Casanova also carried on a running campaign against the more liberal Jesuits and the dangerously radical ideas they expressed in the journal, SIC (*Seminario Interdiocesano Caracas*). No guerrilla priests emerged in Venezuela, but some radical Catholic ideology disturbed the Church hierarchy and conservative laymen.

Caldera's firmness in the face of military and religious criticism drew only minor reactions. When he tried to implement university reforms, however, he inspired recalcitrance and violence, especially in the volatile *Universidad Central de Venezuela*. Political activity accounted in part for UCV's unrest, but the rapid expansion of educational institutions had not kept up with the rising expectations of young high school graduates. Admittedly only a small minority of Venezuelan students made it to the university level, but that vociferous group wanted quality education in the three most important national universities as a ticket to prestigious jobs. In 1974, the Minister of Education announced that the universities only had room for half the 77,000 students who had applied for admission. In the face of a storm of protest, he backed down. Investigation revealed that only about half of those who entered universities continued beyond the first two years. Those who remained crowded into the sometimes less demanding social science and humanities fields, ignoring some of the scientific and technical studies so necessary for economic development. Extreme anxiety for personal goals in a rather dehumanized educational system motivated many students to reject any efforts at reform.[6]

Both AD and COPEI had tried to tackle the political and educational problems at the universities. Late in 1970 the two major parties collaborated on a university reform law which circumscribed university autonomy, more strictly defined a regular, voting student, and limited the terms of office of university authorities such as the rector, academic and administrative vice-rectors, and secretary to four years. Serious disturbances at the *Universidad de los Andes* and UCV had broken out in 1969 and 1970. At UCV, the rector and the students and faculty violently opposed the new reforms. The *Guardia Nacional* and the *Policía Metropolitana* closed UCV, the rector was suspended, and Caldera named a provisional rector. By March 1971, the provisional rector had resigned. A political dead-lock hardened between those who wanted to open the University and create a dialogue on the educational problems and those who insisted on a full-scale housecleaning to remove incompetent officers and teachers before the University reopened. In March the disorders spread to Caracas high schools, and the Governor of the Federal District suspended those establishments as well. Educational issues also coincided with numerous political protests against the United States war in Vietnam. Student disorders spread throughout the nation. The disorder finally subsided, but the implementation of university reforms seemed a pyrrhic victory for the administration. More encouraging was the opening of the *Universidad Simón Bolívar* on the outskirts of Caracas in 1970. From the beginning, the "university of the future" concentrated on technical and scientific fields, strictly limited student and faculty political activity, and set tough admissions standards.

The business community and the oil companies had anticipated a harmonious relationship with Rafael Caldera. COPEI did not have many oil experts and had shown less aggressiveness and interest in petroleum matters than AD had done. Moreover, Pedro Tinoco's presence in the government as Finance Minister reassured the private sector and the oil companies. As head of the *desarrollista* movement since 1945, Tinoco had advocated regulated private capitalism and increased government efficiency, and had headed up the ill-fated alliance of private business and the oil companies which had opposed the 1966 tax reform measures. Industrialist and entrepreneur Eugenio Mendoza had also contributed heavily to Caldera's campaign in exchange for some influence on government appointments in key economic positions.

By the end of the Caldera government, private interests did not have much cause to rejoice. A number of circumstances over which Caldera had little control forced him into a position at least as nationalistic as that of AD. First, stagnating government revenues threatened his ambitious program of public works and housing construction. Secondly, his narrow electoral majority and his decision not to form a coalition gave Congress greater opportunity for obstruction. Oil matters had already become more politicized under Leoni, and a minority President could not recapture executive autonomy. Pérez Alfonzo managed also to push AD policy further to the left when his allies seized the initiative in Congress. No one could dare to be associated with a policy which was characterized as anti-nationalistic. After several years of being on the defensive in oil policy, Caldera began to propose more aggressive measures. Thirdly, the companies had responded to higher taxes and government control by withholding further investment in Venezuela. Venezuelans feared that when concessions ran out in the mid-1980s, the nation might be left with little more than a bit of rusty machinery. The companies also lost sympathy with the Venezuelan public and politicians when Pérez Alfonzo pointed out that they had not passed on to Venezuela the benefits of slight price rises in 1970. Fourthly, Minister Tinoco proved to be a liability. In 1970, Congress criticized the terms of a loan he had arranged with the Chase Manhattan Bank. Tinoco had been Vice President of the Bank's Venezuelan affiliate, and he was accused of a conflict of interest. His tax reform bill drew fire for its regressive nature and his stubborn refusal to raise any levies from the oil companies. By his uncompromising links with international capital and the oil companies, he lost all credibility and could not achieve any success in the increasingly nationalistic Congress. His failure contributed to the falling prestige of the *desarrollistas*. Finally, the upturn in oil prices after 1970, and especially in 1973 as the Middle East situation deteriorated, gave increased confidence to Venezuelan policy-makers. Apparently neither the nation nor the oil companies suffered from the more nationalistic measures the government was passing.

What were these measures? Since Venezuela hoped eventually to terminate the foreign concessions and to replace them with service contracts, a law regulating the terms of service contracts was necessary. By the time the law had passed through Congress, its terms were so stringent that it was unattractive to the companies. Tinoco's tax plan of 1970 called for sales taxes, taxes on luxury goods, taxes on lotteries. Congress balked and finally passed a bill to nationalize the natural gas industry, and the stiff reversion law which required companies to post a bond amounting to 10 percent of the value of investments to guarantee the good condition of their properties on reversion. The nation also supervised industry decisions more closely.

Two government actions, not directly related to oil, angered the business sectors. In 1970, Congress limited to 20 percent the equity which foreigners could hold in Venezuelan banks. The measure intended to open up credit, but some critics levelled the charge that banking control then passed to four strong Venezuelan commercial groups. At any rate, the business community in general did not try to protect the foreign banking interests. But it did protest at the 1972 effort to "democratize capital" by requiring the opening up of ownership of some Venezuelan family businesses to the general public.

A survey in 1973 found that only 38.3 percent of business association leaders thought their interests were "represented" or "well represented" in public policy.[7] Tinoco's failure, the entry into the Andean Pact, increasing nationalism and government regulation of the economy frustrated the business spokesmen who had had high hopes of exercising influence over Caldera. By 1973, they could see little difference between COPEI and AD on economic matters. Indeed, COPEI had probably been pushed further to the left than anticipated. A multiclass and populist system could not afford to abandon either end of the spectrum. The left's return to parliamentary politics through the PCV (1969), MAS (1970), and MIR (1973) meant that some politicians could legally criticize the major parties for close collaboration with the elites.

The unhappy businessmen would have been incredulous at the results of another opinion survey conducted in 1973. It found that a majority of those surveyed thought they had not benefited from the fifteen years of democracy and that government policy satisfied powerful interests before those of the majority. Venezuelans felt little sense of political efficacy.[8] Caldera tried to implement his campaign promise of administrative reform: he saw the civil service law finally pass in 1970, and he breathed new life into the *Comisión de Administración Pública* (CAP) when he had it moved to *Cordiplan*. The CAP and *Cordiplan* tried to attack the overconcentration of wealth and decision-making in Caracas, but with mixed success.

Caldera appointed a former student of his and an energetic member of the "generation of 1958" to take over the CAP and to overhaul the administration. Allan Randolph Brewer-Carías had already made a name for himself in 1969 at the age of twenty-nine. He had graduated in law *summa cum laude* from UCV in 1962, received his doctorate in law there in 1964, and from 1963 was a professor of administrative law at the same institution. By 1969, he had published four weighty studies on administrative law, expropriation, public enterprises, and Latin American economic integration. Few in Venezuela could claim such a strong background in Venezuelan administrative history and law.

As President of the CAP, Brewer-Carías encouraged two major items of legislation. One was the 1969 decree of regionalization and the other was the 1972 decree on administrative regionalization. The first decree divided the nation into eight economic regions, and by 1971 three new development corporations had been created (Zulia; Center-West; North-East) to add to the CVG (1961) and the *Corporación de los Andes* (1964). The region to the far south only merited a *Comisión para el Desarrollo del Sur* (Commission for the Development of the South — *Codesur*), but Caldera gave much more importance to the problem of incorporating this "future" reserve into the Venezuelan development network. The other two regions which lacked regional corporations were the capital and the center, already the recipients of a large portion of government and private credit and services. Brewer-Carías believed that regional economic development had to be accompanied by strengthening regional administration. Thus the 1972 decree called for the establishment of regional offices of various national ministries and institutes. Such decentralization of administration met with opposition by bureaucrats who did not want to see their power delegated or dispersed. Local interests also vied jealously to be the regional center. The most serious problem, Brewer-Carías believed, was that there was little national coordination among the different offices in Caracas. What benefit could the nation obtain by transferring branches of thirteen ministries and eighty-two autonomous institutes to each of the eight regions? Thus, paradoxically, *Cordiplan* and the CAP had first to harmonize and coordinate the work of the national bureaucracy before they could decentralize the functions efficiently. Understandably, Brewer-Carías had made little real headway by 1972, when he resigned his position to take a visiting teaching post at Cambridge University.

Brewer-Carías's ultimate objective was to breathe some life into local and municipal government. He believed that the municipalities and the eight regions constituted a rational ordering of government and administration, unlike the network of states that had sprung from the 1864 constitution but which had never had much autonomy or meaning. He proposed that municipal elections should be held separately from national ones and that candidates should represent districts rather than parties. Caldera opposed the separate local elections by districts, fearing that they would fragment the population too much. Obviously such a system would also strike at the networks of patronage that he and Betancourt had labored on so long and which they thought represented the best hope of Venezuelan stability. In short, Caldera was willing to allow a new territorial and geographic division to be overlaid on the old system, as long as it posed no real threat to party organization or patronage. New regional corporations, coordinating committees, and revitalized state assemblies would provide more political jobs. Encouraging effective local government under local control, on the other hand, might well threaten national party discipline and interests. In some senses, major party structures may have produced a bottleneck to real popular participation by the 1970s, but the old guard defended what had been radical for them, and what had worked for them. Indeed, the newer generation's idealized politico-administrative models may not have been appropriate for Venezuelan society.

The Election of 1973

With each succeeding election, aspirants to the nominations began ever earlier to jockey for position and to compete for the bits of power which the old guard was willing to relinquish. For COPEI, the August 1971 election for secretary general of the party was a dry run which pitted Arístides Beaujón against Pedro Pablo Aguilar and JRC leader Abdón Vivas Terán. Both Beaujón, the incumbent, and Aguilar belonged to the generation of 1945, but Aguilar was an ardent Caldera loyalist, and Beaujón was not. When Aguilar won, Caldera could virtually be assured of imposing his choice for the presidential nomination the following year. At the

March 1972 party convention, his fellow old guard loyalist, Lorenzo Fernández, won over more leftist Luis Herrera Campíns and Beaujón, who subsequently faded from prominence in the party.

The AD choice proved simpler. For a while, Betancourt toyed with the idea of running again, but after his return to Venezuela, he announced in May 1972 that he did not want to run again. His decision cleared the way for his protégé, Carlos Andrés Pérez, to spar with Leoni's protégé Reinaldo Leandro Mora, and old guard member, Gonzálo Barrios. Barrios withdrew before the party convention in August 1972, and Pérez was nominated. Betancourt led the effort to round up the renegades who had left AD in earlier divisions using the slogan "Once an *adeco*, always an *adeco*."

The electoral coalition of MEP, URD, and the PCV helped Betancourt's *Acción Democrática* unity campaign. Called the *Nueva Fuerza* or the *Frente Nacionalista Popular*, the group nominated Betancourt's old antagonist, Jesús Angel Paz Galarraga. The union with the Communists, so long the *bête noire* of AD, drove *mepistas* back to AD. Paz's nomination also lost URD, which had apparently only wanted a coalition if their man, Villaba, were nominated. Villaba again ran separately on the URD ticket. MAS, formed by Pompeyo Márquez and Teodoro Petkoff and many of those who had formed the youth of the PCV in 1970, nominated José Vicente Rangel. There were brief hopes that the two leftist parties could unite, but neither Rangel nor Paz would bow out. MAS probably advanced its eurosocialist tactics and analysis more by retaining its separate identity. Political gadfly Domingo Alberto Rangel counseled the left to cast null ballots as an expression of the belief that formal democracy was worn out and had not solved the national social and economic problems.

Conservative *perezjimenistas* and *desarrollistas* also had a plethora of candidates from which to choose. Pérez Jiménez himself was disqualified in 1972 by a joint AD/COPEI maneuver to pass a constitutional amendment which declared convicted felons ineligible to hold office. Pérez Jiménez showed no talent or desire to manipulate a unified party in his name. Neither M.A. Burelli Rivas nor Pedro Tinoco, Jr., had much credibility or appeal, and General Martín García Villasmil only drew a small following. Conservatives or "independent" candidates appeared to be waning in popularity and appeal.

The campaign was well financed and hard fought. News magazine *Resumen* estimated that AD and COPEI together had spent Bs 318 million compared to the Bs 31 million spent on behalf of the other ten candidates. AD reportedly spent Bs 2.5 million for the sole purpose of retaining the US publicity consultant Joe Napolitan.[9]

Both major parties fully used television, publicity experts hired from US political campaigns, jingles, and gimmicks. Pérez referred to his program as "democracy with energy" and his youthful sideburns and flashy neckties heightened the claim. He charged that COPEI was responsible for the high cost of living, softness toward Communism, a rising crime rate, and administrative inefficiency. His youthful image was aided further by the support of Diego Arría, who had formed an association called *Causa Común* to campaign for Pérez. Arría was another *wunderkind* of Venezuelan politics. He had studied at the London School of Economics and subsequently worked for the Interamerican Development Bank in Washington until 1969. When he returned to Venezuela, Caldera appointed him Director of Tourism in the Ministry of Development and later head of the *Corporación Nacional de Hoteles y Turismo* (*Conahotu*). His jazzy efforts to promote Venezuelan tourism also drew attention to his talents and handsome visage, although in the view of some, his defection from the *copeyanos* showed that he could not be trusted.

Lorenzo Fernández could ill escape his image as a rather dull family man in the midst of all this energy and marketing of the AD candidate. He had to bear the business community's hostility toward Caldera's nationalistic measures and his overtures to Cuba and the Soviet Union. When Augusto Pinochet overthrew and assassinated Chilean President Salvador Allende in September 1973, Fernández's campaign suffered another blow. COPEI's middle and right wing had always sympathized with the more conservative Christian Democrat in Chile, Eduardo Frei, and had been critical of Allende's leftist policies. Caldera recognized Pinochet's government shortly after the coup, an action which offended both the Venezuelan left and adherents to the Betancourt position of non-recognition of *de facto* governments. Thus Fernández lost portions of his support among both the conservative business sector and the leftist youth.

Scandal also flavored the campaign. Allan Brewer-Carías had recommended the purchase of voting machines in time for the 1973 election. Congress and the *Consejo Supremo Electoral* (Supreme Electoral Council—CSE) approved the idea and advertised for bids. The winning company, American Voting Machines, gave bribes or "commissions" to Venezuelan agents to make sure it got the contract. When the news became public, the CSE cancelled the contract in June 1973. Several political parties had been involved in the deal, but no indictments were made. Cynics noted that, despite many calls for an end to administrative corruption, no major figure since Pérez Jiménez had been tried for illicit enrichment.

Two impressive results came from the 1973 election. AD proved still to be the majority party with Pérez's impressive 48.77 percent of the vote. More important, in the field of twelve candidates, AD and COPEI together polled 85 percent of the votes. The two leftist candidates only attracted 10 percent, and the other eight candidates divided up 5 percent. The abstention rate was 3.07 percent of the eligible voters, and only 3.69 percent of the total vote cast was invalid. Also of note, the "Caracas question" appeared to have diminished; the two major parties won handily in Caracas as well as in the rest of the nation.

Reflecting the intense interest in their evolving electoral democracy, Venezuelan social scientists and politicians held a seminar at UCV in January 1974 to analyze the results of the election. They concluded that the parties which supported the system — AD and COPEI — had achieved dominance for a number of reasons: their longer histories, good organization at all levels, control of political organizations, economic resources, and appeal to the emerging middle class. On the finer point of why COPEI had lost, some analysts concluded that voters who wanted to cast an anti-government vote could now be content with voting against one major party and for the other. Fernández's lackluster image, contradictions or apparent opportunism in the platform, and rising prices were specifically harmful. Most voters shared the major parties' concern for bread-and-butter issues, such as jobs, housing, education, and cost of living. The leftist call for ideologically based structural change and the conservative insistence on apolitical economic development were abstractions that did not appeal to most voters.

After the election, Caldera issued a flurry of presidential decrees during his last months in office. He decreed the extension of the labor law to agricultural workers, the end of foreign interest in radio and television stations and electricity companies, and ordered the Creole Petroleum Company to return to the nation two oil fields which were not being exploited, in accord with the petroleum reversion law. Foreign companies had also to turn over 100,000 barrels of petroleum a day to the CVP in lieu of royalties. The CVP then exported the petroleum to Western Hemisphere countries. Caldera had prepared a decree which would have nationalized the petroleum industry if COPEI had won the election. When his party lost, he judiciously decided that such a major action should be effected by Congressional legislation rather than by presidential decree.

The Economy and Income Distribution, 1958–1973

Venezuelans often blamed their political leaders for unemployment, rising prices, inefficient public services, and an economy still entirely dominated by the oil industry. Betancourt, Leoni, and Caldera emphasized political organization and development and evaded structural reforms in the economy and society. It is at least arguable, however, that the Venezuelan Presidents could at best have had only a minimal effect on some of the forces at play: world petroleum prices, rapid population growth with 55 percent of the population under the age of twenty, rapid urbanization, the communications revolution and the expectations it raised, and the corporate trend in the developed world toward multinational subsidiaries and operations. A survey of Venezuelan society and economy by 1973 reveals a number of bottlenecks that limited progress in some areas. The rush of petroleum income after 1973 temporarily postponed the disillusionment which was to accompany a critical assessment of Venezuelan development.

Government programs naturally depended on the expansion of government income. An examination of government revenues between 1958 and 1973 shows only a sluggish expansion of oil revenues because of the low prices. At the same time, the government continued to depend as heavily as ever on petroleum income. In 1970, although the price trend for oil was up, Venezuela was no longer the first world's exporter. Existing reserves had shrunk from seventeen years' supply in 1960 to eleven years' in 1973. The post-petroleum era was looming uncomfortably close at hand. (See Table 1, p. 229)

The structure of trade varied a little, but not significantly. Between 1960 and 1973, lower priced crude oil exports dropped from 94 percent to 85.2 percent of all petroleum exports, but the slight improvement in the market position of refined products was neither striking nor lasting.[10] The value of non-traditional exports and iron ore exports grew more rapidly than that of petroleum, but still provided only a miniscule share of export earnings. If non-traditional exports were ultimately to replace oil earnings as a source of government revenue, they had far to go. (See Table 2, p. 230)

The direction of trade remained much the same. In the 1960s, 50 percent of Venezuelan exports — primarily petroleum — went to the United States, 9 percent to Canada, 22 percent to Latin America, and 19 percent to Europe. By 1969, the United States share had dropped to 42 percent, the Canadian share was up to 13 percent, and the other areas had remained about the same.[11] By 1973, the US share was again 53 percent of Venezuelan exports. Around 70 percent of Venezuela's imports came from the United States, Germany, the United Kingdom, and Japan, throughout the period, with the

United States alone providing over 50 percent.[12]

As oil revenues and trade did not produce enough government income to finance the ambitious development projects, the Venezuelan government increasingly borrowed at home and abroad. The increased debt was hardly alarming in consideration of Venezuela's fiscal conservatism in earlier years, but the national debt increased from Bs 1,168 million to Bs 8,434 million between 1958 and 1973. Debt service increased from Bs 220 million to Bs 1,538 million during the same time. The strength of the Venezuelan currency, tied to the petroleum exports and the US dollar, did not vary. (See Table 3, p. 231)

If the Venezuelan government had little control over trade, oil prices, and currency, was there a difference in the internal allocation of funds between 1958 and 1973? Enrique Baloyra compared the central government expenditure priorities of dictatorships and democracies between 1938 and 1968 and concluded that differences in allocations were minimal. The post-1958 governments had more to spend, at least partly because of their more confrontational style with the oil companies.[13] Nor were there striking differences between AD and COPEI priorities, according to BCV figures on spending in four major policy areas between 1960 and 1973. Social expenditures and defense spending both rose slightly, while economic expenditures fell. These figures reflect central government spending and do not account for the impact of the spending by the autonomous institutes and state corporations. (See Table 4, p. 232)

If we can detect no major change in the structure of income or trade, nor in the government allocation of resources, were Venezuelans nonetheless better off after fifteen years of democractic government? In aggregate terms, the Venezuelan population was in a better situation in 1973 than in 1958. With regard to relative ranking among Latin American nations in terms of the health, education, and communications differential from the United States, Venezuela moved from sixth rank in 1950 to fifth in 1960 and fourth in 1970.[14] Venezuela's *per capita* GNP as a share of the United States GNP went from 20 percent in 1958 to 19 percent in 1972, comfortably above the Latin American average of 10–11 per cent.[15] Gross National Product in constant 1970 dollars had risen from $4,725,000,000 in 1958 to $10,200,000,000 in 1972; the *per capita* GNP in constant dollars rose from $692 in 1958 to $911 in 1968 and $942 in 1971, second only to Argentina ($1,105).[16] The aggregate *per capita* figures might have been more striking had the population not also grown rapidly from 7,524,000 in 1961 to 10,722,000 in 1971, with 45.4 percent of the population under the age of fifteen in 1971, compared with 41.9 percent in 1950 and 44.8 percent in 1961.[17] The urban population grew from 62.5 percent to 73.1 percent of the whole between 1961 and 1971, placing more demands on urban services and national agricultural production.[18]

Income continued to be distributed unevenly both in vertical terms and horizontally between regions. Residents of cities and petroleum zones enjoyed higher incomes than their poorer relatives in the countryside. In 1957, large cities (over 20,000) accounted for 72 percent of all income, while rural areas only earned 9 percent, although they held a majority of the population. In 1972, 86 percent of all earned income went to the cities. In that year, only 13 percent of urban families earned less than Bs 100 a month, but 87 percent of rural families did.[19] Another study made in the late 1960s leaves little room for optimism concerning urban distribution of income. In cities of over 25,000, 57.41 percent of the families earned less than Bs 1,000 a month; that compares well with the 89.22 percent of rural families who earned that amount, but does not suggest that cities are generally middle class in their composition.[20] A United Nations study in the early 1960s concluded that Venezuela had one of the most unequal income distributions in the world.[21] There are few indications to suggest that the situation had improved a decade later. National GNP grew by 6.5 percent from 1962 to 1970, but the growth rate of the lowest 40 percent of incomes only rose by about 3.5 percent.[22] A 1970s United Nations study found that the top 20 percent of Venezuelans earned 65 percent of income, and that the poorest 40 percent of the income-earning population account for only 8 percent of the total earned incomes.[23]

Why could an oil-rich country with a small population and proclaimed social justice goals make so little headway in narrowing the gap between the very wealthy and the very poor? Venezuela unhappily shared some of the problems of the more developed nations along with some of those of the poorest. A conjunction of a number of factors prevented the poor and unskilled from receiving many of the oil benefits. AD and COPEI had not sought to alter the basic economic structure, but had counted on a greater push from the combination of social investments and the import substitution campaign. Yet the capital-intensive economic development could not absorb the traditional workers. Foreigners flowed in, not only as consultants to business and government, but as skilled labor in the steel and petrochemical complexes. The paradox of unemployment and labor shortage coexisting at one time contributed to a smaller percentage of the national income going to salaried workers and employees. In 1958 workers received 54.5 percent of the national income, a figure that rose to 60.8 percent in 1961 and then fell; in 1973 workers received only 46.4 percent of the national income.[24]

Moreover, the secondary and tertiary sectors, already richer than agriculture in 1958 on a *per capita* basis, grew more in GDP after 1958. Agriculture slightly increased its share of the primary sector's GDP, but remained low, especially in consideration of the large number of families supported by the sector. (See Table 5, p. 233)

The average annual remuneration per worker in each sector showed that in 1960–72 trade was the greatest beneficiary. The figures show that during those years each sector saw some improvement, but that agricultural remuneration remained nearly one-quarter that of the industrial sector, one-sixth that of the trade sector, and one-thirteenth that of the petroleum sector. Unless the structure of the employment profile were changed or the income of agriculture greatly raised, there would be little hope of lessening the gap between even the middle groups and the poor.[25]

AVERAGE ANNUAL REMUNERATION PER WORKER BY SECTOR
(*bolívares*)

	1960	1965	1969	1970	1971	1972
Agriculture	1,556	2,084	2,477	2,361	2,411	2,067
Petroleum	25,659	34,563	39,917	25,708	25,348	27,391
Industry	6,170	6,734	7,393	6,999	7,455	7,896
Trade	8,730	7,070	7,205	11,657	12,019	12,370

The number of workers and the percentages of workers in the active tertiary or service sector continued to expand, but the poorly-paying agricultural sector retained a large percentage of the labor force. (See Table 6, p. 234) A small, but increasing, percentage of the working population consisted of women, who had traditionally been confined to poorly-paid service jobs. Low family incomes and the rising aspirations of the middle class, as well as the large number of single or divorced mothers, brought more women into the workplace. In 1950, there were 303,437 women in the salaried labor force; by 1970 the number had more than doubled to 661,945.[26] A significant number of women chose prostitution as a better-paying prospect than commerce or secretarial jobs. A 1973 study of prostitution in Valencia and Puerto Cabello found that 40.9 percent of the women took it up for economic reasons. Fifty-six percent of them said that they had earned less than Bs 600 a month in their previous employment; none had earned over Bs 900. As prostitutes, only 14 percent earned less than Bs 600 a month, and 29 percent reported incomes of over of Bs 1,500.[27]

A final reason why the 1960s saw little redistribution of income in Venezuela was the rising prices of consumer goods and the general cost of living. Venezuela did not import inflation at an alarming rate.

until after 1973, although after 1969 the wholesale prices of imported goods rose more rapidly than national goods. The food index rose more than the general cost of living, reflecting the continuing inadequacy of Venezuelan agriculture, and contributed to the problem of "hunger in a land of plenty."[28] (See Table 7, p. 235)

In sum, the exciting political achievements of the AD and COPEI leaders from 1958 to 1973 were not accompanied by significant progress toward the proclaimed goal of spreading the petroleum wealth more widely. The newly-rich middle and upper income groups became fonder of conspicuous consumption, fed by heavy imports of luxury goods and low taxes. More positive as a sign for the nation and its self-image, the middle and upper groups also spurred a new consumption of and patronage of the arts and literature.

Culture and the Arts, 1958-1973

In 1959 novelists Miguel Otero Silva and Arturo Uslar Pietri began the momentum to establish a state body to set policy and administer funds for cultural programs. Senator Otero Silva pointed out to his colleagues that Venezuelans wagered Bs 18 million a month at the race track, but the state only provided Bs 13 million a year for culture. The new democratic government should be willing to use the petroleum to encourage the arts. In 1960, Congress passed a law which created the *Instituto Nacional de Cultura y Bellas Artes* (National Institute for Culture and Fine Arts — INCIBA), a vague fusion of the existing *Dirección de Cultura* (Directorate of Culture, formed in the Ministry of Education in 1936) and the *Dirección de Cultura y Bienestar Social* (Directorate of Culture and Social Wellbeing, a division of the Ministry of Labor since 1940). INCIBA began to function in 1965 with Mariano Picón Salas at its head and with a modest budget of Bs 11,265,000. Picón Salas, born in 1901, was the foremost essayist, historian and novelist of Betancourt's generation. He had been Minister of Education and held several diplomatic posts in his long public career, and had founded the *Revista Nacional de Cultura* in the 1930s. Unfortunately, he died shortly after being appointed as director of INCIBA. His uncontested stature as a man of letters and his close friendship with Betancourt could perhaps have ensured that INCIBA received the funds and direction it needed in its first few years.

The purpose of INCIBA was to unify and coordinate the state's cultural programs. It was responsible for the development of literary and artistic endeavors, conservation and stimulation of folk and popular culture, sponsoring cultural missions to the interior and abroad, publishing books and journals, creation and judging of art, literary prizes, direction of national museums and libraries, awarding of fellowships, organization of orchestras and other musical groups, the development of theater and film-making, the organization of conferences, and the improvement of the "moral and artistic" quality of radio and television programs. INCIBA proved inadequate for these varied challenges. The budget remained relatively small, and the organization did not in fact have the authority to centralize and supervise all the activities its charter had made it responsible for. The administration of INCIBA was no more efficient than the rest of the state bureaucracy, and various state agencies continued to conduct their own programs without the knowledge or sponsorship of the INCIBA leadership. Without strong Presidential support, it was impossible to regulate television and radio programming. Understandably Presidents Betancourt, Leoni, and Caldera found other matters more pressing, and other allies more trustworthy than artists and intellectuals. During the lifetime of INCIBA (1965–75), cultural development proceeded in spite of, rather than because of, INCIBA's policies. As a first step toward developing a national cultural policy and administration, however, INCIBA paved the way for later organizations.

In culture as in oil, the nation had to struggle to maintain autonomy and authenticity against the greater weight and power of foreign companies. Radio and television in Venezuela gloried in their lucrative role of promoters of merchandise, much of it foreign; additionally, most of the programs were canned ones purchased from the United States. A Congressional investigation in 1964 claimed that nearly 70 percent of Venezuelan television programs lauded violence and brutality. A similar debate in 1970 raised the question of how Venezuelan television could disseminate Venezuelan values when the networks were owned, directed, or administered by foreign broadcasting networks such as the Columbia Broadcasting System. Antonio Pasquali's studies of Venezuelan television and viewing habits convinced the critics that things were worse than they had feared, but the state still did not or could not alter the direction that commercial television had taken.

Pasquali found that the number of sets in Venezuela had risen from 250,000 in 1961 to 822,000 in 1970. People were spending more time in front of the television and less time in other amusements or diversions. Still about 35 percent of the population lay beyond the reach of the broadcast signals, since the stations preferred the more cost-effective urban corridors of the country. Between 1963 and 1967, four commerical networks had increased the percentage of air time they gave to "teledramas," primarily detective and "western" imported dramas. Live Venezuelan shows took up a smaller percentage of air time. An analysis of the television day in 1967 found that 52.2 percent was devoted to imported dramas, 20.3 percent to live programs, and 27.4 percent to commercial advertisements. Much of the live programming went to soap operas, sales promotions, and talk shows of dubious value. The state-operated "Channel 5" provided little relief, since it received inadequate funding for innovative, and thus expensive, productions.[29] Pasquali cites another study which surveyed over 800 children who regularly watched television. A majority of them thought North Americans were the "good guys" and that speaking English was preferable to speaking Spanish.[30]

In the 1960s, Venezuelans who escaped their television sets to go to the movies fared little better. Five motion picture distributors contributed 74 percent of the income of the theaters in the Caracas metropolitan area of 1965 and 89.4 percent in 1973. Four of the five were subsidiaries of foreign companies. The Venezuelan movie market was more lucrative than the relatively small population might suggest. In 1973, gross income from movies was Bs 120 million, about the same as the Netherlands and more than Hungary, Denmark, Norway, Portugal, or Finland.[31] Pasquali estimated that for each Bs 100 spent by the movie-going public, between Bs 19 and Bs 22 went to foreign producers.[32]

Venezuelan artists had long wanted to develop a national film industry, but despite some good efforts by Bolívar Films in the 1950s, the high cost and the lack of directors and technical experience had prevented any continuous national development from taking place. In 1968, the First Festival of Latin American Documentary Films met in Mérida and raised the enthusiasm of a new generation of Venezuelan filmmakers; documentaries in particular pointed out the important role of filmmakers in a developing nation. In 1969, the *Asociación Nacional de Autores Cinematográficas* (ANAC) formed to unite those who were interested in the creative side of filmmaking. Like INCIBA, the ANAC proved unable to accomplish much, but was a valuable starting point to pressure the government for funds and subsidies.

If the technical and financial aspects were still missing, a national cinema had a much better chance in 1973 of producing some excellent Venezuelan works. Rather quietly a national theater had been building since the 1950s. After 1945 Alberto de Paz y Mateos a Spaniard, had formed a theatre group with some of his students from the *Liceo Fermín Toro*. Argentine actress Juana Sujo, who had come to Venezuela to work for Bolívar Films in 1950, stayed and founded the *Escuela Nacional de Arte Escénico*. Chilean Horacio Peterson took charge of the theater affiliated with the *Ateneo de*

Caracas, founded by Anna Julia Rojas, María Teresa Otero, and Josefina Palacios. A Rumanian-French director, Romeo Costea, worked with the *Instituto Venezolano-Francés* and formed a theater group called *"Compas."* A student of Alberto de Paz, Nicolás Curiel, directed the *Teatro Universitario*. From September to November 1959, it became clear that all these seeds had taken root in Venezuelan soil when the First Venezuelan Theater Festival was held in the *Teatro Nacional* in Caracas. Fourteen groups presented plays by fifteen different authors. Critics gave mixed reviews, but the event became the point of departure for the new Venezuelan drama tradition. A second festival was held in 1961, and a third followed from November 1966 to February 1967. By the mid-1970s, playwright and director Isaac Chocrón could claim that Caracas was the third capital of Latin American theater, after Buenos Aires and Mexico City.[33] The burst of enthusiasm for theater, accompanied by improved staging, acting, and directing, coincided with the emergence of a new group of Venezuelan playwrights. Their works were fully Venezuelan in themes and execution; they had grown up working with and in the theater; and they usually combined writing with directing and sometimes acting.

Two of the most acclaimed — Isaac Chocrón and Román Chalbaud — would also turn to filmmaking in the 1970s. Chocrón, born in 1935 in Maracay, became enamored of theater as a child when he put on small dramas and insisted that his friends and neighbors watch. His first major play, *El quinto infierno* (The Fifth Hell — 1961), treated Miss Betsy, a United States woman who had lived in Venezuela and considered it the "fifth hell;" back home in New Jersey, it was pointed out to her by one of her few friends that she carried her own hell within her. Chocrón continued the examination of personal anguish and alienation in a Venezuelan setting with *Animales feroces* (Wild Animals — 1963). The members of a Jewish family living in Venezuela fell upon each other like "wild animals" in an effort to break the emotional ties which united them. Exploring the relationship between the developing and developed world, *Asia y el lejano oriente* (Asia and the Far East — 1966) depicts a town which decides to sell its land to a foreign consortium. Chocrón also showed his respect for his literary precursors in Venezuela when he wrote the libretto for an operatic production of *Doña Bárbara*, which was staged in 1967.[34]

Román Chalbaud, born in 1931 in Mérida, formed with Chocrón a theatrical group in 1967 called simply the *"Nuevo Grupo."* The group dedicated itself to producing Venezuelan and Latin American plays based on written texts and opposed some of the late 1960s experimentation with collective creation or popular participation. Chalbaud wrote poetry and stories as a youth, and he first came in contact with the theater in Alberto de Paz y Mateo's experimental group at *Liceo Fermín Toro*. His first play won him a prize from the *Ateneo* in 1951. Four others soon followed: *Muros horizontales* (Horizontal Walls — 1953), *Caín adolescent* (Adolescent Cain — 1955), *Requiem para un eclipse* (Requiem for an Eclipse — 1958), and *Sagrado y obsceno* (Sacred and Obscene — 1961). The latter one, which he directed as well, established his reputation as one of the best of the new generation. In 1964, *La quema de Judas* (The Burning of Judas) mixed current concerns with popular views of the María Lionza cult and probing questions about morality and immorality. Based on a true story, it treated two brothers, one an honorable soldier and the other an unsavory police informant. Both men were killed in the course of the play, as Chalbaud developed Biblical parallels and paradoxes of contemporary Venezuela where to survive demanded illegal actions. One of Chalbaud's most popular plays, *El pez que fuma* (1969), treated the passions and lives of people who ran a bar and brothel in La Guaira. Again Chalbaud combined a glimpse of vibrant underworld life with a thoughtful consideration of universal human questions and dilemmas.[35]

Novelists also broke out into new directions. Older ones, like Miguel Otero Silva, experimented with new forms and themes. Younger artists like Salvador Garmendia and Adriano González León probed the individual's condition in a new Venezuelan world beset by the materialism and terrorism of the 1960s. These novels were far more complex than Gallegos' nihilistic mood in *Reinaldo Solar*, and they did not share the general confidence of some of the 1930s novels. The hopefulness of the 1930s — that prosperity and democracy would solve national problems — seemed as far away as the innocent games of Tío Tigre and Tío Conejo.

The change in mood is most perceptible in the older writer, Miguel Otero Silva. Between 1955 and 1970, he published four novels that ran the gamut from announcing the death of traditional Venezuela and the birth of its modern successor to expressing his despair about the self-centeredness of young Venezuelans of the 1960s: *Casas muertas* (Dead Houses — 1955), *Oficina No. 1* (Office No. 1 — 1960), *La muerte de Honorio* (The Death of Honorio — 1968), and *Cuando quiero llorar no lloro* (When I want to cry, I don't cry — 1970). *Casas muertas* traced the desperation of Carmen Rosa, a bright young survivor in a *llanos* town whose inhabitants had succumbed to disease. Carmen Rosa acts positively, leaves the "dead houses" with her mother and strikes out for the new oil camps on the eastern coast. The sequel, *Oficina No. 1*, begins with her arrival in the oil camp. The camp and the foreign managers, with all their failings, are vibrant and alive. Labor organizing proceeds in spite of oil company hostility, the dictator falls, and Carmen Rosa's small grocery store thrives. *La muerte de Honorio* brings back the shadow; it is a novel of prisoners and their fantasies in one of Pérez Jiménez's jails. The "new" Venezuela could not prevent a relapse into barbarism, but the human spirit triumphed, even if with the use of myths and self-deception. After a decade of democratic government, Otero Silva became more pessimistic. *Cuando quiero llorar no lloro* treats the lives of three youths named Victorino, one wealthy, another middle class, and the third poor. Like the brothers in *La quema de Judas*, the three men live self-centered and violent lives. One affiliates with urban guerrillas, one is a common thief, and the third is a thrill-seeking sadist and vandal. Higher principles and human values seem foreign to all of them. They are all born on the same day, and all die on the same day, senseless lives and senseless deaths. Reinaldo Solar's impact on the society of his day was perhaps no greater, but he had at least his illusions of wanting a grander future for his nation and his countrymen. By 1970, Otero Silva appeared to be as weary of the violent revolutionaries as of the self-serving democratic politicians and their children.

Salvador Garmendía, born in 1928 in Barquisimeto, perhaps the best known of the younger writers, shares some of Isaac Chocrón's concern for the individual in modern society. He marks a departure from what Venezuelan critics called the reformist novelists of the past. His protagonists, the antitheses of Gallego's heroes, are frequently petty bureaucrats or other "little people" who lead mundane lives. His first novel, *Los pequeños seres* (Little People — 1959), traces a public functionary as he slips back and forth between sanity and madness. Subsequent novels — *Los habitantes* (The Inhabitants — 1961), *Día de ceniza* (Ash Wednesday — 1964), *La mala vida* (The Bad Life — 1967) — and short story collections explored the internal worlds of other ordinary people tortured by their own introspection and by the anonymity of modern Caracas.

Adriano González León's *País portátil* (Portable Country — 1968) combined some of the themes of alienation that Garmendía used with some of the attention to leftist politics that characterized more ideological writers. His first novel, *País portátil* constrasts a close look at modern Caracas with memories of a rural, and peaceful, childhood. The protagonist moves through the city on a political errand for a conspiratorial group, trying all the while to avoid the DISIP. The different levels of life in the city are observed by the protagonist, who remains more of an outsider than a participant. Like Garmendía's writing, the protagonist's reaction to events around him and his memories become the narrative. And, like Otero Silva's three Victorinos, he seems to have few passions or ideals to raise him above the tedium of the mundane or the hostility of the city.

Thus by 1973 fifteen years of democratic government, prosperity and intellectual freedom had produced a number of differing evaluations. The major political parties had achieved a political institutionalization and had survived a guerrilla challenge. The nation had more control of its major national resource than ever before. After the guerrillas returned — and were welcomed — to legal political activity, the level of violence dropped. National *per capita* wealth increased. Press and other media expanded, reflecting both the increased prosperity and the rising level of political interest and of literacy.

Yet notes of gloom were heard. There was little sense of real political participation outside the major political parties. National income was not much more evenly distributed than in 1959. Agriculture still lagged behind national needs, and unemployment continued to plague the nation. Early enthusiasm for import substitution industrialization was dying down, as numerous bottlenecks prevented faster, or more efficient, expansion. Writers and social critics were distressed at the materialism, lack of real culture, inadequate urban services, administrative inefficiency, and corruption which made Caracas a hostile environment for many of its inhabitants. The "agony of modernization" was obvious, even in an oil-rich nation.

Defenders of the system frequently replied that even oil wealth was not adequate to resolve all problems at once. By 1974, it was apparent that the Arab oil embargo was giving Venezuelan policymakers another chance. Undreamed-of revenues began to flood the country. The next decade would bring new possibilities, new problems, and new challenges to Venezuela.

NOTES

1. José Vicente Rangel, *Tiempo de verdades* (Caracas: José Agustín Catalá, 1973), p. 273.

2. Robert J. Alexander, *Rómulo Betancourt and the Transformation of Venezuela* (New Brunswick: Transaction Books, 1982), pp. 581–609.

3. Franklin Tugwell, *The Politics of Oil in Venezuela* (Stanford: Stanford University Press, 1975), pp. 89–90.

4. David J. Myers, "Policy Making and Capital City Resource

Allocation: The Case of Caracas" in John D. Martz and David J. Myers, ed., *Venezuela: The Democratic Experience* (New York: Praeger, 1977), p. 297.

5. Donald L. Herman, *Christian Democracy in Venezuela* (Chapel Hill: University of North Carolina Press, 1980), pp. 120–2.

6. Robert F. Arnove, "Students in Politics," in Martz and Myers, pp. 209–12.

7. José Antonio Gil, "Entrepreneurs and Regime Consolidation," in Martz and Myers, p. 154.

8. Enrique A. Baloyra, "Public Attitudes Toward the Democratic Regime" in Martz and Myers, p. 49.

9. Ramón Velásquez, "Aspectos de la evolución política de Venezuela en el último medio siglo," in Velásquez *et al.*, *Venezuela moderna* (Caracas: Fundación Eugenio Mendoza and Editorial Ariel, 1979), p. 408.

10. Luis Vallenilla, *Oil: The Making of a New Economic Order* (New York: McGraw-Hill Book Co., 1975), pp. 289–90.

11. Loring Allen, *Venezuelan Economic Development: A Politico-Economic Analysis* (Greenwich, Conn.: JAI Press, 1977), pp. 183–4.

12. James Wilkie, *Statistics and National Policy* (Los Angeles: UCLA Latin American Center, 1974), p. 290.

13. Enrique Baloyra, "Oil Policies and Budgets in Venezuela, 1938–1968," *Latin American Research Review* 9 (Summer, 1974): 28–72.

14. Wilkie, p. 481.

15. Ibid., p. 420.

16. Ibid., p. 394.

17. Ibid., p. 183.

18. Ibid.

19. Allen, pp. 120–1.

20. Jeannette Abouhamad, *Los hombres de Venezuela: sus necesidades, sus aspiraciones* (Caracas: Universidad Central de Venezuela, 1970), p. 64.

21. United Nations, Economic Commission for Latin America, *La distribución del ingreso en América Latina* (New York: United Nations, 1970), p. 6.

22. Allen, pp. 120–1.

23. Ibid.

24. Banco Central de Venezuela, p. 35.

25. Mostafa F. Hassan, *Economic Growth and Employment Problems in Venezuela: An Analysis of an Oil Based Economy* (New York: Praeger, 1975), p. 83.

26. Marianne Schmink, "Dependent Development and the Division of Labor by Sex: Venezuela," *Latin American Perspectives* 4 (Winter, Spring, 1977): 160.

27. Cecilia Esaa de Buia, *Problemática de le prostitución en zonas del estado Carabobo* (Valencia: Universidad de Carabobo, 1973), pp. 132–8.

28. George W. Schuyler, *Hunger in a Land of Plenty* (Cambridge: Schenkman Publishing Co., 1980).

29. Antonio Pasquali, *Comunicación y cultura de mases* (Caracas: Monte Avila, 1977), pp. 273–4, 352, 369.

30. Ibid., pp. 359–60.

31. Rodolfo Izaguirre, *El cine en Venezuela* (Caracas: Fundación para la Cultura y las Artes del Distrito Federal, n.d.), pp. 31–2.

32. Pasquali, p. 390.

33. Isaac Chocrón, *Tres fechas claves del teatro contemporáneo en Venezuela* (Caracas: Fundación para la Cultura y las Artes del Distrito Federal, 1978), p. 23.

34. Carlos Miguel Suárez Radillo, *13 autores del nuevo teatro Venezolano* (Caracas: Monte Avila, 1971), pp. 179–81.

35. Ibid., pp. 107–9.

7

THE PETROLIZATION OF THE NATIONAL PROBLEMS, 1974–1983

"Broken carburetors and useless spark plugs float in asphalt lakes like cadavers. We are sinking in our own shadow, in a viscous world where petroleum towers and cross-beams stand out clearly in white, like negatives, against the methane torches. . . .

"As in a dream, we run from ourselves and pursue ourselves. Lunar landscapes with forests of radiator grills and flowers of rearview mirrors. Adjustable spanners and pliers flow into the beaches of empty cans that face a sea of brake fluid. The preternatural light of the refineries watches over the transition from inaminate to animate where electric cables become helicopter-hunting cobwebs."[1]

Luis Britto García

The Arab oil embargo and the correspondingly high prices for oil on the international markets gave Venezuela a fresh opportunity to sow the petroleum after 1973. The late 1960s despair lest the economic and social problems were insurmountable gave way to a wild optimism that the millennium had finally arrived. The major political dilemmas had been resolved in the decade and a half after the revolution of 1958. The fantastic revenues promised the means to solve all other problems. Both the fact of the new wealth and the perception of it affected all aspects of the national life. Politics and foreign policy became more assertive and positive. Money abounded to subsidize more publishing and artistic ventures and a reorganization of the state cultural bureaucracy. Middle-class Venezuelans luxuriated in consumption and display of status symbols from imported food and clothing to the acquisiton of condominiums in Miami, Florida. Neglected regions received more national investment to create poles of development in the interior. It is doubtful that much of the new wealth reached the poorest and least skilled of the population, but massive development projects encouraged the eternal expectation that soon the wealth would indeed trickle down to the poor.

The boom years coincided with the government of *Acción Democrática* President Carlos Andrés Pérez (1974-9). His own energetic and aggressive style seemed especially appropriate for the new era. He ruled by decree for most of his term in order to bypass Congress or any other body which tried to urge caution and deliberation. In his haste, he took some wise initiatives and some foolish ones. He could hardly have foreseen all the consequences of the unprecedented situation. Nor could he have predicted the end of the bonanza.

For end it did as oil prices began to slip again. Economic crisis began when current revenues could not begin to cover the great number of massive, long-term and capital-intensive development projects. It was President Luis Herrera Campíns (1979–84) who had to cope with the downhill plunge of the roller coaster. National commitments shrank; confidence wavered. Belts were tightened among the affluent and those with rising expectations. Just as the wealth had affected all segments of the nation, the relative decline penetrated to all corners and classes. People again expressed concern about a future of declining prices and dwindling reserves. Oil did indeed seem to be the "devil's excrement," a commodity which cursed the nation even as it blessed it.

Petroleum and the Economy

The price of petroleum rose from $2.01 average realized price per barrel in 1970 to $14.26 in January 1974 to $29.40 in 1982 before it began to slip. Venezuela, far from the troubled Persian Gulf, became one of the principal beneficiaries of the price rise. The attention on international petroleum production and reserves strengthened the national concern over the foreign oil companies' role in allowing the Venezuelan industry to decline. In order to ensure control over the future of the industry, Carlos Andrés Pérez determined to nationalize the industry before the 1983 date when most of the concessions would run out. The increased revenues provided him with the resources to effect the nationalization, but the Venezuelans, always cautious with their petroleum decisions, moved deliberately.

As a practice move, they first nationalized the iron industry, effective as of 1 January 1975. Street banners proclaimed *"el hierro es nuestro"* (the iron is ours), a phrase which exalted the national audacity as much as the mineral. However, the agreement with the foreign companies was not quite as audacious as the rhetoric. Orinoco Mining Company (a subsidiary of US Steel) received compensation of nearly $84 million, and Iron Mines of Venezuela (a subsidiary of Bethlehem Steel) received $17.6 million. The nation agreed to sell iron to the parent companies for up to seven years at the minimum price of Bs 59.89 per metric ton. Over 80 percent of Venezuelan iron ore was exported through the middle 1970s, and production had grown from 1.9 million metric tons in 1952 to 15.6 million in 1976. Venezuela's second most important mineral still was insignificant in export earnings compared to petroleum, but hopes were high for the future with the expansion of the steel industry in Guayana and intensified exploitation of coal in Zulia. Venezuela's negotiation of an uncontested settlement with the iron companies provided valuable experience for the more important move to nationalize the petroleum industry.

The way seemed clear to proceed with the nationalization of the petroleum. Even *Fedecámaras* had lost its zest for defending the foreign companies which had proven such untrustworthy allies in earlier tax struggles. Most Venezuelans involved in the planning could agree on the generous $1,000 million compensation to the foreign companies and thought that the creation of *Petroven*, a holding company which would coordinate the activities of the six-teen subsidiaries of the international companies, constituted the most practical organizational solution for the national industry. The most heated discussion focused on Article 5 of the national-ization agreement, a clause which authorized the government to enter into agreements with other agencies or entities on technical or other matters relating to the industry. Critics of the clause, including Juan Pablo Pérez Alfonzo, charged that it masked an intention to leave the national industry still in foreign hands, but under a new guise. Defenders of the clause, like Rómulo Betancourt and Presi-dent Pérez, countered that the government had to retain maximum flexibility for future development. The President had enough'poli-tical clout in general and with Congress to be able to win the battle, but the symbolic value of the nationalization was somewhat tar-nished. The nation did immediately enter into contracts with the foreign companies to provide technical assistance, exploration, and transportation. Some suspected that the companies' quiescence in the nationalization negotiation was an indication that they had improved their financial position through the technical contracts.

Government hopes that petroleum policy could now be removed from the political sphere proved naive. Since 1936, Venezuelan Presidents had tried to use popular pressure to wring concessions from the oil companies. The democratic ideology of the first AD government, with the influence of Pérez Alfonzo, wanted to instruct the public in matters relating to petroleum. The public had still to be taken into account after nationalization. One of the touch-iest issues of the democratic era had been the low, subsidized prices of petroleum for the domestic market. Pérez had little incentive to raise domestic prices in the middle 1970s, but industry spokesmen noted that domestic consumption had been rising rapidly. During an economic downturn, the government might need more petroleum for the higher-priced export market or might need to exact increased revenues from Venezuelan consumers.

The immediate problems after nationalization, however, were both larger and less political. Reserves had fallen, no new exploration had been conducted for years, and industry equipment had not been renewed for a decade or more. *Petroven* began to invest heavily in new explorations and to build up the industry to maintain production at as high a level as possible. Practically no offshore drilling had taken place before 1976, and the national companies moved into the continental shelf area. General (ret.) Rafael Alfonzo Ravard, head of *Petroven,* retained autonomy to direct petroleum investments as he saw fit. He had successfully argued that if the industry were to remain free of the political fray, he must be allowed independence even from the Minister of Mines. There was another good reason for rapid and extensive investment in exploration. In 1976 Venezuela's production consisted of 35 percent light oil, 38 percent medium, and 27 percent of the least valuable heavy crude oil. The percentage of the cheaper heavy crude continued to rise; by 1982, fully 42 percent of the national production was heavy oil, and only 31 percent the more desirable and expensive light oil. New finds could, with luck, add to the reserves of the more valuable product. Least desirable of all was the tar belt along the northern shore of the Orinoco river.New and expensive technology would be necessary to wring a marketable commodity from the region. Banking on the continuation of the high oil prices, the Government planned an investment of Bs. 12 billion between 1981 and 1985 to initiate exploitation in the tar belt. Jealously watching what César Zumeta had called the future of Venezuela, government critics attacked Ravard's decision to turn over the Orinoco fields to foreign companies.

Petroven also programmed large investments for the refining industry and for petrochemicals. Venezuela's existing refineries had been built in an era when there was less of the heavy crude to process, and when they could no longer cope with the domestic demand. The refineries at Amuay, El Palito, and Puerto La Cruz were expanded. In spite of the new investment and reorganization, the petrochemical industry continued to operate at a loss through 1979.

The goverment of Carlos Andrés Pérez sowed happily during good times, and Luis Herrera Campíns had to reap during poor times. Herrera tried to rein in the directors of the autonomous national enterprises and quickly to bring expenditures more in line with the shrinking revenues. It proved easier to spend money quickly, and sometimes carelessly, than it did to stop quickly. Herrera's Minister of Mines, Humberto Caldefon Berti argued that he should make petroleum policy, and that the *Petroven* director should execute the policy. Caldefon initiated a number of organizational reforms which increased his influence in planning and encroached on some of General Ravard's fiefdom. In 1982, the president of the *Banco Central de Venezuela,* Leopoldo Díaz Bruzual, criticized *Petroven* for inefficiency and overstaffing, and the struggle for political control intensified. When General Ravard was out of the country in October 1982, Díaz Bruzual had $5 billion of *Petroven* reserves placed under Central Bank control. Equivalent to an internal coup, the action signalled the end of *Petroven's* financial independence. Ravard had continued to anger Díaz Bruzual and his allies by allowing *Petroven* to make 60 percent of its purchases abroad at a time when the government desperately wanted to control capital flight.[2]

The COPEI government further showed its desperation when it raised domestic oil prices in April 1982. Other measures to encourage conservation included an 80 kilometers per hour (50 m.p.h.) speed limit, restricted hours of service station operation, and an effort to require people to leave their cars in their driveways for one day a week. Unpopular measures all, and widely circumvented.

Venezuela's oil income dropped by 20 percent during the first six months of 1982. Projected budgets for 1983, an election year, had been based on the wishful expectation that they could maintain the export target of 1.7 million barrels per day at the same prices as 1982. A $1 drop in oil prices per barrel brought an annual loss of $500 million for Venezuela, nearly 2 percent of the total government budget. The nation also stood to lose one billion dollars in revenue for every decrease of 100,000 barrels of oil exported. Falling prices, a drop in international consumption, less light oil for export, rising domestic consumption, a desire to conserve the shrinking reserves, and burgeoning foreign debt service augered ill for the 1983 budget and for the ambitious projects plotted in the sixth national plan (1981). Petroleum still accounted for over 90 percent of export earnings, and government dependence on those revenues had climbed during Herrera's term. Petroleum revenues provided 72.2 percent of ordinary revenues in 1979 and 76 percent in 1981.[3]

Clearly oil nationalization had not made the nation more independent. If anything, the commitment to major development projects and the rush of consumer imports had increased Venezuelan dependence. When oil revenues tapered off, financial crisis loomed, and political crisis could follow. The Inter-American Development Bank in 1980 classified the Venezuelan economy as "highly dependent" and ranked it fifth in terms of dependence among twenty-three Latin American and Caribbean nations. In 1970, its rank had been ninth; in other words it had then been less dependent than in 1980. The ranking reflected the relative importance of the external sector in the economies of the region measured as a ratio between the combined value of exports and imports of goods and services and the Gross Domestic Product.[4]

It is logical that a nation which depended heavily on oil exports would not change that dependence even with nationalization of the resource. It is more difficult to comprehend how Venezuela, in the midst of unprecedented revenues, could fall so deeply into debt between 1974 and 1983. As it turned out, even fantastic revenues could not cover the long-term commitments which the government made. In addition to the expensive and necessary investment in petroleum exploration, refining, and petrochemicals, other major projects of Pérez's fifth national plan included the construction of the Paraguaná shipyards, the Paraguaná Fishery Complex, expansion of the Venezuelan merchant fleet, coal exploitation in Zulia, the expansion of the integrated steel industry in Guayana, a new Zulia steel complex, the second stage of the Guri Dam to increase the generation of electricity, aluminum plants, the Caracas metro, railroads, roads, and port modernization. Once investment in and commitments to these massive projects had been made, there was no turning back when revenues dropped. Many of the projects, once begun, enjoyed the same autonomy in financial matters as *Petroven*. Autonomous national institutions could seek loans abroad, and they did so. In the flush days of the mid-1970s, no one vetoed the contracting of short-term loans to cover current operating expenses of firms which could not be expected to show a profit for a decade, if ever. In 1974, the government planned to set aside half of the current oil revenues for long-term and foreign investment through the Venezuelan Investment Fund. Gradually, the ambitious projects, waste, and the increased volume of luxury and capital imports consumed a higher proportion of current revenues. Less was channeled into the Venezuelan Investment Fund, and more foreign loans were sought. The high interest rates and inflation of the United States and Western Europe contributed to inflation and a rising debt service in Venezuela. In 1977, the current account balance showed its first deficit ($3.1 billion) since 1972.

The massive amounts of revenue which poured into the relatively inefficient administrative structure in Venezuela resulted in considerable waste and corruption. Some waste could be attributed to Venezuela's inadequate supply of skilled labor and skilled management. Despite the new civil service law, politicization of the bureaucracy and of the labor unions continued. Wealthy magnates who contributed to political campaigns expected to be paid off with managerial jobs in the state corporations or with a say in policy making. Politicians and businessmen who represented regional interests called for development projects and government offices to be set up in their regions. Deficits in the inefficient and uncontrolled state corporations came to be accepted; in 1977, nearly 40 percent of the state enterprises had deficits which had to be subsidized. If the future shows that the subsidies are merely temporary costs of diversification and development, then the petroleum will have been put to profitable use. But if the subsidies only prop up industries which have no chance of becoming viable, then obviously the hasty decisions of the 1970s will haunt the nation for decades to come.

For Venezuelans, since the time of the Anglo-German blockade of 1902 at the latest, the national debt has been a sensitive issue. When Herrera took office, he announced that the national debt had increased sixfold during Pérez's tenure of office and that the *Acción Democrática* leader had mortgaged Venezuela's future. Pérez denied the charges and claimed that Herrera's figures were exaggerated. In September 1982, the Comptroller General angered Herrera by pegging the national debt at $54 billion, when Herrera claimed that it was only $29 billion.[5] The two totals depend respectively on whether the debt of the national enterprises is included or not. Different state entities continued to contract loans independently throughout 1982. While Herrera was seeking a $600 million loan in March to allow him to bring some order to the national finances, the Venezuelan Development Corporation was independently contracting another short-term loan.[6] The irresponsibility of the national corporations had damaged the government's general credit rating, despite a record of prompt repayments, and accordingly by the end of 1982, the Venezuelan government had to accept the same credit terms as did countries of much higher risk. The terms of a loan contracted in October 1982 were considered especially insulting and became a political issue within the country.[7]

Díaz Bruzual of the *Banco Central de Venezuela* attacked agencies other than *Petroven* in late 1982. The Central Bank took over the largest financial group in Venezuela, the *Banco de Trabajadores de Venezuela*. The Workers' Bank, whose chief shareholder is the AD-dominated *Confederación de Trabajadores de Venezuela* (CTV), had been founded during the Leoni government. It had always depended on the government for capital contributions and cash deposits, but during the bonanza years, it had expanded into new activities as varied as computer services and construction materials. The bank's president wanted to build a financial conglomerate which could make the CTV independent of the government. When the *Banco Central* found a pretext to take over the Workers' Bank, two objectives were served: the BCV gained greater control over an important economic unit, and a CTV move to enhance its autonomy was checked.[8] Government investigations in the first half of 1983 revealed that the bank's officers had mismanaged the institution's funds. The resulting charges of scandal and corruption touched representatives of most of the major political parties.

The rush of petrofunds did not contribute much to Venezuela's lagging agricultural sector. Large commercial farmers received some assistance, which removed them further from the level of the majority of the subsistence farmers. Agricultural production did experience an average 5 percent annual growth under President Pérez, but agriculture's share of the Gross Domestic Product fell from 6.5 to 6 percent. The fifth national plan had projected a rise to 9 percent. In 1971, the nation imported 46 percent of its basic foodstuffs; by the time Carlos Andrés Pérez left office, the share had risen nearly to 70 percent. Food prices rose by 16 percent under Pérez, whose overall strategy for agriculture resembled his strategy for industry and departed from the AD agrarian reform strategy of the early 1960s. That is, Pérez opted to spend money on costly infrastructure projects like irrigation and drainage works in the hope that eventually the benefits would reach the peasants. To avoid consumer reaction, the government continued to subsidize many basic food items. When Herrera came to power, one of his first — and least popular — moves was to "liberate" the prices of 175 consumer food items in an effort to spur production in the countryside. He also removed the tariff exemptions for food items to encourage national agriculture. Between August and October 1979, food prices rose by 9.4 percent. After the removal of tariff concessions for imported foods in January 1980, inflation shot up to 20 percent.[9]

The rapid rise in food prices, interest rates, and housing costs has halted the real gains made by the middle classes in the 1960s and 1970s. That fact, coupled with the national sensitivity to foreign debt will doubtless play a large role in the 1983 Presidential election.

The Presidency of Carlos Andrés Pérez, 1974-1979

The election of Carlos Andrés Pérez in December 1973 brought a new generation and a new style to the Venezuelan presidency. For the first time the old guard generation had relinquished power. Yet Pérez's political career before 1974 had kept him so close to Betancourt that he was practically an honorary member of the generation of 1928.

Born in the Táchira town of Rubio in 1922, Pérez came from a family of the rural middle class. His father and paternal grandparents were Colombian, and they ran a pharmacy in Rubio in addition to owning a small *hacienda*. Pérez recalled heated discussions about the Gómez dictatorship in his youth, and his family had disliked the local German merchants and bankers to whom they owed money. He attended a primary school at which the teachers were Colombian Dominican priests. At an early age, however, he developed a greater interest in politics than in his studies. He sold Colombian newspapers and read them avidly for their political discussions. His father was jailed by the Gómez government, so his own firsthand resentment of the dictator grew. He was only thirteen when Gómez died in 1935, but the radio quickly brought the news to Táchira. Gómez opponents in Rubio, encouraged by the news of demonstrations in Caracas, also launched some public protests against the *gomecistas* who continued to dominate the town. Pérez joined in. He gained some fame by passing around election information and by helping to supervise the local election. He founded the local branch of the *Federación de Estudiantes,* and he asked to join the *Partido Democrática Nacional* in 1937. Spurned for his youth, he began distributing propaganda for the Communist Party. The PDN decided that they had better accept the precocious youth.[10]

After his father's death in the late 1930s, the family was in a precarious economic situation. Some older brothers had graduated from the *Instituto Pedagógico* in Caracas and urged the family to move to the capital. They did in 1939, and Pérez immediately joined the PDN and entered the *Liceo Andrés Bello*. In 1940, he met Rómulo Betancourt for the first time when he returned from exile. Pérez began legal studies at the *Universidad Central de Venezuela* in 1941, but left them almost immediately when his fellow *tachirense* Leonardo Ruiz Pineda asked him to organize the newly founded *Acción Democrática* in Táchira. He was one of the few youths who knew ahead of time about the planned *golpe* of October 18, 1945, and he participated in it. He became Betancourt's secretary on the Revolutionary Junta and later during Betancourt's exile. In the new democratic government after 1958, he was first Congressional Deputy from Táchira and then Betancourt's Minister of the Interior. In the latter post he especially drew the hatred of the left for his persecution of them. In 1969 he became secretary general of *Acción Democrática* and began the rebuilding and reorganization that followed the defeat by Rafael Caldera in 1968. In 1972 Betancourt could no longer stay away from Venezuelan politics and returned from Switzerland. After toying with the idea of running again himself, the old statesman pressed the candidacy of his protégé, Pérez.

Rather like Teodoro Petkoff, Douglas Bravo, and Américo Martín, Carlos Andrés Pérez had given himself wholeheartedly to political activity since his youth. He was ten to fifteen years older than those who considered themselves the "generation of 1958," so Pérez had been able to participate in the founding of *Acción Democrática* and thus secure a leadership position in the party while he was still an adolescent. His political career seemed assured from the early age of twenty-two when he became the private secretary to the president of the Revolutionary Junta in 1945.

All that political promise appeared to be on the verge of fulfillment as he took office as President in 1974. Pérez's astounding electoral victory (48.7 percent) matched Betancourt's victory in 1958. *Acción Democrática* also dominated both houses of Congress. The new oil revenues provided unprecedented opportunities to rectify past mistakes and set the nation firmly on the path to diversified and self-sustaining development. Carlos Andrés Pérez's experience and his energetic style should have enabled him to weather most political storms.

The storms proved too rough even for Pérez to survive unscathed. The enormous revenues raised national expectations that life could be improved immediately and that the future could also be bright through the productivity of the new development projects. As noted already, Pérez's fifth national plan called for a plethora of heavy industries such as steel, petrochemicals, oil refining, shipbuilding, and major new investments in the oil industry. These new or expanded state corporations increased the state's role in the economy, especially after the nationalization of the iron and petroleum industries. In 1976, Pérez decreed incentives for industries to settle in areas of low industrial concentration so as to spread out the benefits from the new development and to avoid the problems of overcrowding in the Caracas-Valencia corridor. Pérez also increased the nationalist thrust of his government by requiring a wide range of foreign manufacturers to sell 80 percent of their stock to Venezuelans within three years. Sears and the Rockefeller-owned supermarket chain CADA were included, as were a number of services such as broadcasting and electric power generating companies. The changes helped to bring Venezuela into harmony with some of the requirements for membership in the Andean Pact.[11]

Pérez and his team were aware of the problems which accompanied the massive revenues pouring into the nation and tried to solve the problem of an overheated economy by reserving half of the revenues for the newly-created Venezuelan Investment Fund. The Fund was supposed to transfer some of the petroleum income to foreign investments, to finance some of Venezuela's long-term domestic capital projects, and to provide foreign economic assistance especially in the Caribbean and the Hemisphere, to help offset the effects to other developing nations of the rising petroleum prices. Venezuela had also recognized that the nation's pool of skilled labor and management to operate these projects was inadequate and so in 1974 Pérez's government created the *Gran Mariscal de Ayacucho* scholarship program to fill this gap by training capable Venezuelan students in new technical fields. Venezuelan universities could not absorb all the extra students for the desired technical fields, so students were sent to United States and European universities. By May 1979, over 20,000 students had received complete scholarships; 39 percent of them remained in Venezuela, and 61 percent studied abroad. Pérez also revived the idea of tax reforms in 1975 when he proposed increased customs duties, luxury taxes, and taxes on income and real estate. If Venezuela was ever to lessen the government's dependence on petroleum income, it seemed reasonable to implement the tax reform while times were still prosperous. *Fedecámaras* and the political opposition blocked the reform measures, but the Congressional Financial Commission finally endorsed a greatly watered-down tax package in late 1977.

President Pérez wanted to be able to respond rapidly to the new situation, and he effected many of his proposals through decree. Since *Acción Democrática* dominated Congréss, he was allowed that freedom. The problems that he faced from the petroleum wealth resembled those of other petroleum nations during the same time. Pérez's response — to initiate enormous development projects rapidly — did not differ much from the responses made by other petroleum nations. He took measures to avoid overconcentration of industry, hyperinflation, and bottlenecks in transportation and education. His premises on how to achieve economic development and a better distribution of wealth were compatible with those of Betancourt, Caldera, and Leoni. Structural changes were unnecessary or undesirable; the business sector had to be placated; capital-intensive and high technology enterprises should receive priority; and thus eventually the prosperity which derived from diversified heavy industry would trickle down to the marginal population. These premises, operating in the new economic context, encouraged monumental expenditures and waste without resolving the dilemma of the isolated marginal and rural populations.

Implementation of policy was hampered by administrative inefficiency. The continuing growth and autonomy of the state enterprises further eroded whatever central direction there had been. In

1980, the Venezuelan state boasted ninety-one administrative entities, seventy-nine state-owned enterprises, and 146 mixed (i.e. private and public) enterprises. Between 1960 and 1975, central government expenditures nearly quadrupled, but shrank from 54 to 21 percent of total public expenditures. State companies, on the other hand, spent nearly twenty-five times more in 1975 than they did in 1960, and their expenditures represented 62 percent of public expenditures in 1975, compared with 23 percent in 1960.[12] This situation was state capitalism with a vengeance and clearly outstripped the managerial talent available in the country. The new law of cities, passed in 1978, gave greater control over local matters to cities and stipulated that all municipalities larger than 50,000 should have a city manager. In the long run the measure could breathe new life into the cities, but in the short run the demand for sixty-five capable city managers would be difficult to meet. In short, the failure to develop a talented, experienced, and apolitical administrative pool in the previous decade and a half ensured that there would be crises of inefficiency in the late 1970s.

Several spectacular scandals damaged the credibility of the regime, as did new allegations of police brutality and some revival of guerrilla activity. In June 1976, Auditor General José Muci Abraham resigned claiming that the government ignored his reports. He had opposed several major purchases as too costly — one by the navy for six frigates from an Italian shipyard — and he had cited irregularities in several autonomous institutions, including the Social Security Institute. His complaints caused prominent *Acción Democrática* leaders to accuse him of exceeding his official responsibilities, so he resigned.[13] In 1977, the head of the government consumer protection agency was removed without reason; he countered that he had become unpopular with influential economic groups due to his having tried to enforce price controls.[14] The most famous case of corruption turned on the purchase of the refrigerated ship, the *Sierra Nevada,* in May 1977. In 1979, after he had left the presidency, Carlos Andrés Pérez became the object of an investigation by the National Congress because of overpayment for the Norwegian ship, valued at just under $12 million. Pérez's government paid $20 million for the vessel, giving ground to the suspicion that he and some of his colleagues had pocketed the difference. The Congress issued a baroque decision which exonerated Pérez from "moral and administrative" responsibility, but found him guilty of fomenting a climate of political corruption. Rather like the Pérez Jiménez case, the Congressional report could not substantiate specific charges of common crimes but logically assumed that the President should bear the blame for general corruption during the period of his government.

Stepped-up guerrilla activity also embarrassed the government into tolerating some excesses on the part of the police and other intelligence services. In June 1974, following the death of an inspector of the *Dirección de Inteligencia Militar* (DIM), other DIM agents were widely believed to have formed a death squad to eliminate leftists. José Vicente Rangel asked President Pérez to investigate the rumors, to which Pérez and the Ministry of Defense agreed.[15] More attention became focused on the guerrillas in February 1976, when they kidnapped William Niehous, general manager of *Owens Illinois de Venezuela*. He was later rescued; see below, p. 216. The Pérez government was chagrined at not being able to recover Niehous and increased the pressure on leftists who might have information about the executive. Nearly four hundred people were detained. In July 1976 the Trotskyist leader of the *Liga Socialista de Venezuela,* Jorge Rodríguez, died of a heart attack while undergoing an interrogation by DISIP. Congress called for the dismissal of the head of the DISIP and a full investigation of police activities. Four policemen were arrested and placed under investigation.[16] The public attention and Congressional investigation contributed to an improvement in the situation until July 1978. In that month, a hit squad of the *Policía Técnica Judicial* (PTJ) killed lawyer Ramón Carmona at two in the afternoon on a Caracas street. PTJ director Manuel Molina Gasperi had allowed a select death squad to develop within the PTJ, and he assisted some of them to leave the country after Carmona's death. Molina Gasperi and his wife, a lawyer, had allegedly become involved in some extortion activities which Carmona was on the verge of revealing on behalf of one of his clients. President Pérez saw that Molina Gasperi was dismissed and that an investigation was begun, but the sensational case damaged the *Acción Democrática* image at the polls in December 1978.

The new concerns over security and the increased power and professionalization of the armed forces encouraged another unpopular move in 1976. Congress passed an Organic Law of Security and Defense, which created a National Council of Security and Defense with a permanent secretary, standing committees, and a national intelligence service. Critics charged that the structure aped the security apparatus so popular with military governments of the Southern Cone; the emphasis on secrecy and the absence of any mention of citizens' rights and guarantees were troubling. No evidence suggested that the armed forces intended to violate the civil liberties that Venezuelans had become accustomed to, but the document was seen in the same light as the excesses of the DIM and the PTJ.

The scandals and the fear of an authoritarian state cut across class lines. Carlos Andrés Pérez also drew criticism because of his style and his allies. His first six months in office saw a shower of decrees, many of them with a populist tone which favored labor. He decreed higher monthly salaries and wages for all people earning less than Bs 5,000 a month; and he implemented heavy penalties for unjustified dismissals in an effort to keep unemployment down. Business interests complained bitterly at the measures, and Carmelo Lauría, Minister of Development and former president of *Fedecámaras,* resigned in July 1974 because of discontent with Pérez's policy. Yet there was no doubt that Pérez befriended influential business interests, especially the so-called "western group" of Maracaibo financiers and entrepreneurs who had bankrolled his campaign. Important members of the group were Enrique Delfino, Ciro Febres Cordero, and Pedro Tinoco, and many of them were connected with the *Banco Hipotecario de Occidente* .These new economic giants largely replaced the Vollmers, Mendozas, and Boultons in terms of political influence, if not in the size of their economic assets. Pedro Tinoco hatched up a plan which illustrated his aggressive efforts to form mixed enterprises with the state, undertakings in which the state usually put up most of the capital and took the greater risk. He, Eugenio Mendoza, and Diego Cisneros formed a company, *Pentacom,* which would invest in petrochemical plants and be affiliated with the Ministry of Energy and Mines. COPEI spokesmen charged that the plan was a means of paying off Pérez's supporters in his presidential campaign, and Pérez backed off and refused to support the plan.[17] Tinoco, ever resourceful, came up with a number of proposals to increase the role of private business in government. Scholars debate the extent to which businessmen influenced government decisions but clearly business and government were becoming more closely allied with each other as the state corporations multiplied and grew. Private interests gave way to state or mixed enterprises as the public sector of the economy grew, but the public enterprises were directed by many people trained in and allied with private businesses.

The fifth national plan called for considerable private investment to complement public investment and to provide more jobs. *Fedecámaras* complained that absenteeism and the restrictions on firing employees damaged their income and their incentives to invest. By 1976, price rises and a series of new economic proposals cut into workers' living standards. However, labor remained relatively quiescent. AD continued to dominate the *Confederación de Trabajadores de Venezuela,* and many labor leaders were loyal *adecos,* unwilling to make trouble for an AD government. Several strikes in 1975 at the newly nationalized iron mines suggested that the AD dominance might be slipping in that region and that workers did not necessarily perceive a difference between striking against a foreign company and against a nationally owned company. The news became worse in October 1975 when the leftist *Movimiento al Socialismo* (MAS) and *Movimiento de Izquierda Revolucionaria* (MIR) swept the elections within the iron miners' union.

Carlos Andrés Pérez's foreign policy, flashy and ambitious, also drew criticism. Like many of the domestic initiatives, the goals of the foreign policy often foundered because of inadequate coordination and a lack of career professionals in the Ministry of Foreign Relations. In addition to maintaining close political ties with the Andean Pact nations, Caracas increased its profile in the Caribbean basin, with special emphasis on the poverty-stricken island mini-states of the eastern Caribbean and the politicized and volatile Central American states. The oil-rich nation bestowed significant financial aid on the region, through multilateral lending agencies such as the Caribbean Development Bank, and unilaterally through special credit arrangements for the purchase of Venezuelan oil.

A new bilateral cooperation with Mexico bloomed, expressed in special Caribbean initiatives and in the founding of the *Sistema Económica Latino Americana* (SELA) in 1975. Pérez appealed to the left in Venezuela by moving toward warmer relations with Cuba, and Venezuela restored diplomatic relations in December 1974. But he lost ground when a 1974 Venezuelan initiative to remove the Organization of American States sanctions against Cuba failed to win the necessary two-thirds vote. In Venezuela, the loss was generally attributed to diplomatic bungling, and Foreign Minister Schacht Aristeguieta stepped down shortly thereafter. Pérez's warmth toward Cuba caused uneasiness among some of the anti-Communist old guard of AD. In 1977, Betancourt forced the AD executive committee to refuse official sanction for the planned visit to Cuba by AD youth to attend the World Youth Festival and Betancourt also published a strong letter criticizing the AD youth leaders and Pro-Venezuela who were promoting the delegation. Pérez's strong advocacy of Panama's stance in seeking control over the Canal and his support for the *sandinista* guerrillas who were seeking to overturn the dictatorship of Anastasio Somoza rounded out the higher profile for Caracas in the Caribbean. If some Venezuelans considered the policies improvised and too friendly to the left, there were Caribbean leaders, like Eric Williams of Trinidad, who characterized Venezuelan actions as "subimperialism."

Pérez's Caribbean policy constituted one aspect of his general efforts to assume continental and Third World leadership. He traveled abroad more than any other Venezuelan President had done, even including Moscow on one of his itineraries in 1976. The Minister of State for International Economic Affairs, Manuel Pérez Guerrero, took a lead in some of the North/South economic discussions, and Andrés Aguilar Mawdsley assumed a high profile in the United Nations Law of the Sea conferences.

Relations with the two most important hemispheric nations — Brazil and the United States — blew hot and cold. Pérez preferred to leave aside Caldera's concern over Brazilian expansionism, but in mid-1976 the Venezuelans viewed with alarm an apparently increased Brazilian military and economic presence along the shared border. Pérez publicly criticized Brazil's nuclear policy and expressed Venezuelan resentment at US Secretary of State Henry Kissinger's announced intention to work closely with Brazil in hemispheric and world matters. Tempers had cooled by 1978, however, and Venezuela joined Brazil and other nations of the Amazon basin in signing a treaty for Amazonian cooperation. The treaty exhorted all nations to work together to develop the region, but its effect was little more than symbolic. Venezuelan spokesmen did reflect more interest in geopolitical theories as they asserted that Venezuela was simultaneously a Caribbean, an Andean, an Amazonian, and an Atlantic nation.

Venezuela bitterly resented the United States Trade Act amendment in 1974 which denied the benefits of the Generalized System of Preferences to any OPEC nation. The Trade Act was a reprisal for the Arab embargo of 1973, and did not take into account the fact that Venezuelan oil had continued to flow to the United States during the crisis. Nor was Caracas pleased with the designation of oilman Harry Shlaudeman as US ambassador to Venezuela. In 1976, the discriminatory trade clause was lifted, Shlaudeman was replaced, and relations became somewhat more friendly.

In some of his foreign initiatives, Pérez was both encouraged and supported by *Acción Democrática's* closer association with a more active Socialist International. The former West German Chancellor Willy Brandt, who was elected president of the Socialist International in 1976, encouraged more contact with Third World nations. With a strength of more than a million, *Acción Democrática* has been the largest affiliate, although much of the AD membership views the socialist members of Socialist International with suspicion and feels more comfortable with the social democratic or labor parties which are members. The Socialist International strongly supported the *sandinista* campaign against the Somoza regime in Nicaragua, as did Pérez.

Political jockeying for position for the 1978 elections began nearly as soon as Pérez had taken office. COPEI, alarmed by the large AD margin of victory and by the prospect that AD would receive credit for the nationalization of oil and iron, took a consistently critical stance. Pérez sidestepped much of their obstructiveness in Congress by governing by decree, but the constant criticism took its toll. The *Movimiento al Socialismo* (MAS) also remained critical, especially about administrative corruption, but gave some support to Pérez in the course of his term. MAS continued to grapple with a political image problem; they wanted to distance themselves from the Communist Party, but had to fall to the left of AD. Rómulo Betancourt tried to limit effectiveness of the strategy by a series of strong attacks on MAS, charging that they were dangerous Communists who were trying to infiltrate the armed forces. Some other AD attacks on MAS were so strident that Betancourt called MAS leaders together in early 1976 to assure them that no generalized political oppression was planned.[18]

By early 1977, the two major parties were settling on their candidates for the upcoming election. Luis Herrera Campíns seemed assured of the COPEI nomination, despite Rafael Caldera's lukewarm endorsement. Party unity would give them some advantage over *Acción Democrática,* which had been wracked by contention since 1975. Betancourt's disapproval of Pérez's association with non-party technocrats, his leftist foreign policy, and his freewheeling style had become more open. Betancourt supported Luis Piñerúa for the presidential nomination. Although Pérez did not openly endorse any candidate, he probably favored the bid of Jaime Lusinchi (elected President in 1983). Betancourt and Piñerúa retained control of most of the party machinery and won by a 2-1 margin in a direct election among the party members, one-third or more of whom did not vote at all.[19] The left, as usual, was divided. MAS nominated José Vicente Rangel again; MIR backed Américo Martín; the MEP endorsed Luis Beltrán Prieto Figueroa; and the PCV nominated Héctor Mujica. In 1977, there had been hope that at least MIR and MAS could collaborate to support Rangel, but that alliance fell apart as the election day approached.

Betancourt apparently acted as an *éminence grise* during the last year and a half of the campaign, sponsoring virulent attacks on Pérez and trying to help some minor candidates who could take votes from COPEI's Herrera Campíns. Renny Ottolinia, a popular television personality, declared himself a presidential candidate in August 1977 and, reminiscent of earlier "independent" candidates, he criticized the principal political parties for their corruption and incompetence. Other than a vague appeal to the poor and those disillusioned with Pérez, Ottolinia's platform was scarcely note-worthy. Businessmen who were known to be allies of Betancourt financed his campaign. It was thought that his candidacy would draw votes from both MAS and COPEI and that it would thus help the AD candidate, Piñerúa.[20] However, he died in a plane crash in March 1978. After Ottolinia's death, Minister of Information Diego Arria resigned to launch his own presidential campaign. More impressive than his candidacy was his new newspaper *El Diario de Caracas* ,which benefited from advice by Pierre Salinger, once press secretary to US President John F. Kennedy. Betancourt was less pleased with Arria, who had been closely associated with Carlos Andrés Pérez; he believed that support for Arria would subse-quently limit AD's control of Congress. Some AD strategists, with the approval of Betancourt, hit on the idea of encouraging Jorge Olavarría, editor of the news magazine *Resumen*, to run in order to draw votes from Arría. Olavarria had had encouragement from Betancourt to attack Pérez's team in his editorial columns. In 1977, he was sent to prison because his former wife accused him of misappropriating her property; he believed the imprisonment was harassment by Pérez's government. He finally took refuge in the Nicaraguan embassy, and in 1978 was living in exile in Miami. He refused the invitation to run for the presidency, but he kept up the journalistic attacks on Pérez and the alleged corruption of the regime. The last issue of *Resumen* before the election made revela-tions about the Carmona case and demanded Pérez's impeach-ment; the issue was confiscated by the government, and Pérez threatened to charge Olavarría with libel.[21]

The last months of the campaign took on their now customary carnival atmosphere. Joe Napolitan, the US media advisor who had taken Pérez in hand in 1973, tried to sell Luis Piñerúa, but had dull material to work with. Joseph Garth advised Luis Herrera and depicted him as a serious and dignified statesman. Herrera broke out of the mold on occasion with his folksy *llanos* sayings and aphorisms, which may have heightened his appeal. Even Diego Arria engaged a US pollster and expert, Patrick Cadell.[22]

Herrera Campíns came out the winner, with 46.6 percent of the vote to Piñerúa's 43.4 percent.Arria was disappointed with less than 2 percent, and MAS candidate José Vicente Rangel took 5 per-cent of the vote, an improvement on his performance in 1973. The election results reflected popular concern about the charges of corruption, but even more, the experience with the declining quality of public services and the perception that the government could not or would not remedy the situation. To the extent that Piñerúa was seen as Betancourt's candidate, the election was a defeat for the old politican. Those like Betancourt who believed that the strength and stability of Venezuelan democracy rested on the strength of the two major parties could take heart from the 90 percent of the vote shared by AD and COPEI. The election results may have vindicated Carlos Andrés Pérez in his belief that Jaime Lusinchi would have been the better candidate. Aside from that small comfort, he must have been disheartened by the nearly universal vilification of himself and his administration. One cannot but conclude that, flawed as his administration was, the reasons for Pérez's sharp drop in popularity were chiefly political. Arguably, Carlos Andrés Pérez's government was no more corrupt, inefficient, or repressive than the governments which preceded him, if one discounts the greater revenues available. There is little to suggest that any other Venezuelan could or would have handled the petroleum windfall with any more wisdom. COPEI, fearful of becoming a permanent minority party, did not maintain criticism at the more genteel level of the early 1960s. MAS, with growing strength and credibility, hammered constantly at the non-ideological issues of corruption and violation of human rights. Most damaging to Pérez's reputation, however, was the intergenerational struggle in *Acción Democrática* between him and Betancourt.

Betancourt did not accord Pérez the same freedom he had accorded to Raúl Leoni. Through daily contact with party members but not with Pérez, Betancourt jealously sought to keep his creation, *Acción Democrática,* on the path he had set out for it. He did not like Pérez's administrative team, younger men whose contact with the party had frequently been minimal. Betancourt especially distrusted Gumersindo Rodríguez, director of *Cordiplan* and a former member of the leftist MIR. When Rodríguez published a survey of national problems and possible solutions to them, Betancourt may have considered the document a repudiation of his own work.[23] Betancourt also deplored Pérez's willingness to strengthen relations with Fidel Castro's Cuba and disliked the Third World stance in general, believing that Venezuela had enough problems to solve at home before setting out to aid other nations.[24] He did support Pérez in the oil nationalization debate, but the debate caused another division in the old guard when Pérez Alfonzo attacked Article 5. Betancourt also questioned the wisdom of directing such a large percentage of revenues to long-term projects instead of to immediate benefits.[25] Betancourt's willingness to sponsor attacks on Pérez and his uncompromising insistence on his own theses probably hurt Pérez and *Acción Democrática* as much as the overt party division in 1968 had done. Betancourt's intransigence contributed to the political humiliation of one whose youth and energy might have helped to hold the party together after his death.

The squabbles and their results bring to mind the political uncertainty which followed Guzmán Blanco's resignation nearly a century earlier. Unwilling to designate one political heir or to resist the temptation to intervene in national politics, Guzmán Blanco galvanized the civil wars and chaos of the 1890s.

The Presidency of Luis Herrera Campíns, 1979–1984

Like Carlos Andrés Pérez, Luis Herrera Campíns belonged to the second generation of leaders in the two major parties. Herrera's climb within COPEI, however, was less spectacular than that of Pérez in AD; he met and became inspired by party leader Rafael Caldera in 1940, campaigned for him in 1946 and 1947, but remained somewhat distant from the power centers of the party in the 1940s. He did assume leadership within the *Juventud Revolucionaria Copeyano,* a youth group which he helped to found in 1947.

Herrera was born into a middle-class family in the *llanos* town of Acarigua in 1925. When his father, an accountant, died in 1941, the family had already moved to Barquisimeto, where the boy attended the prestigious *Colegio La Salle.* Like Pérez, he has some vague childhood memories of the Gómez dictatorship and the terror it inspired. After General Gabaldón's uprising in 1929, rumors flew that he was going to Acarigua. Gómez's troops took over the town and made an impression on the young child. He also remembered the violence in Barquisimeto in 1936 after Gómez's death, but he took no active political role in the furor of the late 1930s. His childhood and youth had been devoted to playing baseball with home-made gloves and bats and to study.[26]

He turned to journalism and teaching in the 1940s. After he joined COPEI shortly after its founding in 1946, he became the director of the party's weekly newspaper COPEI. He was jailed briefly under the dictatorship for denouncing the press censorship. In 1952, his university education was interrupted by student strikes, some of which he had helped to organize. He went into exile in Europe, studied law at the University of Santiago de Compostela in Spain, and read extensively from Social Christian theorists like Jacques Maritain and Teilhard de Chardin. On his return to Venezuela in 1958, he was considered one of the more intellectual members of COPEI. His political career until his nomination for the presidency had been primarily focused in Congress, as a Deputy and a Senator, although he continued to provide some leadership on ideological and philosophical matters within the party. He had had strong support from the labor and youth sectors of the party for the presidential nomination in 1973, but had been outmanuevered by Rafael Caldera and his protégé, Lorenzo Fernández. His turn finally came in 1978, but he had a more difficult job than Carlos Andrés Pérez.

His electoral victory was not so great, and COPEI was not able to control Congress. The June 1979 municipal elections did go to COPEI, further embarrassing former President Pérez, but the new system of separate municipal elections ensured that the political agitation continued for a longer period. Herrera hesitated to leap into the office immediately upon his election and lost some momentum. He even had trouble designating his cabinet, because so many prominent *copeyanos* wanted to begin to plan for the 1983 presidential election. Only two of his cabinet had served in government before: Interior Minister Rafael Andrés Montes de Oca and Education Minister Enrique Pérez Olivares. Several new ministries were created, and the Ministry of State for International Economic Affairs was abolished.[27]

The new minister with the longest title was Mercedes Pulido Briceño who accepted the post of Minister of State for the Participation of Women in Development. Luis Alberto Machado held the other new cabinet post, the Ministry for the Development of Intelligence; he enthusiastically endorsed educational theories which claimed to expand human intelligence and analytical ability. The Venezuelan press did not treat him kindly, and he became the subject of ridicule for one of his pet projects: teaching some young Peman Indians how to play the violin in ten weeks. Another new ministry which had been established under Carlos Andrés Pérez was the Ministry of Youth. Having noticed that 44.8 percent of the population was under the age of fifteen, the government had decided to launch an effort to discourage delinquency and make some contacts in the younger age groups for the political parties. Herrera's Youth Minister, Charles Brewer-Carías, satisfied the President's love of sport when he encouraged activities such as scuba diving, mountain climbing, running, and camping.

On more substantial matters, Herrera revealed his familiarity with Social Christian theory when he spoke of the communitarian society and of improving the lives of the poor in Venezuela. He promised a greater effort toward health services, especially in the countryside, and in education; he did raise the number of years of obligatory schooling from six to nine and initiated a program of building new schools to house the burgeoning school age population. Sports and recreation would also receive attention, including preparation for the Pan American Games to be held in Caracas in 1983. Noting an 800,000-unit housing deficit in the country, he pledged to aim for the construction of 644,500 new *"soluciones habitacionales"* during his presidency. Wags joked at his language, saying. they already had a "habitational solution;" what they needed was a house. One of the most passionate indictments against Carlos Andrés Pérez had been the decline in urban services-especially in Caracas. Herrera promised to improve the delivery of services and urban planning. And although pacification of the guerrilla threat was not as intense an issue as it had been in 1969 when Caldera took office, it also received some attention from Herrera. He said less about foreign affairs, but seemed more comfortable with a less aggressive stance than Pérez's. Despite his own origins in the left wing of COPEI, Herrera was markedly cooler toward the *sandinista* government in Nicaragua and toward Castro's Cuba.

Herrera's greatest problem was that he, like Pérez, had been elected on a platform of fiscal conservatism. Fearful of the large and growing debt, the public wanted a semblance of order in the administration. In theory, they wanted the waste, corruption, and mismanagement of funds to be replaced by a sober and judicious government which could plan well and implement well. At the same time, few Venezuelans would condone a high unemployment rate, rising prices of basic consumer items, rising taxes, or heavy exchange controls. Herrera had inherited an administration which had grown out of control through the autonomous institutes and state corporations, and he had inherited the popular expectation that sooner or later the people should see some benefits from the petroleum wealth. His quick removal of government subsidies on many food items and his reimposition of tariffs on food and other consumer items aimed at curbing imports and encouraging domestic production. The measures also produced an immediate and sharp rise in the cost of living.

By late 1982, it seemed apparent that Herrera had made little progress in reining in the profligate administration, although he had to bear the political cost of rising prices. The public generally did not give his administrative team high marks for efficiency. Interior Minister Montes de Oca especially drew criticism for spending much of his time enhancing his political image rather than on the work of the government. Worst of all, the national debt and the debt service continued to grow. In September 1982, *Resumen* estimated that Pérez had left a debt of Bs 110 billion and that Herrera had increased it to more than Bs 200 billion.[28] Not a good record for an administration which had promised austerity.

Labor, hurt by the rising prices and the government's effort to hold wages steady, caused problems for Herrera. President of the *Banco Central de Venezuela* Leopoldo Díaz Bruzual lectured petroleum workers for their demands in January 1982. He pointed out that their average monthly salaries of Bs 9,000 was nearly three times the average income of people in the public administration. The number of workers in the petroleum industry had grown in recent years, but their productivity had not. Other ministers such as Minister of Mines and Energy Humberto Calderón Berti hastened to smooth over some of Díaz Bruzual's harsh words, leaving an impression of division in the administration.[29] In March 1982, the *copeyanos* separated from the *Federación Campesina Venezolana* and charged that the FCV was corrupt and run by professional labor organizers, mostly *adecos*. A *Resumen* article stressed the magnificence of the Caracas headquarters of the FCV, a modern building which had cost Bs 15 million; Armando González, President of the FCV, received the reporter in a luxurious office and was noted to have a diamond tietack. González, a textile worker in the 1930s, had never been a farmer and had spent most of his career as a labor bureaucrat[30].

Charges of syndicate corruption were hardly new or unique to Venezuela. The level of labor-related violence did rise during Herrera's presidency. The two major parties struggled to maintain control of the influential steel workers' unions in Guayana, but the left made considerable inroads. Since 1979, the left had dominated the *Sindicato Unico de Trabajadores de la Industria Siderúrgica y Similares* (SUTISS) which was affiliated with the CTV federation *Fetrametal*, dominated by AD. SUTISS took to court a charge that *Fetrametal* had made a corrupt deal with the management of the national steel industry in the negotiation of the new collective contract. Violence broke out several times between the rival unions, and the steel industry was troubled by the conflict for much of Herrera's presidency.[31] It might be added that COPEI often experienced more difficulty with labor than AD, because most of the unions have been dominated by AD. The steel workers' conflict, however, represented a new and effective challenge by the left.

Urban services fared little better under Herrera than they had under Pérez. In January 1982 Allan Brewer-Carías characterized the Caracas situation as one of crisis.[32] From time to time, disagreements over the terms of collective contracts of transportation workers left *caraqueños* stranded until some compromise could be reached. Public transportation fares rose, and the city's only hope of deliverance lay in the metro, which was scheduled to open in 1983. One urban expert pointed out that part of the traffic problem was related to the lack of planning when new Caracas suburbs were developed. In 1980, there were plans for 10,000 new middle-class apartments in one high-density area. Allowing two cars per family, each car with an average length of four meters, the resulting parade of eight kilometers of cars would funnel into a six-kilometer freeway with three lanes. He predicted that within three years no one would be able to move at peak hours.[33] Complaints also continued about the telephone service in the capital; new lines were desperately needed. In a conflict with American Telephone and Telegraph, the Venezuelan company stopped paying for international calls, a sum which totaled over $1 million a month. ATT hesitated to offend its best Latin America customer until the bill reached $14 million. Then US operators were instructed to refuse to put through collect calls to Venezuela. The resulting uproar quickly had its effect, and the Venezuelan company resumed payments in August 1982.[34]

Despite Herrera's alleged sympathy for the poor, Venezuelans did not sense in him a real concern for their problems or an ability to do something without thought of political gain. As the financial picture darkened in 1982, Herrera proudly touted the Bs 2.2 billion which would be spent to prepare the facilities for the Pan American Games. Another lavish program both acknowledged the government's failure in food production and drew criticism for being politically motivated. In his New Year's Eve speech of December 1981, Herrera announced a system of food bonds, or stamps, to provide nutritional needs for families which earned less than Bs 1,500 a month. He estimated that 2,500,000 Venezuelans would qualify for the Bs 100 subsidy and that the total yearly cost would be Bs 2,907 million. There was talk of setting up a new autonomous institution to administer the program. Cynics referred to the program as the *"bono-voto,"* since it would probably only be in operation for about a year before the 1983 election.In fact, the program still had not been approved by June 1983, but COPEI presidential candidate Rafael Caldera added it to his list of campaign promises.

Pacification of the guerrillas proved a more complicated issue than Herrera had thought. In June 1979, William Niehous, the Owens-Illinois executive who had been kidnapped in 1976, was recovered. He was found on an abandoned ranch by two members of the PTJ along with two of his captors. The captors were killed, and Niehous was immediately rushed out of the country, as a humane gesture to return him to his family. From the United States Niehous stated that he had never seen the faces of his captors, and he was not available for an investigation by Venezuelan courts. Given the general suspicion of official police bodies, Venezuelans believed that there had been some sort of cover-up to shelter politicians in influential places. In late 1982, guerrillas again made the news when a surprise raid in the east resulted in the deaths of twenty-three of the rebels. Venezuelans were both startled at the news of the guerrilla group's size, and rather uneasy at the army's inability to take any prisoners.

Accord with Guyana and Colombia on the long-standing boundary disputes came no closer, and by 1982 Herrera appeared to have abandoned the negotiations. Relations with Cuba worsened after misunderstandings and rhetorical flourishes followed the efforts of numerous Cubans to seek diplomatic asylum in the Venezuelan embassy at Havana in the spring of 1980. Caribbean policy in general was complicated by Herrera's singleminded support for fellow Christian Democrat José Napoleón Duarte in El Salvador. The left characterized the policy as merely following the United States position, always a sensitive accusation. The Andean Pact negotiations made little progress, so the Venezuelan businessmen who had opposed the clauses on joint industrial planning had little to worry about. The high point of Herrera's foreign policy probably came in the spring of 1982, when he supported Argentina in the conflict with Great Britain over the Malvinas (Falkland) islands. Most of the Latin American nations including Cuba were able briefly to share a sense of unity and of outrage at the United States alliance with the British.

Venezuelan public opinion polls did not give Herrera a very high rating when he took office. The 24 percent positive rating he earned in May 1979 had slipped to only 15 percent by December 1980.[35] There were few victories in 1981 or 1982 to raise his popularity. Herrera also suffered from the same problem that had plagued Pérez; the founder of his political party began to undercut him. COPEI struggled to decide on a suitable "pre-candidate" for the 1983 election virtually as soon as the votes had been counted in 1978. Herrera favored his friend, Rafael Montes de Oca, but Rafael Caldera, then in his late sixties, felt the stirrings of ambition and sought the nomination for himself. Herrera was eclipsed almost from the moment he took office.

Acción Democrática also began early to avenge the defeat suffered in 1978. David Morales Bello competed with Jaime Lusinchi for the role of party leader and presidential nominee. Rómulo Betancourt's death in September 1981 meant that the continuing struggles between the newer generations, the discredited Carlos Andrés Pérez, and the few remaining old guard members like Gonzalo Barrios would be unresolved. Betancourt's ghost hovered over the struggle, as the new party boss realignment which he had sponsored before his death succeeded in swinging the labor wing and most of the party to Lusinchi. When Lusinchi won 75 percent of the vote in the party's internal primary in January 1982, he assured his nomination and provided an indirect defeat for Carlos Andrés Pérez. Relations between Pérez and Lusinchi had cooled since the 1978 campaign, and Pérez sided with Morales Bello against Lusinchi and the old guard. Pérez himself did not participate directly in the partisan maneuvers this time.[36]

MAS began with a strong endorsement of their founder and theorist, Teodoro Petkoff. An enormous reception for him in the spring of 1980 drew representatives from all parties and even the US ambassador, William Luers. It seemed as if MAS had finally achieved respectability. Petkoff's popularity was rising in mid-1983 as Venezuelans focused on the weaknesses of both Caldera and Lusinchi. Yet he still seemed more the favorite of party insiders than of labor or the general public. As one Venezuelan political pundit said, "Can you see some illiterate *campesino* from Acarigua voting for someone named Petkoff?" The other major leftist party of the "new generations" — MIR — also had its problems. It divided between two founding members and former guerrillas: Américo Martín and Moisés Moleiro. Martín and his followers supported Petkoff, while Moleiro and his followers endorsed the leftist coalition which nominated José Vicente Rangel. MAS in late 1982 put out the traditional call for the unity of the left, but it seemed likely that the varied personalities would continue to maintain their ideological and personal separateness.

Jorge Olavarría, editor of *Resumen*, rounded out the field of highly visible pre-candidates. Supported by the leftist political party *Causa R*, Olavarría used his magazine to harry the government without mercy on charges of corruption, inefficiency, and political pandering. He further asserted his leftist sympathies, previously unsuspected, when he supported the leftist SUTISS in the Guayana steel disputes. In late June, alleging an irreconcilable break with some of the *Causa R* leaders, Olavarría dropped out of the race.

By 1983, then, both major parties had made an effort to handle the monumental problems associated with the new oil revenues and the anomaly of a strongly centralized government which had no fiscal control over its subordinate agencies. Neither Pérez nor Herrera had been able to form a capable and honest administrative team or to implement administrative reforms. Neither had been able to use the oil revenues in the short run to break some of the economic development bottlenecks which had grown up since World War II. Despite their best efforts, agriculture languished, and the poor made little headway to a more secure subsistence. They both presided over an active foreign policy, especially in the region, but had to face the increasing politicization of foreign policy. Neither seemed to be able to break the impasse on the Colombia and Guyana border disputes.

Herrera and Pérez were victims of history and of their nation's compressed political and economic development. They reaped the harvest from the accumulated problems which previous administrators had not been able or willing to solve. Ironically, great wealth strained the system's weak links more than the average revenues of earlier years had done. Closely tied to the founders of modern politics in Venezuela, Herrera and Pérez had learned to deal with political and ideological dilemmas. Their experience had not prepared them to be efficient managers of complex modern businesses lodged within a complex modern state.

The Cultural Boom

The increased income fueled a cultural boom in Venezuela. Writers, musicians, poets, artists, filmmakers, and historians expressed some of the same self-confidence in their art that diplomats voiced in foreign policy. Greater government revenues allowed massive subsidies for high-cost artistic enterprises such as film-making, national symphony orchestras and national ballet companies. Caracas promoted national artists and groups at home and abroad; the new, aggressive diplomatic projection included sending Venezuelan artists abroad to represent the depth and variety of the naional culture. As in other aspects of the national life, the 1980s brought a certain contraction and a questioning whether even the increased government sponsorship had contributed to a development of an authentic national culture. There can be no doubt, however, that the cultural explosion of the 1970s awakened a general interest in national history, themes, and problems.

At Juan Liscano's urging, the government abolished the ineffectual *Instituto Nacional de Cultura y Bellas Artes* (INCIBA) in 1975. After preliminary studies and recommendations, a new autonomous institution was born to assume the direction and coordination of cultural activities: the *Consejo Nacional de la Cultura* (CONAC). CONAC had a tighter administrative structure, assumed more responsibilities than INCIBA, and had larger budgets. Feuds continued between artists and interests, however, and the new law and institute did no more than begin to address the question of the national direction of culture.

In 1974, the celebration of the one hundred and fiftieth anniversary of the Battle of Ayacucho touched off a new sponsorship of historical studies. The *Biblioteca Ayacucho* was established to publish inexpensive editions of Latin American classics with lengthy introductions. The *Academia Nacional de la Historia,* the *Instituto de Estudios Hispanoamericanos* of UCV, the *Instituto de Investigaciones Económicas y Sociales* of UCAB, and the *Centro de Estudios Latinoamericanos "Rómulo Gallegos,"* among other universities and associations, sponsored historical research teams and increased their publishing activities. Especially notable was the greater interest of scholars in the history of the modern period; UCV's Institute of Historical Research initiated a unique long-term multidisciplinary study of the Castro/Gómez period (1899–1936). *El Nacional,* under the directorship of historian Ramón Velásquez, offered several prizes a year for the best unpublished works on Venezuelan history and subsidized their publication.

Another of Velásquez's projects, the *Fundación para el Rescate del Acervo Documental Venezolano* (Foundation for the Redemption of the Venezuelan Documentary Heritage — *Funres*), came to life in 1975, also at the urging of Virginia Betancourt, director of the Biblioteca Nacional and daughter of the former President. *Funres* aspired to comb archives and libraries all over the world to compile and microfilm material relating to Venezuela. Eventually, Venezuela's *Biblioteca Nacional* would be the depository for a near-definitive collection of documentation on the country's history and culture. With the assistance of a team of collaborators at Northwestern University, (Illinois, USA), bibliographic citations were collected and programmed for retrival through use of computers. In addition to microfilming documents in the United States, British, Dutch, Spanish, French, German, and other national archives, *Funres* also copied and deposited in the *Biblioteca Nacional* complete files of ministerial *Memorias* and sponsored the copying of files of the regional newspapers of Venezuela.

The interest in national history was manifested too in the rash of films made in the 1970s. The films, many made with government credit, enjoyed great popularity and were financially successful. A list of some of the most popular films and their directors shows that most took their inspiration also from national literature:
Cuando quiero llorar no lloro (1973, Mauricio Wallerstein, Mexican director)
La quema de Judas (1974, Román Chalbaud)
Juan Vicente Gómez y su epoca (1975, Manuel De Pedro)
Fiebre (Fever — 1975, Juan Santana)
País portátil (1977, lvan Feo)
El pez que fuma (The Fish that Smokes — 1977, Román Chalbaud)
Se llamaba SN (It's Called SN — 1977, Luis Correa)
El cabito (The Little Corporal — 1977, Daniel Oropeza)

The films often provoked considerable debate over their depiction of events and personalities. Some Venezuelans criticized the showing of *Juan Vicente Gómez y su epoca* as a rendering of homage to the old dictator and indirectly as a glorification of dictatorship. In 1980, Alfredo Anzola's *Manuel* prompted a heated discussion of the role of the Church in Venezuela and of the morality of the younger, more socially conscious priests. The plot portrays Manuel, a priest in an eastern coastal town, who joins with the townspeople and the local fishermen to try to block the construction of a large apartment and tourist complex which would destroy the livelihood and the tranquility of the town. His chief ally is a young married woman, with whom he eventually has an affair. Irate letters to the newspapers objected less to the political content of the film than to the portrayal of a priest as an adulterer. Needless to say, the controversy helped the box office, and, perhaps more important, the film focused on the national situation rather than on Hollywood or New York.

Film-makers also turned to the production of more complex documentary film. In 1975, a showing of new documentaries suggested the range of topics and approaches that Venezuelans were trying out. *Se mueve* (It's Moving — Ivan Feo and Antonio Llerandi) explored body movement through dance and stylized activities. *Campona* (Jesus Enrique Guedez) showed the lives and legends of the small eastern town of Campona, which had originated as a community of escaped slaves. The director showed the present-day poverty of the town as poignantly as he developed the oral historical tradition of its people. The Uruguayan Mario Handler, in *Dos puertos y un cerro* (Two Ports and a Hill), contrasted the life of the port of La Guaira where all manner of manufactured goods entered the country with the port of Puerto Ordaz, near the iron mines of Cerro Bolívar, from which the iron ore was exported. The graphic contrast between the two ports made the point of Venezuela's economic dependence. Other films treated children's games, the theater, newspapers and manipulation of the news, baseball, painting classes, and Avila mountain as a place of recreation and inspiration to national artists. Filmmaker Carlos Oteyza won fame and some critisicm for his documentary *Mayami nuestro* (1982), which depicted Venezuelan tourists and their frantic shopping sprees in Miami, Florida.

Even with the increased profitability of national films and with the improved technical and artistic levels, the film industry still had to struggle. Film-making demanded enormous credits, which became less available as Venezuela's economic malaise set in. Moreover, the film distributors, especially in Caracas which comprised 60 percent of the national market, often preferred to show foreign films and to exclude Venezuelan films or to allow them only brief runs. One of the last actions of Carlos Andrés Pérez as President in February 1979 was to try to remedy the situation. He decreed that "special" foreign films which would be expected to make large profits (such as *Superman* in 1979–80) had to be accompanied by a Venezuelan short film, which would receive 2 percent of the box office receipts. The money was supposed to go to a fund to promote and subsidize national film production. President Pérez also decreed that national films had to remain in distribution for at least eighteen weeks. The distributors protested and retaliated by refusing to show any of the major foreign films throughout much of 1980. The struggle with the distributors continued, but the hopeful signs were the higher quality of Venezuelan productions, their inspiration in national themes and literature, and the willingness of the state to advance credits for the business.

Theater in the 1960s had provided the base on which the film industry had grown. Theater also continued to be popular in the 1970s and 1980s, and CONAC supported various theater groups. The Fifth International Festival of Theater in Caracas in 1981 cost Bs 5 million and hosted twenty-two theater groups from eighteen countries. The outstanding Venezuelan production for the festival was *Fin de round* directed by Rodolfo Santana. The play followed a boxer who came from a poor *barrio* and eventually became the world champion. His friends from the *barrio* simultaneously fought for life in the *barrio*, most of them turning to crime. Popular *salsa* music accompanied the play.

Even television and radio made some advances in displaying national rather than foreign productions. Decrees forced radio stations to play more Venezuelan music and to set aside more hours of the week for educational or cultural programs. By 1982, Venezuela only imported 35 percent of its television programs, in contrast to the 50 percent of imported production in 1973. During the decade, Venezuela became one of the major Latin American television producers, along with Mexico, Brazil, and Argentina. Some of the Venezuelan shows were exported to other countries in Latin America.[37]

Venezuelans were even more proud of the international attention paid to some of their musical groups. The Maracaibo Symphony Orchestra, founded in the early 1970s, imported talented musicians from all over the world. Under the directorship of Eduardo Rahn, they built up an impressive repertory, one quarter of which had been written by Latin American composers. CONAC and the state government of Zulia supported the orchestra as well as the First

Festival of Latin American Contemporary Music, held in Caracas in November 1977. Thirty-six composers from all over the world attended to conduct seminars and give concerts. Caracas also supported a Metropolitan Opera and hosted an opera season. In May 1979 the Caracas Opera Company put on *El caballero de Ledesma* , written by Venezuelan Eric Colón. The opera told the story of the sack of Caracas in 1595 by an English pirate; Alonso Andrea de Ledesma confronted the pirate band alone on the *Avila* and died. Colón, director of the José Angel Lamas Music School, employed a chorus and other traditional forms to present the Venezuelan subject.

The most impressive cultural initiative may well have been the formation of the *Ballet Internacional de Caracas* in 1974. It had the advantage of internationally recognized Vicente Nebrada as artistic director and Zhandra Rodríguez as prima ballerina. A truly international company, it employed Canadians, Swedes, Russians, and United States citizens, among others. Yet Nebrada, Rodríquez, and the Venezuelans in the dance company and the orchestra also ensured that the tone was Venezuelan at heart. The company went on tour in Latin American and the United States in the late 1970s, usually to the accompaniment of critical acclaim. Some of the ballets made use of Venezuelan music — such as *Nuestros valses* (Our Waltzes) with music by Teresa Carreño — or Venezuelan folk dances such as the *joropo* which contributed a flair to the ballet *La Luna* (The Moon).

Two major artistic retrospectives honored traditional and contemporary Venezuelan artists. Jesús Soto received international recognition for his pioneering kinetic sculptures and paintings when the Hirshhorn Gallery in Washington, DC, offered a retrospective exhibition of his work in 1975. In Caracas, 1979 was proclaimed the "Year of Reverón," and the Government sponsored a retrospective of the La Guaira artist's work as well as the publication of books, films, and other exhibitions to analyze his life and work. Alfredo Boulton's *Reverón* was the most impressive publication.

Novelists seemed less prolific than in the 1960s and early 1970s, but some impressive new works were added to the national bibliography. Miguel Otero Silva turned to history for inspiration when he wrote *Lope de Aguirre: principe de la libertad* (Lope de Aguirre: Prince of Liberty — 1979), a fictionalized treatment of the life of one of the *conquistadores* of Venezuela. Of the same generation, Arturo Uslar Pietri added to his cycle of novels which treated twentieth-century Venezuela and its dictators in *Oficio de difuntos* (Ministry of Corpses — 1976). The younger generation of 1958 saw their representative Luis Britto García (born 1940) achieve major recognition with *Abrapalabra* (1980). The experimental form of the book allowed the author to examine the whole of the Venezuelan experience from the conquest to the guerrilla conflict to the urban jungle of pollution and noise. In 1979, the manuscript won the coveted prize of the Cuban *Casa de las Americas* .Other writers also experimented with a mixture of history and fiction. Historian Ramón J. Velásquez contributed to the fierce interest in the Gómez period with his *Confidencias imaginarias de Juan Vicente Gómez* (1979). As the title suggests, the book consists of an extensive monologue in the style of Gómez's speech, and it conveys the old dictator's reasoning and prejudices during his long period of rule.

Uslar, Otero Silva, Britto García, and perhaps even Velásquez may have been heavy for popular taste. Psychiatrist and historical novelist Francisco Herrera Luque brought Venezuelan history to the masses in the 1970s and became a publishing phenomenon. In 1973, his *Boves el Urogallo* about the violent Wars for Independence broke all publishing records in the country. He followed his success with *En la casa del pez que escupe el agua* (In the house of the fish which spits water — 1976), which covered the period from the 1870s to the death of Gómez and included some of the same families which had been in *Boves el Urogallo*. His most ambitious work appeared in 1979, the two-volume *Los amos del valle* (The Masters of the Valley). It focused on the oligarchy which grew up in the Caracas valley during the colonial period and depicted it as cruel and greedy. Herrera Luque's books were eagerly awaited and received. They possessed little literary merit, with their simple and colorful prose, but the author's passion for history and his training in psychiatry made an absorbing mixture and contributed to the effort to interest the Venezuelan youth in their national history. Over 50 percent of the population had been born in the 1960s and could remember little even of the guerrilla conflict of those years. Older Venezuelans who had struggled to overthrow the dictators and to forge the democratic compromise had cause to worry about the younger generations who took both the democratic system and the oil affluence so much for granted.

The Future as History

The most recent decade of Venezuelan history has thrown the problems of a developing nation into sharp relief. Venezuela continues to be blessed by a wealth of resources, an advantageous geographic location, and a relatively homogeneous and small population. Yet neither a gradual increase in government revenues until 1973 nor the massive rush of funds after 1973 has been sufficient in itself to break the economic bottlenecks and launch a self-sustaining economic growth. Dependence on oil revenues, and on the price of oil in the international market, has grown. Venezuela has also become more dependent on imported intermediate industrial products, raw materials, and consumer products. The modern capital-intensive industries which have promised an economically diversified economy have to date not become profitable. Some of them may never do so, remaining costly monuments to the western model of industrialization and development. The rapid population growth in recent years has placed a great demand on the government for services such as schools and health care for the young.

Although the society is culturally homogeneous relative to that of, say, Mexico or Peru, great gaps exist between the rural and urban cultures. Life in Caracas bears little resemblance to that in Bruzual on the Orinoco or even San Cristóbal in the mountains of Táchira. In some ways, the quality of life and community may be higher in Bruzual or San Cristóbal or Carúpano; there is less pollution, noise, crime, anonymity. There is also less health care education, and electricity, and there are fewer job opportunities. The effort at developing community pride and structures still has not checked the dominance of Caracas in nearly all aspects of political and economic life. As in many developing nations, the greatest threat to national unity and pride is the great disparity between the wealthy and the poor; and also as in many developing nations, the disparity in Venezuela is both vertical and horizontal. The wealthier half of the population participates fully in the modern economy and lives fairly well, although the second quarter of the population probably has a fairly weak hold on a secure economic future. The poorer half of the population experiences an uncertain present and even more uncertain future. Since the metropolitan area of Caracas and the north-central industrial corridor stretching from Caracas to Valencia controls most of the national jobs, power, and wealth, the poverty is horizontal as well. Some regions are quite wealthy, others quite poor.

Venezuela's political democracy has had great success in providing stability and an opportunity for a degree of political participation for a large share of the population. Yet the Pact of Punto Fijo of 1958 has suffered some erosion in the last decade as the old guard of politicians faces challenges to its system and to its dominance. Challenges come from the left, which did not participate in the original pact, and from the politicians who have matured within the major parties since 1958. The universal vote and the structures of political democracy are not sufficient in themselves. The system must be made to work. The administration has to implement policies and channel services to all sectors and regions of the country with a minimum of waste and corruption if it is to retain the confidence of the population. The left and the young technocrats have become restless enough now to assert that they can provide an administrative stability and coherence that the generation of Betancourt and Caldera could not. To date, the armed forces have not argued for their unique mission and ability to rule. They have, however, taken a great interest in the delicate boundary negotiations and in the nation's frontier policy. Some geopolitical theories have made them sensitive to the advisability of projecting a national presence beyond the borders and of rejecting any shrinkage of the national territory. The left, especially the MAS, has advocated drawing the military men more actively into politics. The weakening of the political rules of the game which were negotiated in 1958 may leave a situation in which the preference of the armed forces carries greater weight.

Venezuela was first thrust on to the international stage by the oil industry and in more recent times has taken initiatives to remain at the center of the action. Yet, much of Venezuela's aggressive foreign is defensive at the core, trying to maintain oil prices and markets and to diversify exports. Nor can the issue of national security be overlooked by a mineral-rich nation with a long, exposed coastline. The grandest objective — to be the linchpin which unites the Caribbean and the South American continent — must remain a dream if the domestic economic and political problems remain unresolved.

Artists and writers have contributed in the last hundred years to the country's having a greater sense of a national identity. And in the last decade the mass media and films have appealed to a wider segment of the population and have fomented an enthusiasm for the study of history. Music, dance, painting, and theater have been fed by the creole past and the universal, western culture of the present. A self-conscious national identity has still probably not overcome the economic and cultural gap between Caracas and the hinterlands. And much of the rich folk culture of the rural areas and small towns has been lost or has failed to connect with the elite culture which owes its inspiration more to the contemporary urban scene. The continuing development of arts and literature probably depends considerably on the continuation of state subsidies in a nation with such a small population.

What choices and paths for Venezuela in the next decade or so? Historians may be excused from the risky job of predicting the future. Venezuelan writer and critic Juan Liscano sums up thoughts on the future in the following words:

"This country, leader for the moment of the Third World, will continue being a leader while petroleum constitutes the principal source of energy. 'Afterwards' will depend on what we have done during the epoch of abundance."[38]

NOTES

1. Luis Britto García, *Abrapalabra* (Caracas: Monte Avila, 1980), p. 585.
2. *Latin America Weekly Report*, 8 Jan. 1982.
3. Ibid., 19 March 1982; *The Washington Post*, 22 Feb. 1983.
4. Inter-American Development Bank, *Economic and Social Progress in Latin America: The External Sector* (Washington DC: Inter-American Development Bank, 1982), p. 24.
5. *Latin America Weekly Report*, 17 Sept. 1982
6. Ibid., 9 April 1982.
7. Ibid., 29 Oct. 1982.
8. Ibid., 3 Dec. 1982.
9. John D. Martz, "Approaches to Agricultural Policy in Venezuela," *Inter-American Economic Affairs*, 34 (Winter, 1980), pp. 43-5, 49.
10. Alfredo Peña, *Conversaciones con Carlos Andrés Pérez* (Caracas: Editorial Ateneo de Caracas, 1979), vol. 1, passim.
11. *Latin America*, 10 May 1974.
12. José Antonio Gil Yepes, *El reto de las élites* (Madrid: Editorial Tecnos, 1978), p. 91.
13. *Latin America*, 25 June 1976.
14. Ibid., 8 July 1977.
15. Ibid., 28 June 1974.
16. Ibid., 30 July 1976.
17. Ibid., 25 April 1975.
18. Ibid., 20 Feb. 1976.
19. Ibid., 29 July 1977.
20. Ibid., 26 Aug. 1977.
21. Ibid, 8 Dec. 1978; 5 May 1977; 27 Jan. 1978.
22. Ibid, 26 May 1978.
23. Robert J. Alexander, *Rómulo Betancourt and the Transformation of Venezuela* (New Brunswick, NJ: Transaction Books, 1982), pp. 632-3.
24. & 25. Ibid.
26. Alfredo Peña, *Conversaciones con Luis Herrera Campíns* (Caracas: Editorial Ateneo de Caracas, 1978), pp. 13-31 passim.
27. *Latin America*, 16 March 1979.
28. *Resumen*, 19 Sept. 1982, p. 38.
29. Ibid., 3 Jan. 1982, p. 17.
30. Ibid., 21 March 1982, p. 30; 28 March 1982, pp. 32-4.
31. *Latin America Weekly Report*, 19 March 1982.
32. *Resumen*, 3 Jan. 1982, pp. 33-42.
33. *El Diario de Caracas, "Arquitectura y construccion"* supplement, 18 May 1980, p. 23.
34. *Newsweek*, 16 Aug. 1982, p. 9.
35. *Resumen*, 22 March 1981, p. 10.
36. *Latin America Weekly Report*, 29 Jan. 1982.
37. *Campus Report* (Stanford University), 19 Jan. 1983, p. 9.
38. Juan Liscano, "La cultura en los últimos cincuenta años," in Ramon J. Velásquez *et al., Venezuela Moderna* (Caracas: Editorial Ariel and Fundación Eugenio Mendoza, 1979), p. 961.

PRESIDENTS OF VENEZUELA SINCE 1871

Antonio Guzmán Blanco	1871–7
Francisco Linares Alcántara	1877–8
Provisional Presidents	1878–80
Antonio Guzmán Blanco	1880–4
Joaquín Crespo	1884–6
Antonio Guzmán Blanco	1886–8
Juan Pablo Rojas Paúl	1888–90
Raimundo Andueza Palacio	1890–2
Provisional Presidents	1892–4
Joaquín Crespo	1894–8
Ignacio Andrade	1898–9
Cipriano Castro	1899–1908
Juan Vicente Gómez	1908–29
Juan Bautista Pérez	1929–31
Juan Vicente Gómez	1931–5
Eleazar López Contreras	1935–41
Isaías Medina Angarita	1941–5
*Rómulo Betancourt	1945–8
Rómulo Gallegos	1948
*Carlos Delgado Chalbaud	1948–50
*Germán Suárez Flamerich	1950–2
Marcos Pérez Jiménez	1952–8
*Wolfgang Larrazábal	1958
Rómulo Betancourt	1959–64
Raúl Leoni	1964–9
Rafael Caldera	1969–74
Carlos Andrés Pérez	1974–9
Luis Herrera Campíns	1979–84
Jaime Lusinchi	1984–

*Presided over a junta or collegiate government

STATISTICAL TABLES

1

PETROLEUM AND GOVERNMENT INCOME
(*millions of bolívares*)

	Govt. Income (millions Bs.)	Govt. Income from Petroleum (millions Bs.)	Petroleum as % of Ordinary Revenues	Average realized price per barrel (US $)
1958	4,705	2,559	54.4	2.48
1959	5,441	3,102	57.0	2.19
1960	4,967	2,891	58.2	2.08
1961	5,792	3,129	54.0	2.10
1962	5,910	3,103	52.5	2.06
1963	6,597	3,474	52.7	2.03
1964	7,133	4,654	65.2	1.94
1965	7,265	4,720	65.0	1.88
1966	7,751	4,912	63.4	1.88
1967	8,539	5,666	66.4	1.85
1968	8,775	5,791	66.0	1.86
1969	8,661	5,443	62.8	1.81
1970	9,498	5,708	60.1	1.84
1971	11,637	7,643	65.7	2.35
1972	12,192	7,884	64.7	2.52
1973	16,054	11,182	69.7	3.71
1974	42,558	36,448	85.6	10.53
1975	40,898	31,655	77.4	10.99
1976	38,130	28,024	73.5	11.25
1977	40,474	29,421	72.6	12.61
1978	40,123	25,810	64.3	12.04
1979	48,339	33,377	69.0	17.69
1980	62,697	45,331	72.3	26.44
1981	92,656	70,886	76.5	29.71

Sources: Banco Central de Venezuela, *La economía venezolana en los últimos treinta y cinco años* (Caracas: Banco Central de Venezuela, 1978), pp. 82, 273; *Anuario de series estadísticas 1981* (Caracas: Banco Central de Venezuela, 1982), pp. 72, 343.

2

VALUE OF VENEZUELAN EXPORTS FOB
(*millions of US $*)

	Petroleum	Iron	Rest of the economy
1958	2,299	120	53
1959	2,128	129	60
1960	2,149	158	50
1961	2,213	125	46
1962	2,343	113	51
1963	2,336	93	71
1964	2,341	107	55
1965	2,306	123	54
1966	2,221	123	60
1967	2,333	118	82
1968	2,342	103	79
1969	2,280	130	88
1970	2,380	147	113
1971	2,905	142	103
1972	2,929	131	142
1973	4,450	170	164
1974	10,762	273	255
1975	8,493	269	214
1976	8,802	256	284
1977	9,225	168	268
1978	8,705	139	330
1979	13,673	140	547
1980	18,301	149	825
1981	19,094	170	814

Sources: Banco Central de Venezuela, *La economía venezolana en los últimos treinta y cinco años* (Caracas: Banco Central de Venezuela, 1978), p. 326; *Anuario de series estadísticas 1981* (Caracas: Banco Central de Venezuela, 1982), pp. 29, 31, 47.

3

VENEZUELAN DEBT AND DEBT SERVICE
(*millions of bolívares*)

	External	Internal	Floating	Total	Service on National Debt
1958	680	488		1,168	220
1959	501	824		1,325	282
1960	986	1,186	406	2,578	543
1961	814	1,557	406	2,777	1,381
1962	746	1,424	406	2,576	1,318
1963	691	1,323	216	2,230	924
1964	855	925	150	1,930	904
1965	1,083	989	56	2,128	547
1966	1,332	1,003	19	2,354	556
1967	1,546	1,283		2,829	510
1968	1,881	1,647		3,528	568
1969	2,183	2,200		4,383	525
1970	2,931	2,560		5,491	693
1971	3,770	2,712		6,482	1,471
1972	4,340	2,870		7,210	1,361
1973	5,201	3,233		8,434	1,538
1974	4,709	5,467		10,176	2,226
1975	6,123	6,778		12,901	2,374
1976	14,146	8,251		22,397	4,578
1977	20,275	14,464		34,739	5,622
1978	31,186	17,913		49,099	5,792
1979	35,326	19,207		54,533	7,967
1980	41,516	19,237		60,753	11,801
1981	40,795	25,859		66,654	15,081

Sources: Banco Central de Venezuela, *La economía venezolana en los últimos treinta y cinco años* (Caracas: Banco Central de Venezuela, 1978), pp. 280–3., *Anuario de series estadísticas 1981* (Caracas: Banco Central de Venezuela, 1982), pp. 92, 104.

Statistical Tables

4

GOVERNMENT EXPENDITURES BY SECTOR (%)

	Services	Defense	Social	Economic	*Other	Total expenditures (millions Bs)
1960	7.4	6.6	26.1	40.1	16.8	6,147
1961	6.3	8.2	24.5	34.3	26.7	7,075
1962	6.3	8.1	26.1	29.2	30.4	6,258
1963	8.1	9.3	26.4	31.8	24.4	6,590
1964	7.3	9.1	29.3	31.0	23.4	7,100
1965	7.1	10.0	32.7	31.1	19.1	7,400
1966	7.5	9.9	33.2	29.7	19.7	7,924
1967	7.6	10.2	35.4	29.9	18.9	8,605
1968	9.1	9.7	29.3	33.1	18.8	9,014
1969	7.7	8.9	29.5	36.2	17.7	9,826
1970	8.0	8.7	32.2	33.5	17.6	10,295
1971	7.8	9.7	30.3	31.2	21.0	11,915
1972	7.7	10.2	31.5	30.2	20.4	12,842
1973	7.6	9.1	33.3	31.9	18.1	15,042
1974	4.2	4.9	18.3	63.1	9.5	40,059
1975	5.9	5.7	20.4	51.0	17.0	40,370
1976	7.2	8.7	27.2	42.1	14.8	39,468
1977	7.3	4.7	28.8	39.9	19.3	52,041
1978	8.7	5.4	28.9	35.3	21.7	49,905
1979	9.4	6.3	32.2	19.3	32.8	47,569
1980	10.3	4.7	30.7	27.2	27.1	68,551
1981	8.8	3.7	28.3	34.4	24.8	92,132

Sources: Banco Central de Venezuela, *La economía venezolana en los últimos treinta y cinco años* (Caracas: Banco Central de Venezuela, 1978), p. 277; Banco Central de Venezuela, *Anuario de series estadísticas 1981* (Caracas: Banco Central de Venezuela, 1982), p. 74.

*Includes interest and amortization of public and administrative debt, transfers to regional governments, acquisition of financial assets and funds to finance exports and OPEC.

5

SECTORAL COMPOSITION OF GDP

	Total GDP*	Agriculture	Petroleum	Mining	Total Primary	Secondary	Tertiary
1958	24,164	1,576	6,708	379	8,663	4,871	10,630
1959	26,065	1,642	7,154	420	9,216	5,461	11,388
1960	27,103	1,974	7,325	463	9,762	5,365	11,976
1961	28,475	1,995	7,493	358	9,846	5,441	13,188
1962	31,050	2,071	8,214	333	10,618	5,790	14,642
1963	33,177	2,175	8,336	282	10,793	6,078	16,306
1964	36,407	2,357	8,734	390	11,481	6,826	18,100
1965	38,543	2,484	8,915	425	11,824	7,332	19,387
1966	39,444	2,605	8,653	427	11,685	7,556	20,203
1967	41,033	2,746	9,093	411	12,250	7,951	20,832
1968	43,167	2,837	9,278	366	12,481	8,763	21,923
1969	44,782	3,025	9,222	454	12,701	9,039	23,042
1970	50,159	3,502	9,453	649	13,604	10,943	24,789
1971	51,748	3,592	8,849	611	13,052	11,739	26,425
1972	53,380	3,543	8,173	576	12,292	12,766	28,007
1973	56,955	3,730	8,573	743	13,046	13,890	29,581
1974	60,285	3,958	7,455	852	12,265	14,585	32,611
1975	63,416	4,236	5,891	817	10,944	15,828	35,678
1976	68,353	4,083	5,800	675	10,558	17,930	38,781
1977	74,796	4,403	5,505	572	10,480	19,530	42,678
1978	77,161	4,682	5,330	581	10,593	20,767	44,097
1979	77,742	4,792	5,897	627	11,316	20,901	43,127
1980	76,612	4,837	5,481	637	10,955	20,580	42,470
1981	77,369	4,766	5,317	619	10,702	20,511	43,460

Source: Banco Central de Venezuela, *La economía venezolana en los últimos treinta y cinco años* (Caracas: Banco Central de Venezuela, 1978), pp. 37,41, *Anuario series de estadísticas 1981* (Caracas: Banco Central de Venezuela, 1982), p. 294.
*Millions of *bolívares* at constant 1957 prices through 1969, then at constant 1968 prices for 1970–81.

6

DISTRIBUTION OF LABOR FORCE (%)

	1950	1961	1971	1981*
Professionals, technicians	3.96	5.91	8.69	n.a.
Managers, administrators, directors	6.98	1.66	2.83	n.a.
Office employees	4.19	7.23	9.14	n.a.
Sales employees	3.14	10.52	11.42	22.00
Farmers, cattlemen, fishermen, hunters	41.11	32.73	22.75	13.9
Miners, stonecutters	0.34	0.84	0.68	1.2
Communications and transportation employees	4.88	7.05	6.10	6.9
Artisans and factory workers	22.70	21.31	22.13	14.8
Services, sports and leisure employees	11.90	11.92	14.91	25.4
Looking for work for first time	0.80	0.83	1.36	0.9

Sources: Chi-Yi Chen and Michel Picouet, *Dinámica de la población: caso de Venezuela* (Caracas: Edición UCAB-ORSTOM, 1979), p. 464; Banco Central de Venezuela, *Anuario de series estadísticas 1981* (Caracas: Banco Central de Venezuela, 1982), pp. 406–7.

*The figures for 1981 are for the first six months of that year; they are not strictly comparable with the earlier series since they do not specify professionals, technicians, managers, administrators, directors, and office employees. "Sales employees" includes employees in commerce and financial institutions. Additionally in 1981, construction workers are a separate category (8.3 percent) as are workers in the sectors of electricity, gas, water, and sanitary service (1.1 percent).

7

WHOLESALE PRICE INDICES
(*base year 1968*)

	National products	Imported products	Food	General index of wholesale prices
1958	87.3	65.7	82.1	78.3
1959	90.4	66.7	85.9	80.4
1960	90.1	68.0	84.6	81.0
1961	90.6	69.9	85.7	82.3
1962	90.3	77.4	85.7	86.2
1963	90.2	82.7	87.3	88.9
1964	95.0	83.4	95.5	92.8
1965	98.2	91.5	96.2	95.7
1966	98.1	95.5	96.9	97.0
1967	98.5	98.1	97.3	98.3
1968	100.0	100.0	100.0	100.0
1969	101.2	102.1	101.4	101.6
1970	101.7	105.2	101.8	103.1
1971	104.1	110.4	104.2	107.7
1972	106.9	115.4	108.6	110.4
1973	114.6	122.4	120.2	117.8
1974	133.9	142.8	136.1	137.5
1975	146.3	161.1	154.8	156.3
1976	165.3	170.9	169.7	167.5
1977	185.8	183.5	*184.6	184.9
1978	199.8	196.5	198.5	198.5
1979	220.6	211.4	216.9	216.8
1980	271.2	244.3	278.2	260.3
1981	312.0	273.3	314.2	296.3

Sources: Banco Central de Venezuela, *La economía venezolana en los últimos treinta y cinco años* (Caracas: Banco Central de Venezuela, 1978), pp. 290–1, 302; Banco Central de Venezuela, *Anuario de series estadísticas 1981* (Caracas: Banco Central de Venezuela, 1982), pp. 439–42.

*The index for food from 1977 through 1981 is for "processed food," which includes: oils and fats, animal food, meat, sweets, crackers, ice cream, fruits, flours and meals, fish, sugar cane products, dairy products, and miscellaneous.

BIBLIOGRAPHY:
TWENTIETH-CENTURY VENEZUELA

The following list is a selective one of books and dissertations consulted. The reader should refer to general indexes such as the *Handbook of Latin American Studies* and to John Lombardi, Germán Carrera Damas, and Roberta Adams, *Venezuelan History: a Comprehensive Working Bibliography* for further sources.

Abouhamad, Jeannette. *Los hombres de Venezuela: sus necesidades, sus aspiraciones*. Caracas: Universidad Central de Venezuela, 1970.

Acción Democrática. *Acción Democrática: doctrina y programa*. Caracas: Acción Democrática, 1963.

——. *Rómulo Betancourt: pensamiento y acción*. Mexico: n.p., 1951.

Aguirre, Jesus M. and Bisbal, Marcelino. *El nuevo cine venezolano*. Caracas: Editorial Ateneo de Caracas, 1980.

Alexander, Robert J. *The Communist Party of Venezuela*. Stanford, Calif.: Hoover Institution Press, 1969.

——. *Rómulo Betancourt and the Transformation of Venezuela*. New Brunswick, NJ: Transaction Books, 1982.

——. *The Venezuelan Democratic Revolution*. New Brunswick, NJ: Rutgers University Press, 1964.

Allen, Henry J. *Venezuela: A Democracy*. New York: Doubleday, Doran & Co., 1941.

Allen, Loring. *Venezuelan Economic Development: A Politico-Economic Analysis*. Greenwich, Conn.: JAI Press, 1977.

Alvarez, Frederico et al. *La izquierda venezolana y las elecciones del 1973*. Caracas: Síntesis Dosmil, 1974.

Aranda, Sergio. *La economía venezolana*. Mexico: Siglo Veintiuno Editores, 1977.

Armas Chitty, J.A. de. *"El Mocho" Hernández: papeles de su archivo*. Caracas: Instituto de Antropología y Historia, Universidad Central de Venezuela, 1978.

——. *Vida política de Caracas en el siglo XIX*. Caracas: Editorial América Libre, 1976.

Arnove, Robert F. *Student Alienation: A Venezuelan Study*. New York: Praeger, 1971.

Baloyra, Enrique A. and Martz, John D. *Political Attitudes in Venezuela: Societal Cleavages and Political Opinion*. Austin: University of Texas Press, 1979.

Banco Central de Venezuela. *La economía venezolana en los ultimos treinta y cinco anos*. Caracas: Banco Central de Venezuela, 1978.

Belrose, Maurice. *La sociedad venezolana en su novela, 1890–1935*. Maracaibo: Centro de Estudios Literarias, Universidad del Zulia, 1979.

Bernstein, Harry. *Venezuela and Colombia*. Englewood Cliffs, NJ: Prentice-Hall, 1964.

Betancourt, Rómulo. *América latina: democracia e integración*. Caracas: Editorial Seix Barral, 1978.

——. *Venezuela, política y petróleo.* 3rd ed. Caracas: Editorial Senderos, 1969.

——. *Venezuela's Oil.* London: George Allen and Unwin, 1978.

Blanco Muñoz, Agustín. *La conspiración cívico militar: Guairazo, Barcelonazo, Carupanazo y Porteñazo.* Caracas: FACES-UCV/ Editorial Ateneo de Caracas, 1980.

——. *La lucha armada: hablan 5 jefes.* Caracas: FACES-UCV/Editorial Ateneo de Caracas, 1980.

——. *La lucha armada: hablan 6 comandantes.* Caracas: FACES-UCV/ Editorial Ateneo de Caracas, 1981.

——. *El 23 de enero: habla la conspiración.* Caracas: FACES-UCV/ Editorial Ateneo de Caracas, 1980.

Blank, David Eugene. *Politics in Venezuela.* Boston, Mass.: Little, Brown & Co., 1973.

Boersner, Demetrio. *Venezuela y el caribe: presencia cambiante.* Caracas: Monte Avila, 1978.

Bond, Robert Duane. "Business Associations and Interest Politics in Venezuela: the FEDECAMARAS and the Determination of National Economic Policies." Ph.D. dissertation, Vanderbilt University, 1975.

——, ed. *Contemporary Venezuela and its Role in International Affairs.* New York: Council on Foreign Relations and New York University Press, 1977.

——. "Venezuela, Brazil, and the Amazon Basin." In *Latin American Foreign Policies: Global and Regional Dimension*, edited by Elizabeth G. Ferris and Jennie K. Lincoln. Boulder, Colo.: Westview Press, 1981.

Bonilla, Frank. *The Failure of Elites.* Cambridge, Mass.: MIT Press, 1970.

Bonilla, Frank and Silva Michelena, José A. *A Strategy for Research on Social Policy.* Cambridge, Mass.: MIT Press, 1967.

Brewer-Carías, Allan. *Estudios sobre la reforma administrativa.* Caracas: Universidad Central de Venezuela, 1980.

——. *Política estado y administración pública.* Caracas: Editorial Ateneo de Caracas and Editorial Juridica Venezolana, 1979.

——. *Cambio político y reforma del estado en Venezuela.* Madrid: Editorial Tecnos, 1975.

—— and Izquierdo Corser, Norma. *Estudios sobre la regionalización en Venezuela.* Caracas: Universidad Central de Venezuela, 1977.

Briceño, Olga. *Cocks and Bulls in Caracas: How We Live in Venezuela.* Boston, Mass.: Houghton Mifflin Co., 1945.

Brito Figueroa, Federico. *Historia económica y social de Venezuela.* 2 vols. Caracas: Universidad Central de Venezuela, 1966.

Buitrago Segura, Luis. *Caracas la Horrible.* Caracas: Editorial Ateneo de Caracas, 1980.

Burggraaff, Winfield J. *The Venezuelan Armed Forces in Politics, 1935–1959.* Columbia: University of Missouri Press, 1972.

Calderón Berti, Humberto. *La nacionalización petrolera: visión de una proceso.* Caracas: n.p., 1978.

Cãnizales Márquez, José. *Así somos los venezolanos.* Caracas: Editorial Fuentes, 1979.

238   *Bibliography: Twentieth-Century Venezuela*

Cannon, Mark W.; Fosler, R. Scott; and Witherspoon, Robert. *Urban Government for Valencia, Venezuela.* New York: Praeger, 1973.

Carpio Castillo, Rubén. *Geopolítica de Venezuela.* Caracas: Editorial Ariel-Seix Barral Venezolana, 1981.

Carrera Damas, Germán. *Historia contemporánea de Venezuela: bases metodológicas.* Caracas: Universidad Central de Venezuela, 1979.

——. *Una nación llamada Venezuela.* Caracas: Universidad Central de Venezuela, 1980.

Carreras, Charles. "United States Economic Penetration of Venezuela and the Effects on Diplomacy: 1895–1906." Ph.D. dissertation, University of North Carolina, 1971.

Castellanos, Rafael Ramón. *La sublevación militar del 7 de abril de 1928.* Caracas: Italgrafica, 1978.

Castro Rojas, Gaspar. *Como secuestramos a Niehous.* Caracas: Editorial Fuentes, 1979.

Chen, Chi-Yi and Picouet, Michel. *Dinámica de la población: caso de Venezuela.* Caracas: Edición UCAB-ORSTOM, 1979.

——. *Desarrollo regional-urbano y ordenamiento del territorio: mito y realidad.* Caracas: Universidad Católica Andrés Bello, 1978.

——. *Economía social del trabajo.* Caracas: Instituto de Investigaciones Económicas, Universidad Católica Andrés Bello, 1969.

Chocrón, Isaac. *Tres fechas claves del teatro contemporáneo en Venezuela.* Caracas: Fundación para la Cultura y las Artes del Distrito Federal, 1978.

Clinton, Daniel Joseph [Thomas Rourke]. *Gómez, Tyrant of the Andes.* New York: Greenwood Press, 1936.

Cortina, Alfredo. *Breve historia de la radio en Venezuela.* Caracas: Dirección General de Cultura de la GDF y Fundarte, 1978.

Crist, Raymond and Leahy, Edward. *Venezuela: Search for a Middle Ground.* New York: Van Nostrand Reinhold Co., 1969.

Dehollain, Paulina and Pérez Schael, Irene. *Venezuela desnutrida.* Caracas: Equinoccio, n.d.

Díaz Rangel, Eleazar. *Miraflores fuera de juego.* Caracas: Editorial Lisbona, 1978.

Donnelly, Vernon C. "Juan Vicente Gómez and the Venezuelan Worker, 1919–1929." Ph.D. dissertation, University of Maryland, 1975.

Doyle Joseph. "Venezuela 1958. Transition from Dictatorship to Democracy." Ph.D. dissertation, George Washington University, 1967.

Duffy, Edward. "The Politics of Expediency: US-Venezuelan Relations under Gómez." Ph.D. dissertation, Pennsylvania State University, 1969.

Ellner, Steve. *Los partidos políticos y su disputa por el control del movimiento sindical en Venezuela, 1936–1948.* Caracas: Universidad Católica Andrés Bello, 1980.

Equipo Proceso Político. *CAP 5 años: un juicio crítico.* Caracas: Editorial Ateneo de Caracas, 1978.

Ewell, Judith. *The Indictment of a Dictator: The Extradition and Trial of Marcos Pérez Jiménez.* College Station: Texas A & M University Press, 1981.

Friedman, John. *Regional Development Policy: A Case Study of Venezuela.*

Cambridge, Mass.: MIT Press, 1966.

Fuenmayor, Juan Bautista. *Historia de la Venezuela política contemporánea.* 5 vols. to date. Caracas: n.p., 1978-9.

——. *1928-1948: veinte años de política.* 2nd ed. Caracas: n.p., 1979.

Fundación John Boulton. *Política y economía en Venezuela, 1810-1976.* Caracas: Fundación John Boulton, 1976.

García Ponce, Guillermo. *El país, la izquierda y las elecciones de 1978* Caracas: n.p., 1977.

García Ponce, Servando. *La imprenta en la historia de Venezuela.* Caracas: Monte Avila, 1975.

Gil Yepes, José Antonio. *The Challenge of Venezuelan Democracy.* New Brunswick, NJ: Transaction Books, 1981.

Gilmore, Robert. *Caudillism and Militarism in Venezuela, 1810-1910.* Athens, Ohio: Ohio University Press, 1964.

González Abreu, Manuel. *Venezuela foranea.* Caracas: Universidad Central de Venezuela, 1980.

Groves, Roderick. "Administrative Reform in Venezuela, 1958-1963." Ph.D. dissertation, University of Wisconsin, 1965.

Hassan, Mostafa. *Economic Growth and Employment Problems in Venezuela: An Analysis of an Oil Based Economy.* New York: Praeger, 1975.

Heaton, Louis E. *The Agricultural Development of Venezuela.* New York: Praeger, 1969.

Herman, Donald. *Christian Democracy in Venezuela.* Chapel Hill: University of North Carolina Press, 1980.

Herrera Campíns, Luis *et al. Sociedad comunitaria y participación.* Caracas: Editorial Ateneo de Caracas, 1979.

Hood, Miriam. *Gunboat Diplomacy 1895-1905: Great Power Pressure in Venezuela.* London: George Allen and Unwin, 1975.

Izaguirre, Rodolfo. *El cine en Venezuela.* Caracas: Dirección General de Cultura de la Gobernación del Distrito Federal and Fundación para la Cultura y las Artes del Distrito Federal, 1978.

Izard, Miguel. *Series estadísticas para la historia de Venezuela.* Mérida: Universidad de Los Andes, 1970.

Kamen-Kay, Dorothy. *Venezuelan Folkways.* Detroit: Blaine-Ethridge Books, 1976.

Karst, Kenneth; Schwartz, Murray; and Schwartz, Audrey. *The Evolution of Law in the Barrios of Caracas.* Los Angeles: Latin American Center, UCLA, 1973.

Kelley, Russell L. "The Venezuelan Senate: A Legislative Body in the Context of Development." Ph.D. dissertation, University of New Mexico, 1973.

Kolb, Glen. *Democracy and Dictatorship in Venezuela, 1945-1958.* Hamden, Conn.: Archon Books, 1974.

La Belle, Thomas. *The New Professional in Venezuela Secondary Education.* Los Angeles: Latin American Center, UCLA, 1973.

Lanz Rodríguez, Carlos. *El caso Niehous y la corrupción administrativa.* Caracas: Editorial Fuentes, 1979.

Larrazábal, Oswaldo. *10 novelas venezolanas*. Caracas: Monte Avila, 1972.
Larrazábal, Radames. *Monopolios Nacionales*. Valencia: Vadell Hermanos, 1978.
Levine, Daniel H. *Conflict and Political Change in Venezuela*. Princeton: Princeton University Press, 1973.
——. *Religion and Politics in Latin America: The Catholic Church in Venezuela and Colombia*. Princeton: Princeton University Press, 1981.
Levy, Fred D., Jr. *Economic Planning in Venezuela*. New York: Praeger, 1968.
Lieuwen, Edwin. *Petroleum in Venezuela: A History*. Berkeley: University of California Press, 1954.
——. *Venezuela*. 2nd ed. New York: Oxford University Press, 1965.
Liscano, Juan. *Rómulo Gallegos y su tiempo*. Caracas: Monte Avila, 1979.
Liss, Sheldon. *Diplomacy and Dependency: Venezuela, the United States, and the Americas*. Salisbury, NC: Documentary Publications, 1978.
Lombardi, John. *Venezuela: The Search for Order, the Dream of Progress*. New York: Oxford University Press, 1982.
——; Carrera Damas, Germán; and Adams, Roberta *et al. Venezuelan History: A Comprehensive Working Bibliography*. Boston: G.K. Hall & Co., 1977.
López Guiñazu, Antonio. "Modernization in Venezuela, 1950–1961." Ph.D. dissertation, Colorado State University, 1970.
Machado, Luis A. *El derecho a ser inteligente*. Caracas: Seix Barral, 1978.
——. *La revolución de la inteligencia*. Caracas: Seix Barral, 1975.
Margolies, Luise, ed. *The Venezuelan Peasant in Country and City*. Caracas: EDIVA, 1979.
Marrero, Levi. *Atlas geográfico y económico: Venezuela visualizada*. Caracas: Cultura Venezolana, 1978.
Marsland, William D. and Amy. *Venezuela Through its History*. New York: Thomas Y. Crowell Co., 1954.
Martín, Américo. *Los peces gordos*. Valencia: Vadell Hermanos, 1979.
Martínez Terrero, José. *La publicidad en Venezuela*. Valencia: Vadell Hermanos, 1979.
Martz, John D. *Acción Democrática. Evolution of a Modern Political Party in Venezuela*. Princeton: Princeton University Press, 1966.
—— and Myers, David J., ed. *Venezuela, the Democratic Experience*. New York: Praeger, 1977.
Mayobre, José Antonio. *Las inversiones extranjeras en Venezuela*. Caracas: Monte Avila, 1970.
Medina, Jose R. *50 años de literatura venezolana*. Caracas: Monte Avila, 1969.
Moleiro, Moisés. *La izquierda y su proceso*. Caracas: Ediciones Centauro, 1977.
——. *El partido del pueblo: crónica de un fraude*. 2nd ed. Valencia: Vadell Hermanos, 1979.
Morón, Guillermo. *A History of Venezuela*. London: George Allen and Unwin, 1964.

Nieves, David. *La tortura y el crimen político*. Caracas: Poseidon, 1979.

Nuñez Tenorio, J.R. *La izquierda y la lucha por el poder en Venezuela*. Caracas: Editorial Ateneo de Caracas, 1979.

Pasquali, Antonio. *Communicación y cultura de masas*. Caracas: Monte Avila, 1977.

Peattie, Lisa Redfield. *The View from the Barrio*. Ann Arbor: University of Michigan Press, 1970.

Peña, Alfredo. *Conversaciones con Américo Martín*. Caracas: Editorial Ateneo de Caracas, 1978.

——. *Conversaciones con Carlos Andrés Pérez*. 2 vols. Caracas: Editorial Ateneo de Caracas, 1979.

——. *Conversaciones con Douglas Bravo*. Caracas: Editorial Ateneo de Caracas, 1978.

——. *Conversaciones con José Vicente Rangel*. Caracas: Editorial Ateneo de Caracas, 1978.

——. *Conversaciones con Luis Beltrán Prieto*. Caracas: Editorial Ateneo de Caracas, 1979.

——. *Conversaciones con Luis Herrera Campíns*. Caracas: Editorial Ateneo de Caracas, 1978.

——. *Conversaciones con Uslar Pietri*. Caracas: Editorial Ateneo de Caracas, 1978.

——. *Corrupción y golpe de estado*. Caracas: Editorial Ateneo de Caracas, 1979.

——. *Democracia y golpe militar*. Caracas: Editorial Ateneo de Caracas, 1979.

Pérez Alfonzo, Juan Pablo. *Hundiéndonos en el excremento del diablo*. 3rd ed. Caracas: n.p., 1976.

Pérez Alfonzo, Juan Pablo. *El pentágono petrolero*. Caracas: Ediciones Revista Política, 1967.

Pérez-Esclarín, Antonio. *La gente vive en el este*. Caracas: Editorial Fuentes, 1974.

Petkoff, Teodoro. *Corrupción total*. Caracas: Editorial Fuentes, 1979.

——. *Razón y pasión del socialismo*. Caracas: n.p., 1973.

——. *Socialismo para Venezuela?* Caracas: Editorial Fuentes, 1972.

Petras, James F.; Morley, Morris; and Smith, Steven. *The Nationalization of Venezuelan Oil*. New York: Praeger, 1977.

Picón Salas, Mariano. *Comprensión de Venezuela*. Caracas: Monte Avila, 1976.

——; Mijares, Augusto; and Díaz Sánchez, Ramón. *Venezuela Independiente: Evolución política y social, 1810–1960*. Caracas: Fundación Mendoza, 1975.

Piño Iturrieta, Elías. *Positivismo y gomecismo*. Caracas: Universidad Central de Venezuela, 1978.

Planchart, Enrique. *La pintura en Venezuela*. Caracas: Universidad Simón Bolívar, Editorial Equinocio, 1979.

Pocaterra, José Rafael. *Memorias de un venezolano de la decadencia*. 2 vols. Caracas: Monte Avila, 1979.

Pollak-Eltz, Angelina. *Aportes indígenas a la cultura del pueblo venezolano*. Caracas: Universidad Católica Andrés Bello, 1978.

——. *Cultos afroamericanos*. Caracas: Universidad Católica Andrés Bello, 1977.

Porras, Eloy. *Juan Pablo Pérez Alfonzo: el hombre que sacudió el mundo*. Caracas: Editorial Ateneo de Caracas, 1979.

Powell, John Duncan. *Political Mobilization of the Venezuelan Peasant*. Cambridge, Mass.: Harvard University Press, 1971.

Rabe, Stephen G. *The Road to OPEC: United States Relations with Venezuela, 1919–1976*. Austin: University of Texas Press, 1982.

Ramírez Faría, Carlos. *La democracia petrolera de Rómulo Betancourt a Carlos Andrés Pérez*. Buenos Aires: El Cid Editor, 1978.

Rangel, Carlos. *Del buen salvaje al buen revolucionario*. Caracas: Monte Avila, 1976.

Rangel, Domingo Alberto. *Los Andinos en el poder*. Caracas: Vadell Hermanos, 1975.

——. *Capital y desarrollo*. 2 vols. Caracas: Universidad Central de Venezuela, 1969–70.

——. *Elecciones 1973: el gran negocio*. Valencia: Vadell Hermanos, 1974.

——. *Gómez, el amo del poder*. Caracas: Vadell Hermanos, 1975.

——. *Los mercaderes del voto: estudio de un sistema*. Valencia: Vadell Hermanos, 1973.

——. *La oligarquía del dinero*. Caracas: Editorial Fuentes, 1972.

——. *El proceso del capitalismo contemporáneo en Venezuela*. Caracas: Universidad Central de Venezuela, 1968.

Rangel, José Vicente. *Expediente negro*. Caracas: Editorial Domingo Fuentes, 1969.

——. *Tiempo de verdades*. Caracas: n.p., 1973.

——; Petkoff, Teodoro; and Lairet, Germán. *El año chucuto*. Caracas: Colección Parlamento y Socialismo, 1975.

Ray, Talton F. *The Politics of the Barrios of Venezuela*. Berkeley: University of California Press, 1969.

Reyes, Antonio. *Cuando el marido es el presidente*. Caracas: Publicaciones Seleven, 1979.

Roche, Marcel. *Rafael Rangel: ciencia y política en la Venezuela de principios de siglo*. Caracas: Monte Avila, 1978.

Rodríguez, Manuel Alfredo. *El capitolio de Caracas: un siglo de historia de Venezuela*. Caracas: Ediciones del Congreso de la República, 1974.

——. *Tres decadas caraqueñas*. Caracas: Monte Avila, 1975.

Rodríguez Campos, Manuel. *Venezuela 1902: la crisis fiscal y el bloqueo*. Caracas: Universidad Central de Venezuela, 1977.

Rodulfo Cortes, Santos. *Antología documental de Venezuela, 1492–1900*. Caracas: n.p., 1960.

Rodwin, Lloyd *et al*. *Planning Urban Growth: The Experience of the Guayana Program of Venezuela*. Cambridge, Mass.: MIT Press, 1969.

Rojas, Armando. *Historia de las relaciones diplomáticas entre Venezuela y los Estados Unidos, 1810–1899*. Caracas: Ediciones de la presidencia de la República, 1979.

Salazar Martínez, Francisco. *Tiempo de compadres: de Cipriano Castro a*

Juan Vicente Gómez. Caracas: Librería Piñango, 1972.

Salazar-Carrillo, Jorge. *Oil in the Economic Development of Venezuela*. New York: Praeger, 1976.

Salcedo-Bastardo, J.L. *Historia fundamental de Venezuela*. 8th ed. revised. Caracas: Universidad Central de Venezuela, 1979.

Salinger, Pierre. *Cuadernos venezolanos: viajes y conversaciones con Carlos Andrés Pérez*. Caracas: Seix Barral, 1978.

Schael, Guillermo J. *Caracas: la ciudad que no vuelve*. Caracas: n.p., 1968.

Schuyler, George. *Hunger in a Land of Plenty*. Cambridge, Mass.: Schenkman Publishing Co., 1980.

Shoup, Carl. *The Fiscal System of Venezuela*. Baltimore, Md.: Johns Hopkins Press, 1959.

Silva Michelena, Jose A. *The Illusion of Democracy in Dependent Nations*. Cambridge, Mass.: MIT Press, 1971.

—— and Sonntag, Heinz R. *El proceso electoral de 1978: su perspectiva historica estructural*. Caracas: Editorial Ateneo de Caracas, 1979.

Siso Martínez, J.M. *150 años de vida repúblicana*. Caracas: Ministerio de Educación, 1968.

Sonntag, Heinz R. *et al. Psiquiatría y subdesarrollo. Reflexiones en base al caso de Venezuela*. Caracas: El Cid, 1977.

Stambouli, Andrés. *Crisis político: Venezuela, 1945-1958*. Caracas: Editorial Ateneo de Caracas, 1980.

Suárez Figueroa, Naudy. *Programas políticos venezolanos de la primera mitad del siglo XX*. 2 vols. Caracas: Universidad Católica Andrés Bello, 1977.

Suárez Radillo, Carlos M. *13 autores del nuevo teatro venezolano*. Caracas: Monte Avila, 1971.

Sullivan, William. "The Rise of Despotism in Venezuela: Cipriano Castro, 1899-1908." Ph.D. dissertation, University of New Mexico, 1974.

Tarre Murzi, Alfredo. *El estado y la cultura*. Caracas: Monte Avila, 1972.

Tennassee, Paul Nehru. *Venezuela, los obreros petroleros y la lucha por la democracia*. Caracas: EFIP-Editorial Popular, 1979.

Toro Jiménez, Fermin. *La política de Venezuela en la conferencia interamericana de consolidación de la paz: Buenos Aires, 1936*. Caracas: Universidad Central de Venezuela, 1977.

Tugwell, Franklin. *The Politics of Oil in Venezuela*. Stanford, Calif.: Stanford University Press, 1975.

Uslar Pietri, Arturo. *De una a otra venezuela*. Caracas: Monte Avila, 1972.

——. *Letras y hombres de Venezuela*. 4th ed. Madrid: Edime, 1978.

——. *Tierra venezolana*. Caracas: Minsterio de Educación, 1965.

Valente, Cecilia. *The Political, Economic, and Labor Climate of Venezuela*. Philadelphia: Industrial Research Unit, Wharton School, University of Pennsylvania, 1979.

Vallenilla, Luis. *Oil: The Making of a New Economic Order: Venezuelan Oil and OPEC*. New York: McGraw-Hill, 1975.

Velásquez, Ramón J. *La caída del liberalismo amarillo: tiempo y drama de Antonio Paredes*. 2nd ed. Caracas: n.p., 1973.

——. *Confidencias imaginarias de Juan Vicente Gómez*. Caracas:

Ediciones Centauro, 1979.
—— et al. *Venezuela moderna: medio siglo de historia 1926–1976*. Caracas: Fundación Eugenio Mendoza and Editorial Ariel, 1979.

Venezuela 1979: Examen y futuro. Caracas: Editorial Ateneo de Caracas, 1980.

Venezuela, panorama 1969: una mirada al futuro. Caracas: Creole Petroleum Company, 1970.

Vivas Gallardo, Freddy. *Venezuela en la sociedad de las naciones, 1920–1939. descripción y análisis de una actuación diplomática*. Caracas: Universidad Central de Venezuela, 1981.

Watters, Mary. *A History of the Church in Venezuela, 1810–1930*. Chapel Hill: University of North Carolina Press, 1933.

Wise, George. *Caudillo: A Portrait of Antonio Guzmán Blanco*. New York: Columbia University Press, 1951.

Wright, Winthrop R. "Elitist Attitudes toward Race in Twentieth-Century Venezuela." In *Slavery and Race Relations in Latin America*, edited by Robert Brent Toplin. Westport, Conn.: Greenwood Press, 1974.

Ybarra, T.R. *Young Man of Caracas*. New York: Ives Washburn, 1941.

Zapata, J.L. et al. *CAP, cero en agricultura*. Maracaibo: Fondo Editorial IRFES, 1977.

Ziems, Angel. *El gomecismo y la formación del ejército nacional*. Caracas: Editorial Ateneo de Caracas, 1979.

GLOSSARY OF SPANISH TERMS

Adeco: popular designation for member of *Acción Democrática* party.

Amplia base: broad base, used to refer to political coalitions.

Andino: person from the Andean region of Venezuela.

Andradista: political follower or ally of President Ignacio Andrade (1898–9).

Aprista: member of populist political party (APRI) founded in Peru by Raúl Haya de la Torre in the 1930s.

Astucia: cunning or astuteness.

Audiencia: court of law.

Barrio: city district or neighborhood, usually used in Venezuela to designate lower income neighborhoods.

Bicho: general name for small insects; often used in Venezuela metaphorically.

Bolívar: Venezuelan unit of currency; for most of the twentieth century until 1983, about 4.3 to the US dollar.

Brujo (bruja): witch.

Cambio: change; Rafael Caldera (1969–74) used the term to refer to his COPEI government, since it was the first Christian Democratic government in Venezuela.

Campesino: rural dweller, usually of modest economic means.

Campo: countryside.

Caraqueño: resident of Caracas.

Casta: term used primarily in the colonial period and nineteenth century to refer to groups of mixed racial heritage.

Caudillo: strongman, dictator, or leader.

Causa Común: common cause; name of Diego Arria's political party in the 1978 election.

Colegio: high school; also a body of persons in the same profession.

Comadreja: weasel.

Conquistador: conqueror, usually in reference to sixteenth-century explorers and settlers.

Consulado: merchants' guild.

Continuismo: practice of a politician, party, or dictator to continue in office, often without more than a façade of electoral legitimization.

Contrapunto: a singing contest in which each singer tries to outdo the other in clever lyrics without missing a beat of the rhythm; common entertainment in the *llanos*, or plains.

Copeyano: member of the COPEI political party.

Crespistas: followers of President Joaquín Crespo (1894–8).

Criollista: refers to literature, or customs, deriving from local people, places, history rather than from European themes; comes from the word *criollo* (creole) for a person of Spanish parentage who was born in America.

Desaparecido: literally, disappeared; used to refer to persons who have vanished at the hands of death squads or who have been detained by police or intelligence agents in some undisclosed jail, usually for political offenses.

Desarrollista: "developmentalist;" one who places the greatest value on economic development and less value usually on political and social development.

Frailejón: espeletia plant common to the cold regions of the Andes above 3,000 meters in altitude.

Golpe: a seizure of political power by force; *golpe de estado* or *coup d'état*.

Gomecista: follower of dictator Juan Vicente Gómez (1908–35).

Guerrilla: member of a small force of irregular soldiers.

Hacendado: owner of a large rural estate.

Hacienda: a large rural estate.

Hectare: unit of surface measure equivalent to 10,000 square meters or 2.471 acres.

Joropo: typical folk dance of the Venezuelan *llanos*, or plains.

Junta: board or council; often a collegiate governing body which holds executive political power.

Latifundia: an agrarian structure characterized by large landed estates.

Ley fuga: literally "law of flight;" refers to the irregular practice of executing prisoners with the fabricated rationale that they had tried to escape.

Liceo: high school.

Llanero: person from the central plains, or *llanos*.

Llanos: central plains region of Venezuela.

Lopecista: follower of President Eleazar López Contreras (1936–41).

Mantuanos: members of Venezuelan colonial élite, lit. wearers of lace *mantillas*.

Margariteños: people from the island of Margarita.

Medinista: follower of President Isaías Medina Angarita (1941–5).

Mepistas: follower of Luis Beltrán Prieto Figueroa, founder of the party *Movimiento Electoral del Pueblo* (MEP).

Mestizo: person of mixed racial descent.

Minifundia: an agrarian system characterized by many owners of small plots of land.

Mirista: member of the *Movimiento de Izquierda Revolucionaria* (Movement of the Revolutionary Left—MIR).

Mocho: maimed; nickname of José Manuel Hernández.

Movimiento: movement, activity.

Oriente: east; often refers to eastern coastal region of Venezuela.

Páramo: cold, desolate heights of Venezuelan Andes.

Pardo: mulatto; of mixed African and Spanish descent.

Perezjimentista: follower of President Marcos Pérez Jiménez (1952–8).

Proclama, Proclamación: proclamation; announcement of political program.

Rancho: small farm; also modest house or hut in rural or urban areas.

Salsa: sauce; contemporary music of the Hispanic Caribbean.

Serape: a type of long scarf or cloak.

Sombrero: broad-brimmed hat.

Supermercado: supermarket.

Tachirense: person from Táchira state in the western Andean region of Venezuela.

Tarea: task; day's labor.

Tertulia: group which meets regularly for discussion; salon.

Tío Conejo: Uncle Rabbit.

Tío Tigre: Uncle Tiger.

Trienio: three-year period; specifically used to refer to the 1945–8 period dominated by *Acción Democatica*.

Toros Coleados: form of bullfighting practiced in the *llanos* in which the bull is thrown by his tail.

Viveza: liveliness; cleverness; perspicacity.

INDEX

Abrapalabra (Britto García), 224
Acción Democrática, 77, 85, 89; Betancourt's government, 127–46; divisions of, 126, 128, 164, 211; and labor, 82–3, 92, 96, 102, 122, 130, 168, 206–7; Leoni's government, 157–64; in opposition, 91–2, 107, 167; Pérez's government, 200–12; petroleum policy of, 68, 101–2, 135–7, 159–60, 194–6; role in 1945 revolt, 94–6; rural strength of, 96, 99, 122, 125, 128, 130–1, 139; scandals 1974–8, 204–6; social program of, 104–6, 139–42; in *trienio*, 94–107
Academia de Bellas Artes, 49
Academia Nacional de la Historia, 22, 31
Acción Electoral, 91
Acción Femenina, 84
Acción Nacional, 91
Actualidades, 49, 85
AD en Oposición, 152. See also ARS
African slavery, 3, 8
agrarian reform: and AD, 96, 99, 105, 130, 139–40; in 1950s, 106
agriculture, 4, 7, 14–15, 17, 96; cacao, 4, 7, 56, 70–1; coffee, 7, 38, 40, 56, 70–1; credit, 70–1, 140; decline of in 1920s, 55–6; livestock, 56; production, 139, 184, 200; remuneration of, 139, 183
Agrupación Cultural Femenina, 84, 150
Agrupación Revolucionaria de Izquierda, 90
Aguilar, Pedro Pablo, 176
Aguilar Mawdsley, Andrés, 208
Aguirre, Manuel, 84
air force, 54. See also armed forces
Alcántara, Linares, 48
Allen, Henry, 80
Allende, Salvador, 178
"*Alma Llanera*," 80
Amazon Cooperation Treaty, 207
American Telephone and Telegraph, 216
Ana Isabel, una niña decente, 117
Andean Pact, 163, 169, 202, 217
Andrade, Ignacio, 25, 26, 39, 47
Andueza Palacio, Raimundo, 22, 38, 39, 47
Angel, Jimmy, 79

Angel Falls, 79
Animales feroces (Chocrón), 187
Anzola, Alfredo: *Manuel*, 221
Araya Peninsula, 15
Arcaya, Ignacio Luis, 144
Arcaya, Pedro, 70
Arguello, José N., 73
Arias, Rafael, 118
armed forces, 42, 53–4, 83, 94, 161; and geopolitics, 109, 145, 164, 169, 170, 208; and military conspiracies, 54–5, 74, 94–6, 106–7, 119, 124–5, 132; and national security, 122, 158, 205; and politics, 77, 95–6, 106–7, 132, 171, 226; professionalization, 53–4, 127, 131.
Arria, Diego, 178, 210
ARS, 128, 131
art: *Círculo de Bellas Artes*, 49, 87; muralists, 31–2, 48–9; Reverón, Armando, 49, 88, 223; Soto, Jesus, 223
Asia y el lejano oriente (Chocrón), 187
Asociación de Escritores, 81
Asociación Latinoamericana de Libre Comercio, 162
Asociación Nacional de Autores Cinematográficas, 186
Asociación Nacional de Empleados, 81
Asociación Venezolana de Mujeres, 84
Asociación de Maestros, 141
Asociación Venezolana de Periodismo, 81
asphalt, 29, 42
Audiencia, 5
autonomous institutes, 99–100, 143, 198, 203–4

Ballet Internacional de Caracas, 223
Banco Agrícola y Pecuario, 71, 99, 105, 140
Banco Central de Venezuela, 75, 99, 197, 199
Banco de Trabajadores de Venezuela, 199
Banco de Venezuela, 56
Banco Industrial, 75
Banco Obrero, 72, 99, 141
banking laws, 174
Baptista, Leopoldo, 48